IMAGES
of America

JOHNSTOWN

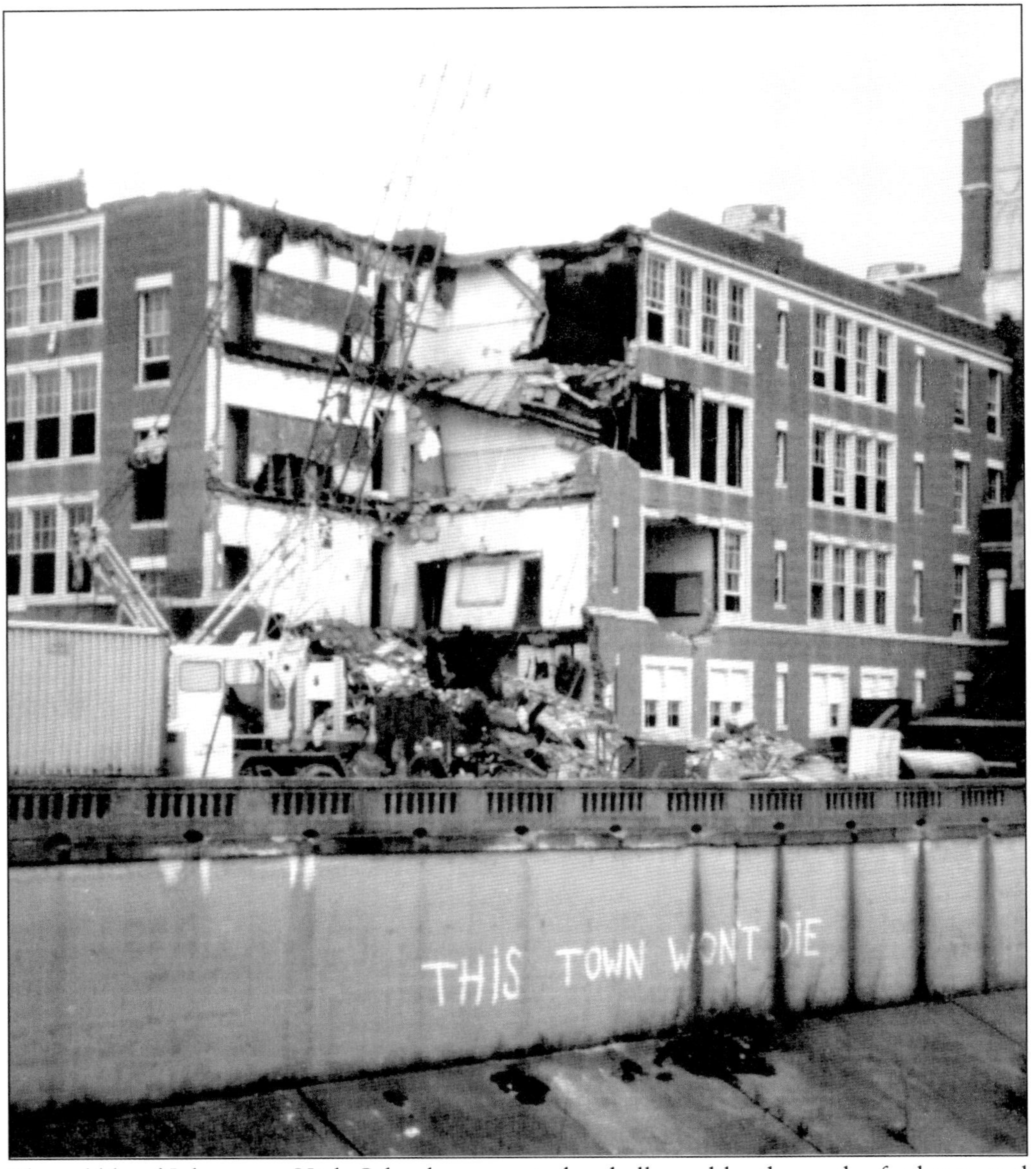

The rubble of Johnstown High School appears to be challenged by the work of a brave soul who scrawled the defiant words "This Town Won't Die" on the riverbank below the cranes and dump trucks. It was always a tradition for graduating classes to send someone over the concrete wall to draw a symbol of the high school. Usually, the artwork would be the school's Trojan head mascot. However, after the 1977 flood, when things seemed grimmest, as businesses were closing or relocating and the population migrating to other parts of the country, the tradition turned from lighthearted high school slogans to the serious promise of those who were determined to remain. When demolition of the high school began in 1985, again, someone jumped onto the riverbank to refresh the words that had appeared eight years before. Although the phrase is faintly visible today, there is no doubt that the sentiment remains. It is with that spirit that we affectionately dedicate this book to those who came before, those who live in Johnstown now, and those who have yet to call Johnstown home. (Author's collection.)

IMAGES
of America

JOHNSTOWN

Lyndee Jobe Henderson and R. Dean Jobe

ARCADIA
PUBLISHING

ISBN 978-0-7385-3493-0

Published by Arcadia Publishing
Charleston, South Carolina

Printed in the United States of America

Library of Congress Catalog Card Number: 2003114319

For all general information contact Arcadia Publishing at:
Telephone 843-853-2070
Fax 843-853-0044
E-mail sales@arcadiapublishing.com
For customer service and orders:
Toll-Free 1-888-313-2665

Visit us on the Internet at www.arcadiapublishing.com

ACKNOWLEDGMENTS

Thanks to Larry Henderson for the hours he spent working with the photographs. We honor and thank the following people and organizations for contributing photographs, information, and time to this project: Barb Cover and Jim Cover Jr. (Cover's Frame Shop); Jeanne and Robert Buck; Robert Snavely; the Reverend Wilbert A. Boerstler; Robert Geist; David Geist; Merle and Martha Showalter; Gary Henderson (Henderson Funeral Home); Terry Alwine; Ray Clites; Ellyn Henderson; Pamela Mayer (publisher of the *Tribune-Democrat*); the Johnstown Area Historical Association, Robin Rummel (archivist), and Richard Burkert (executive director); the Cambria County Historical Society, Kathy Jones (curator), Fremont J. McKenrick, and the board of directors; the Ferndale Historical Society; the Clara Barton National Historic Site (National Park Service); Phyllis Jobe; Marilyn McDermott; Ross Henderson; Lisa Konkol; Park O. Cover (Cover Studio); Herbert Pfuhl; the reference librarians at the Cambria Library System, Johnstown; R. Keith Rager; Rick and Diane Safko Buck; the Johnstown High School archives; William L. Glosser; Sr. Mary Parks; Bill Jones; and Doug Richardson of the Johnstown Flood National Memorial. Special thanks go to editor Erin Loftus and the staff at Arcadia Publishing.

Every attempt was made to verify the ownership of the photographs contained in this publication. Please notify the author if you are aware of a discrepancy.

Contents

FOREWORD

Greater Johnstown is a massive subject to distill into 200 photographs. Considering its limited space, this book cannot be a comprehensive historical record. Admittedly, there are many missing pieces here. Ethnic groups, social and fraternal organizations, churches, sports teams, and businesses are represented to a small degree. Our goal was to share rare, never-before-published photographs. Because of the limited number of images available on the early history of Johnstown, this was not always possible.

The method of determining which photographs to include was guided by one simple precept: wherever possible, in lieu of buildings, choose faces. Rather than filling the pages with the exteriors of factories, we selected images that showed the people; the faces of mothers and fathers, and children at play; homes and neighborhoods that form the surrounding community; and events that molded the city and touched the nation. This book is a snapshot of the past and a small portion of the history that Johnstown residents share.

—Lyndee Jobe Henderson

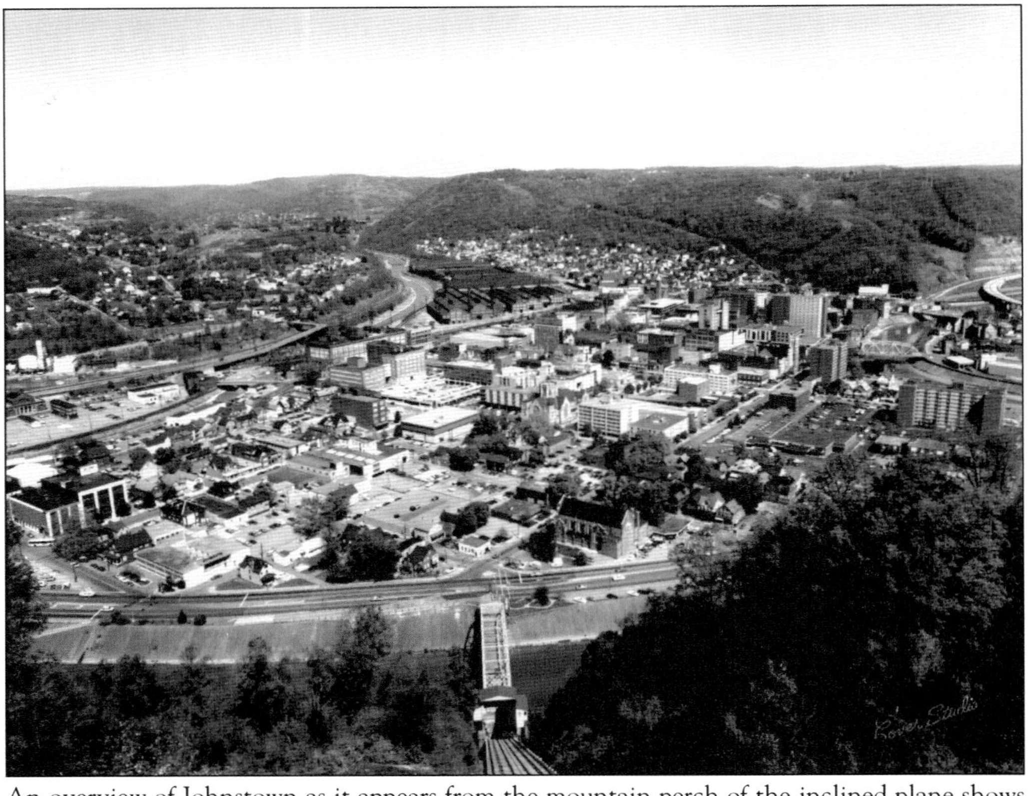

An overview of Johnstown as it appears from the mountain perch of the inclined plane shows the outline of the land and the town nestled between mountains and guarded by two rivers. (Courtesy of Jim Cover Jr.)

INTRODUCTION

Every city harbors its history in a variety of places, hidden on dusty library shelves or in dark basements, where long-lost journals protect the records of bygone days. Family legends are sometimes embellished beyond the truth. Intriguing photographs contain smiling faces of precious children on one side but no date or information on the other. Historians study images, anxious to discover that faint pencil mark or neatly scrolled script of an earlier time that might provide a hint of the story behind the artifact.

The first accounts of Johnstown's founding fall into that same trap. A death date is reported in an ancient obituary, recorded improperly on a gravestone, or accidentally misprinted in a later book, and before long, facts, dates, and story accuracy become suspect. Because the early settlers of Johnstown were understandably more concerned with survival than with maintaining records, very few specific events and dates before the 1800s can be verified. In fact, the birth and death dates of founder Joseph (Schantz) Johns are in question, as are his place of birth, his time of arrival in America, and the path that brought him to the valley that would one day bear his name.

We can, with good conscience, say that Johns was a farmer who followed the religious principles of the Amish. Described as standing at five feet six inches with a stocky build, there are no photographs, sketches, or paintings of Johns, which is understandable because of his staunch faith. There is one obvious trait we can deduce from our founder's actions: he was a man with a vision. He did not create the town to make a profit—many early accounts indicate that his lots were sold for less than the going price in other area towns. There is reasonable doubt that he intended to elevate his own stature, as his religious views prohibited him from holding political office or acting in a manner that appeared anything less than humble in the eyes of God.

The events that led to Johns's ownership of the parcel that he originally called Conemaugh began with the signing of the 1768 Treaty of Fort Stanwix, between the Iroquois Indians and the heirs of William Penn. The agreement permitted the pioneers' entrance into parts of Pennsylvania that were formerly off-limits for settlement. Within five months of the treaty, paperwork was drawn for warrants of purchase.

The 249-acre stretch of timber, mountains, and valley between the Conemaugh and Stonycreek Rivers was initially owned by Charles Campble, as recorded in a survey dated April 3, 1769. As land speculators bargained among themselves, the ownership passed hands several times before Joseph Johns secured the original Campble land. The date of his purchase appears to be September 30, 1793, and early accounts report that he built a log home at what would later be named Levergood Street and moved his family from his Somerset farm to this new address.

During his first seven years of ownership, Johns cleared timber, farmed, and hunted. He also delved into designing a town with the foreknowledge that a new county called Cambria would be created. History hints that he aspired to have Conemaugh named the new county seat. However, when the charter for Cambria County was drawn, the verbiage clearly stated that the county seat would be located in the center of the county. Thus, Conemaugh lost its bid for county seat to midpoint Ebensburg.

There is discussion as to whether or not this defeat spurred Johns to sell off his interests. Nonetheless, by May 1807, he had completed all transactions and moved to a farm outside of Davidsville.

Peter Levergood owned Conemaugh when the Pennsylvania state legislature voted to rename it Johnstown after Joseph Johns. With the discovery of ore and the foresight of Peter

Levergood, the town began a transformation. Aware that Johnstown would be a major link in the Pennsylvania Canal system, Levergood steered the town toward a new prosperity.

Once the canal connected Johnstown to Philadelphia and Pittsburgh, economic growth accelerated the town from a moderately successful one to a burgeoning commercial location. The railroad only improved the town's financial outlook, and Johnstown began to attract major companies and hardworking people. Soon, the steel industry commanded the landscape with numerous buildings. Nights became bright and glowing. Homes and buildings were dressed in a steel-born patina.

The population grew, attracting immigrant workers who often arrived by train. These immigrants had few English words in their vocabulary and virtually no money or possessions, but they had a work ethic that would make Johnstown's steel, mining, and railroad industries essential to the community, the state, the nation, and the world. Pride drove these people to outproduce better-equipped and larger factories in Pittsburgh. They were determined to own a piece of the American Dream.

As everyday life hummed around them, the people of Johnstown dealt with the nuisance of flooding. On May 31, 1889, the water that surrounded them became a fierce enemy coupled with a dam that loomed over the mountain ridge beyond. The Johnstown flood became one of the most heavily reported and written about disasters in national history. The mettle of the survivors is a testament to their strength. When disaster struck other towns, Johnstown sent money and workers to help, repaying the outpouring it had received in its time of need.

The steel industry and the businesses spawned by it helped Johnstown recover. The local economy was bolstered during wartime, as mills received government purchase orders for everything from bullets to rails. At the same time, Johnstown suffered the losses of fine young soldiers who never returned.

The cycle repeated with another huge flood in 1936 and an economic recovery during World War II. Johnstown battled through the ups and downs. The construction of a major flood-control project filtered money into the town during the Depression era and provided jobs for unemployed steelworkers and miners.

During the 1960s and 1970s, the U.S. steel industry continued to struggle. Unemployment in Johnstown soared above 20 percent. In a domino effect, the troubled steel industry rippled change to local spin-off businesses that depended on the mills.

The once-in-10,000-years 1977 flood shattered the security of the city. Again, townspeople faced the loss of life, homes, and jobs. This became a turning point for many. Some longtime businesses closed. The population continued to shrink, as many searched for employment elsewhere. The era of "Johnstown, the steel giant" ended with the familiar mill whistle echoing the final shift. For those who remained, there was the challenge to bring Johnstown into a new time, with a new economic frontier based on technology, communications, and tourism.

Today, as the economy fights to come back, education has resurfaced as a priority. Residents voted to build a new high school, which opened in 2003. *Money* magazine rated Johnstown as Pennsylvania's best-kept secret because of its quality of life, low taxes, and low crime rate. *Forbes* magazine ranked Johnstown as the most-affordable city in the nation.

Johnstown is a study in contrasts. With the closing of the larger steel mills and coal mines, the air is clearer and the streets are cleaner. The rivers and surrounding countryside are recovering from years of heavy industry. Only a fraction of Johnstown's 13 miles of mills are operating in smaller but more efficient production. The workforce is learning the languages of engineering, communications, medicine, and science, as new technology businesses replace the old. It is another adjustment, but one that Johnstown is bound to make. Truly, the future looks bright.

One

Down in the Valley

Considered the first permanent settler, Amish farmer Joseph Johns formally founded the settlement of Conemaugh in 1800. Johns attempted to sell his town's parcels at bargain-basement prices, but early demand waned as other farmers were not particularly interested in the small city lots that he had created in his master plan. In fact, the land was more valuable because of what was below ground. It was not until George King discovered ore deposits and began building furnaces to process ore into iron that interest surged in the town. However, Mother Nature kept many of the early businesses in check, as spring flooding often washed away budding enterprises that required waterpower and were located along the Conemaugh and Stonycreek Rivers. These events discouraged businessmen, who abandoned their stake and moved elsewhere.

When Conemaugh was snubbed as the best choice for the county seat of the newly formed Cambria County, Johns sold the town to Peter Levergood. Eventually, the Pennsylvania state legislature voted to rename Conemaugh after its founder, and Johnstown was born. Ownership of the town passed from person to person until Peter Levergood repossessed it through a failed loan. This time, rather than selling the town again, Levergood held his investment as state officials discussed the potential of building a canal using Johnstown's waterways. When the canal became a reality, the transportation route fed people, goods, and profitability into the community. Johnstown was transformed from a sleepy farm hamlet into a bustling business center. The population began to grow with the creation of jobs. Early settlers enjoyed a standard of living not experienced in most river communities. Development meant building schools, ample stores, and decent transportation. The stage was set for Johnstown to become an industrial leader.

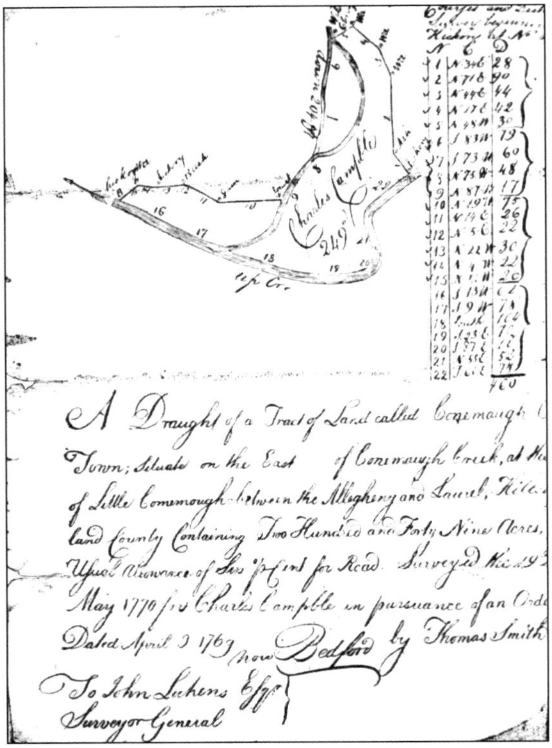

A Draught of a Tract of Land called Conemaugh
Town; situate on the East of Conemaugh Creek, at the
of Little Conemaugh between the Allegheny and Laurel Hills
land County Containing Two Hundred and Forty Nine Acres,
Usual Allowance of Six p Cent for Road. Surveyed the 29
May 1770 for Charles Campble in pursuance of an Ord
Dated April 3 1769 now Bedford by Thomas Smith

To John Lukens Esq
Surveyor General

Referred to as the Campble deed, this April 3, 1769, document is the original survey of the land that Joseph Johns purchased by warrant on November 3, 1800. Johns named the 249 acres Conemaugh. (Courtesy of the Cambria County Historical Society.)

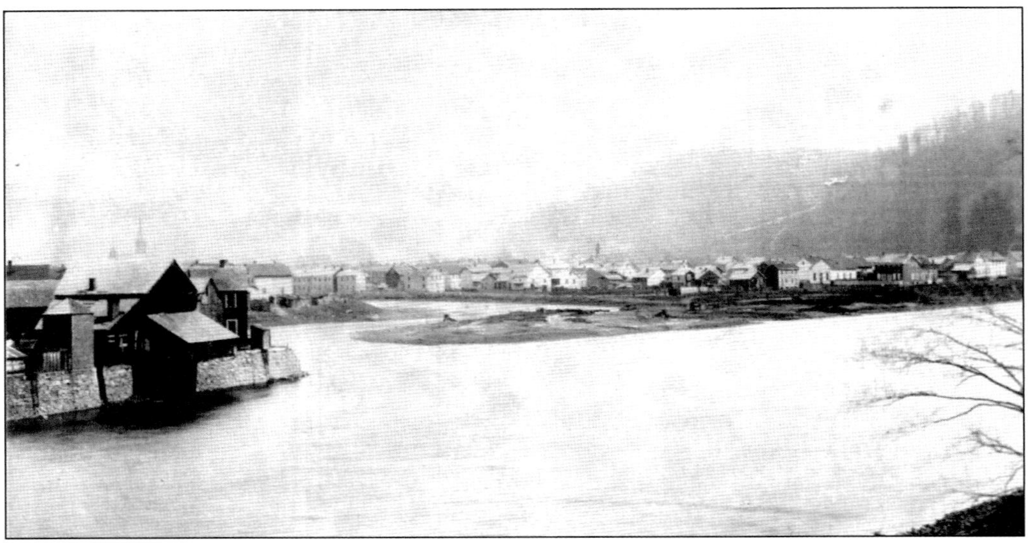

In honor of Joseph Johns, the state legislature voted to change the name from Conemaugh to Johnstown 34 years after the town was founded. By the time of this photograph, *c.* 1870, the land was covered with houses as far as the eye could see—in stark contrast with the once dense forest. (Courtesy of the Johnstown Area Heritage Association archives.)

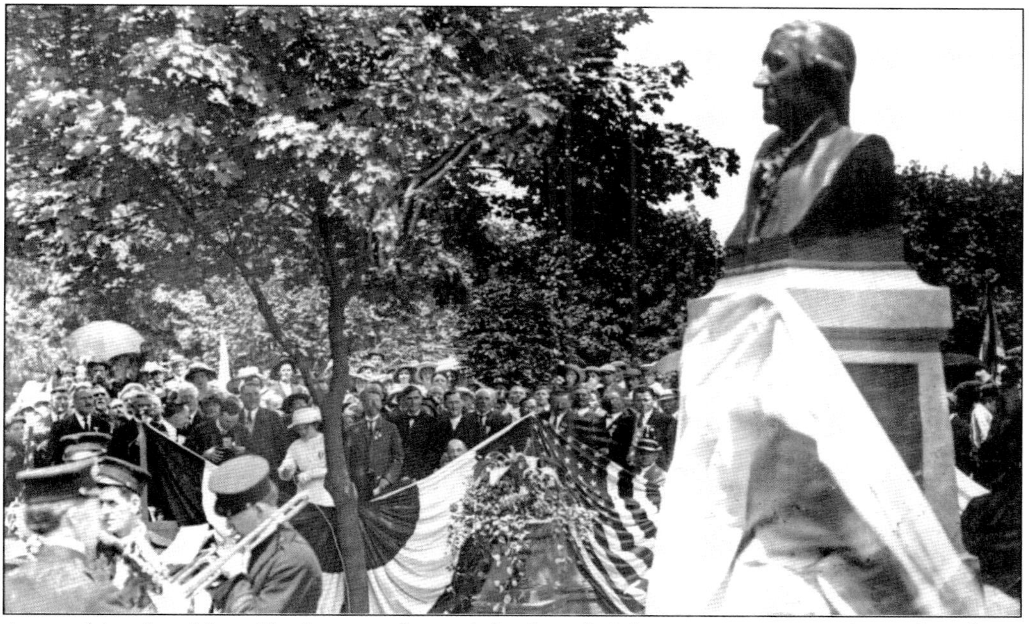

A marching band heralds the unveiling of the Joseph Johns monument in Central Park on June 16, 1913. The German-American Alliance of Pennsylvania commissioned sculptor J. Otto Schweitzer to create the polished granite statue to honor Johns on the 100th anniversary of his death. Full of symbolism, the monument has a plain base honoring Johns's Amish faith and two water fountains (one flowing from each side of the pedestal) representing the Conemaugh and Stonycreek Rivers. Subscriptions were sold to cover the $3,000 project. (Courtesy of the Cambria County Historical Society.)

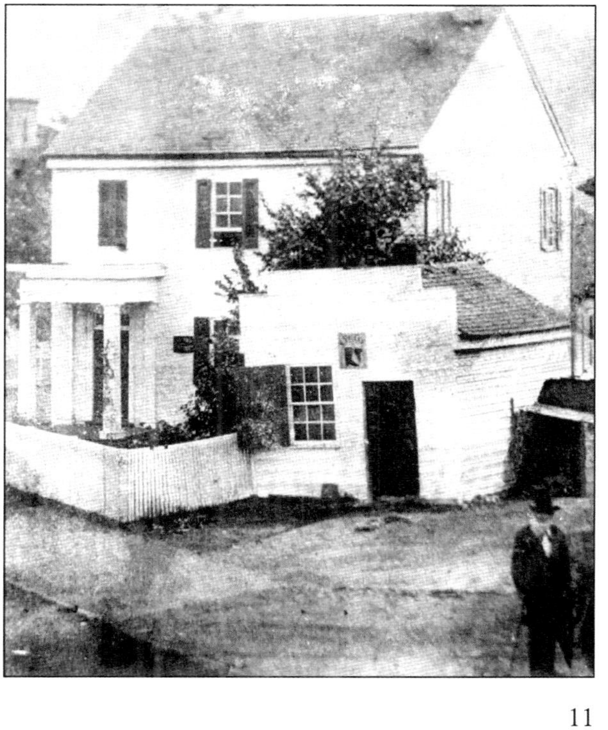

Peter Levergood moved Conemaugh into the age of canal travel and, ultimately, financial viability. Levergood bought Conemaugh in 1811, sold it in 1813, and reclaimed it five years later. His donation of land for the canal system secured Conemaugh's economic future. On April 14, 1834, the state legislature changed the town's name from Conemaugh to Johnstown, and Levergood served as burgess in 1845 and 1846. Levergood's farmhouse stood on Bedford and Levergood Streets until the 1889 flood. (Courtesy of the Johnstown Area Heritage Association archives.)

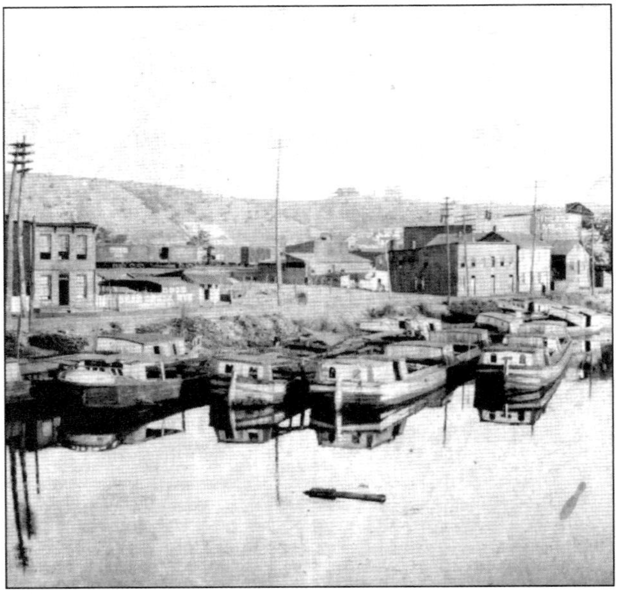

The Pennsylvania Canal system opened in stages, initially connecting Pittsburgh with Johnstown in 1830. Upon completion of the inclines and railroad system of the Allegheny Portage Railroad over the state's eastern Allegheny Mountains in 1834, the movement of goods and people flowed from Philadelphia to Pittsburgh, with Johnstown serving as the midpoint. Packet boats, such as these, floated along the canal basin where the now defunct Gautier works of Bethlehem Steel is located. (Courtesy of the Johnstown Area Heritage Association archives.)

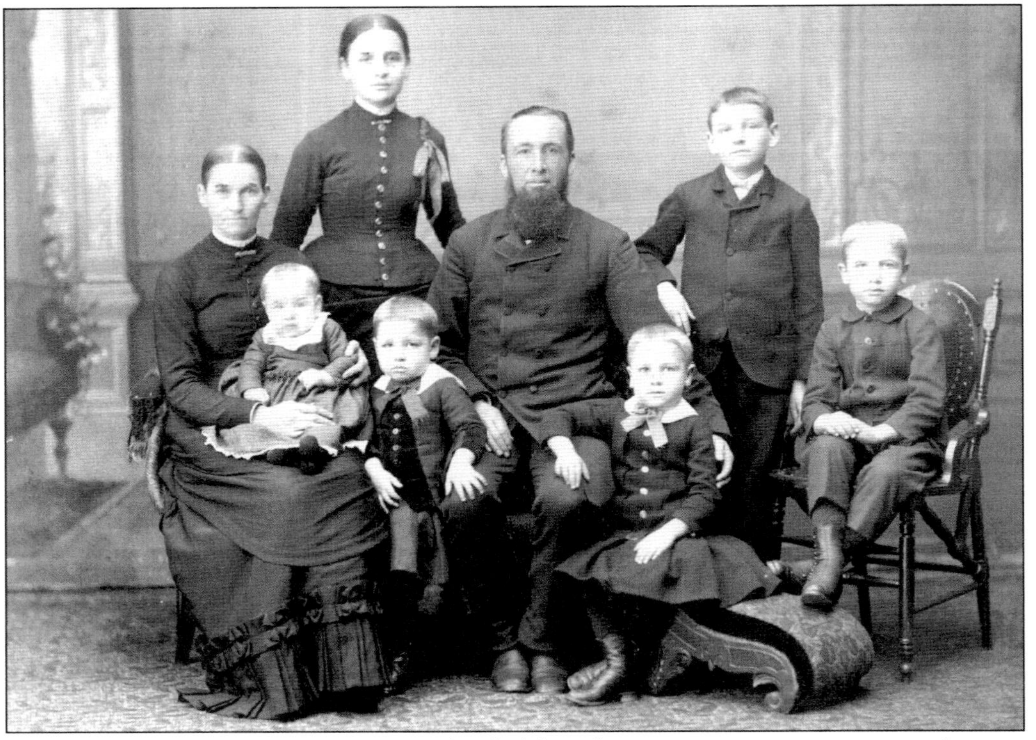

With improvements in transportation, the fledgling farming community transitioned into a burgeoning economic town. Families were enticed to the growing area, which promised jobs for skilled laborers, shopkeepers, and the like. In the 20-year period between 1820 and 1840, the population expanded from 200 to more than 1,000 residents. Early on, Johnstown served as a steppingstone for new residents on the path to the American Dream. (Courtesy of the Johnstown Area Heritage Association archives.)

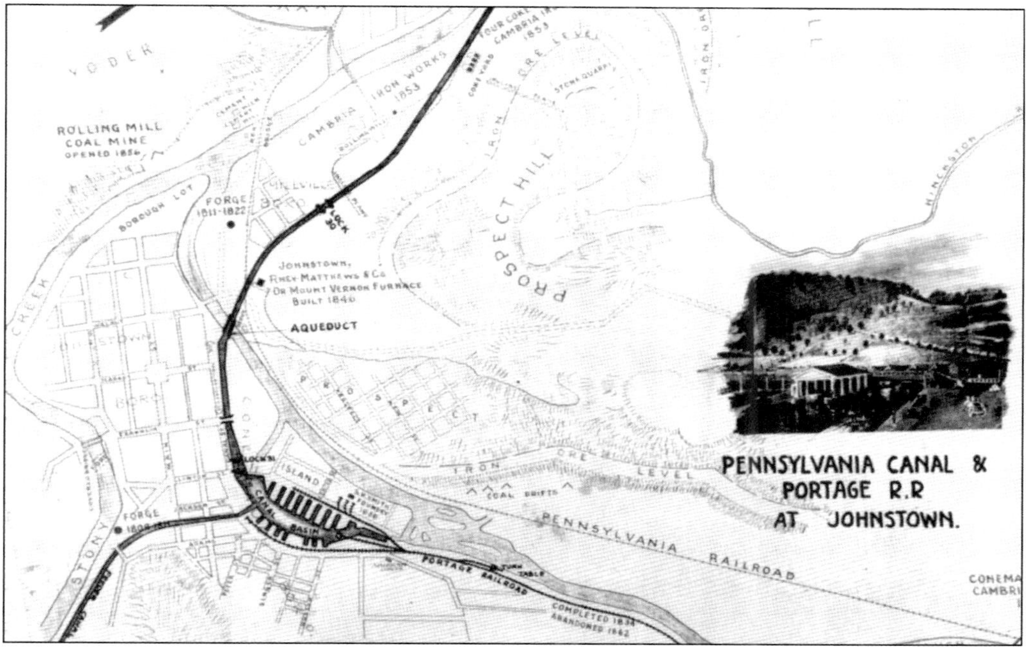

The Pennsylvania Canal and Portage Railroad systems are highlighted on this map, along with early notable businesses such as iron furnaces and forges, which thrived along the waterway as early as 1808. When the canal system closed in 1858 due to competition from the workhorse Pennsylvania Railroad, Johnstown barely felt a loss, as the town had established itself as an integral part of the national transportation and manufacturing scene. (Courtesy of the Johnstown Area Heritage Association archives.)

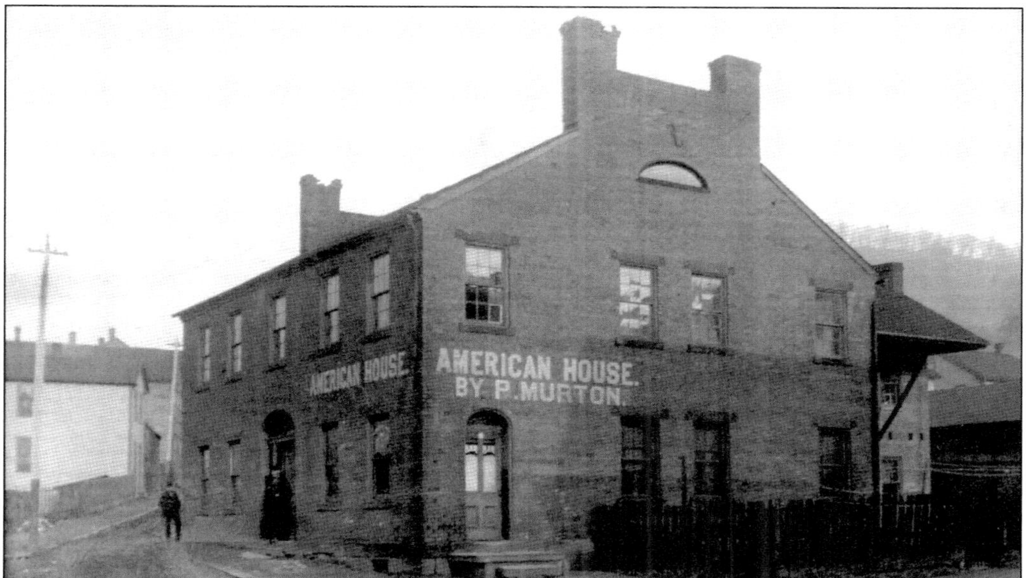

P. Murton's American House became a popular local hotel. One happy customer described it as "a fine place to stop in [the] Portage Railroad days." (Courtesy of the Johnstown Area Heritage Association archives.)

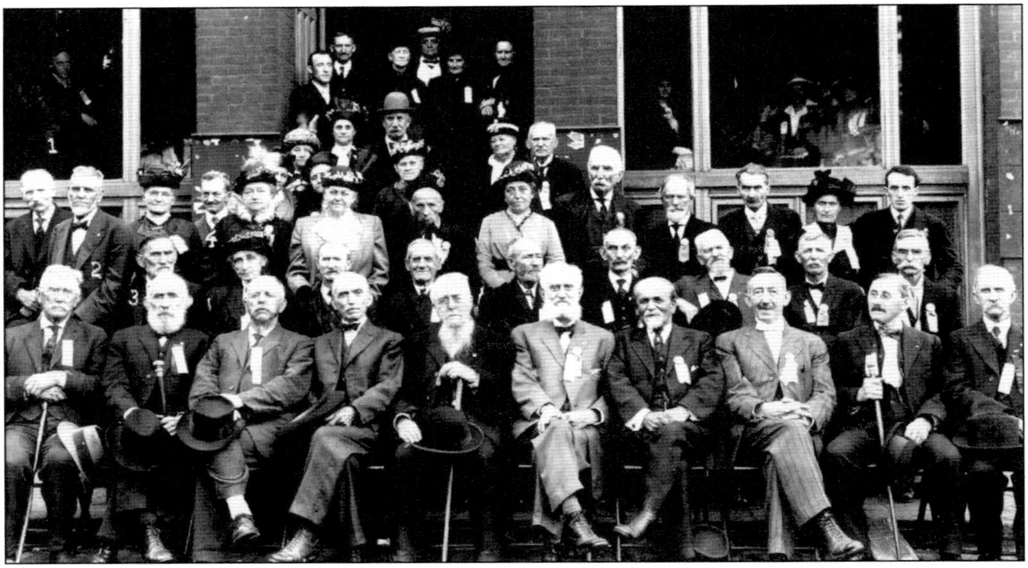

The solitary and physically difficult life on the river created a strong fraternity among river crews. Boatman reunions were not to be missed, although the 1889 flood interrupted the meetings for several years. At the popular Capital Hotel *c.* 1900, these men from Pittsburgh, Blairsville, Greensburg, and the greater Johnstown area share a camaraderie born of common experience. It can be assumed that this group is quite sober, as the Capital Hotel was noted for not maintaining a bar on the property. (Courtesy of the Johnstown Area Heritage Association archives.)

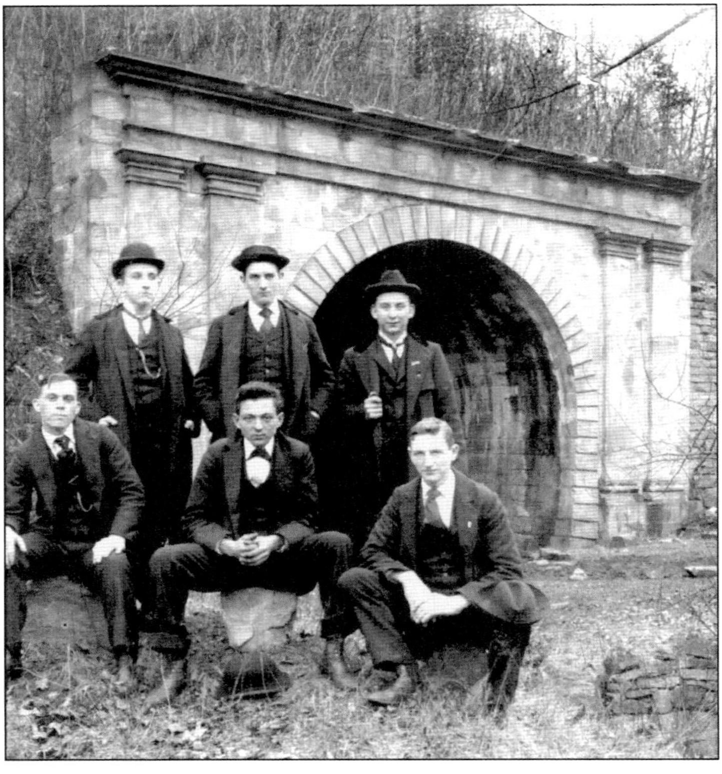

Hikes to Staple Bend Tunnel were popular *c.* 1910. Designated as Inclined Plane No. 1, Staple Bend was the first railroad tunnel built in the United States. Workmen carved the 901-foot-long tunnel through the solid-rock mountain from opposite sides, chipping away some 18 inches a day from each end until they met in the middle. Located four miles outside Johnstown, the tunnel was sealed off for many years before being renovated and reopened by the National Park Service on July 5, 2001, as the Allegheny Portage Railroad National Historic Site. (Courtesy of the Johnstown Area Heritage Association archives.)

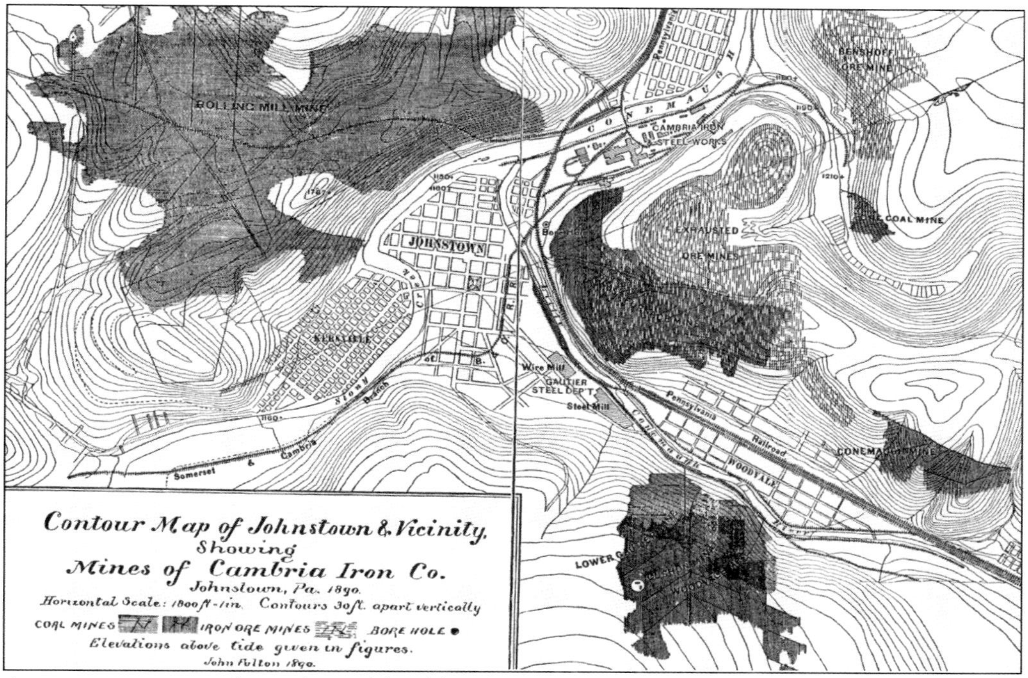

A turning point in the industrial livelihood of Johnstown came with the discovery of iron ore and coal hiding deep under the rolling landscape. Excavator John Fulton recorded this geological survey in 1890 for the Cambria Iron Company. (Courtesy of the Johnstown Area Heritage Association archives.)

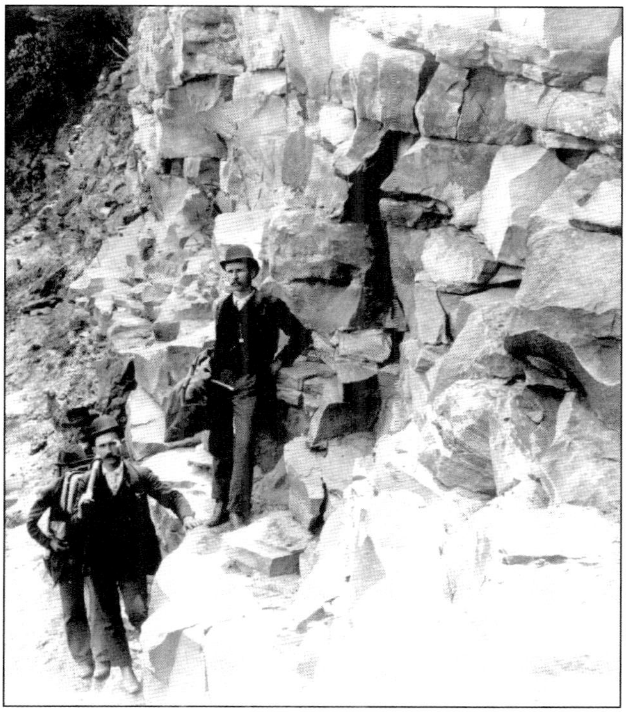

As was the custom *c.* 1880, these men wear full suits—complete with vests, derbies, and pocket watches—as they climb the rocks along a riverbed. Lugging picks and equipment, they are potentially scouting for coal or ore veins. (Courtesy of the Johnstown Area Heritage Association archives.)

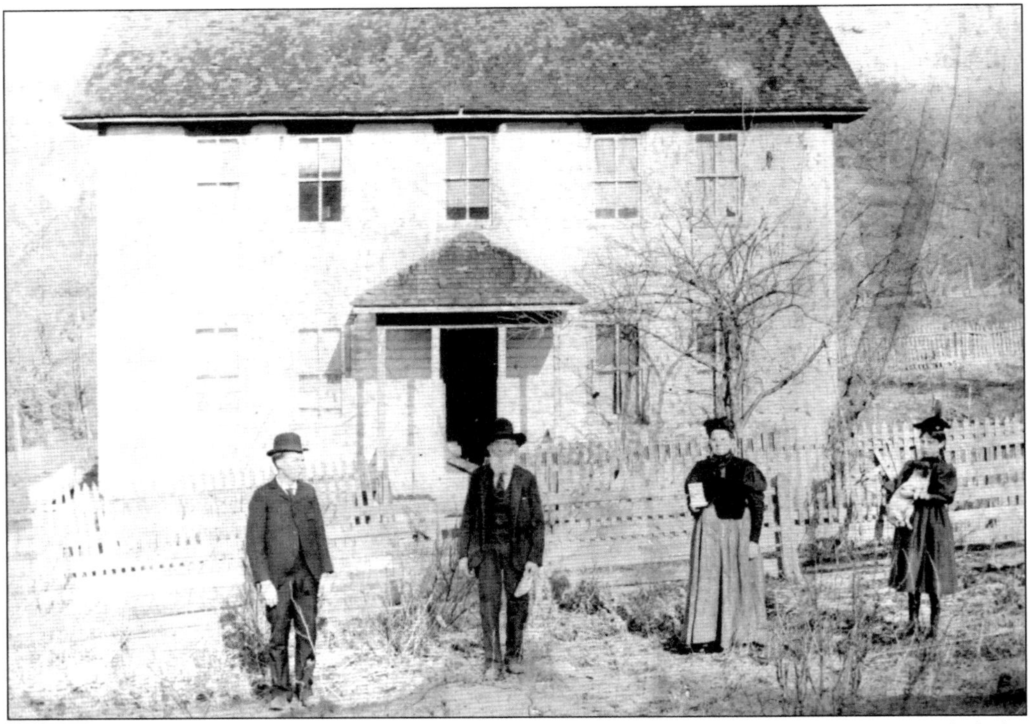

By the 1880s, many Johnstown families had attained a fine standard of living that included a nice home and attire of proper fashion. Having a large home also gave the woman of the house the option of taking in boarders to earn additional income. Yards were tidy, with picket fences to keep animals from straying into the vegetable gardens growing out back. (Courtesy of the Johnstown Area Heritage Association archives.)

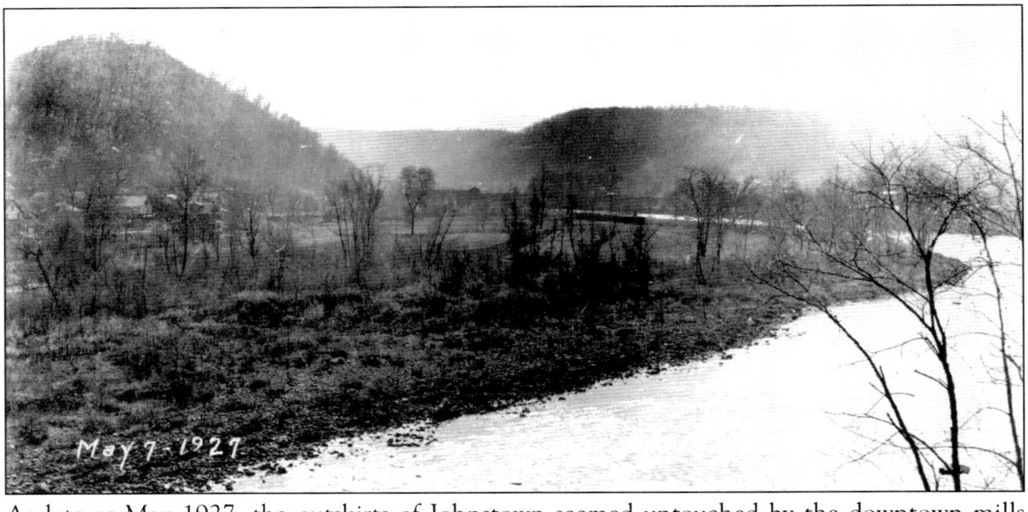

As late as May 1927, the outskirts of Johnstown seemed untouched by the downtown mills belching black smoke. In this view looking toward Riverside, the bend in the Stonycreek contains a few farmhouses and barns and appears pristine, just as it did when early settlers arrived in the area. What cannot be detected in this peaceful scene is the discoloration of the water from the industries that supported the region. (Courtesy of Jeanne D. Buck.)

Two

A Company Town

By the 1860s, Johnstown was already a company town. As the steel industry boomed, Johnstown became a powerhouse manufacturing mecca. Mining was an integral part of the steelmaking process. Railroads were built at a record pace. Skilled workers such as pattern makers, blacksmiths, and carpenters were in high demand. Later, unskilled immigrants hoping to escape the poverty of their homeland flocked to Johnstown in hopes of securing a piece of the American Dream.

Cambria Iron Company expected long hours from its workers, including back-to-back shifts. Wages were low for some of the most backbreaking and dangerous work. The struggle of Johnstown workers for and against unions became a centerpiece for the nation, and yet, in the early years, the only time the mills ceased operation was after the 1889 flood. Whether or not it was ever expressed, workers understood that they could be replaced for insubordination, accidents, or careless behavior.

In return for their loyalty and labor, workers were given health care at the nation's first company-owned hospital, which provided the best medical treatment in the area. Wood, Morrell and Company served as the company store for Cambria Iron employees, offering a wide variety of items for outright purchase or on credit. Lorain Steel Company sponsored summertime picnics for employees and family members.

Probably the most important relationships, though, were forged between the workers themselves. Together, they created a unit for the good of the company. Sons followed fathers into the workforce, often in the same mill or mine.

Creative individuals such as William Kelly, who invented the Kelly converter to improve the strength of steel, were fostered in this atmosphere. Improving production, speed, and quality were as important as production quantities. No matter the job, employees met the challenges before them and took great pride in their work.

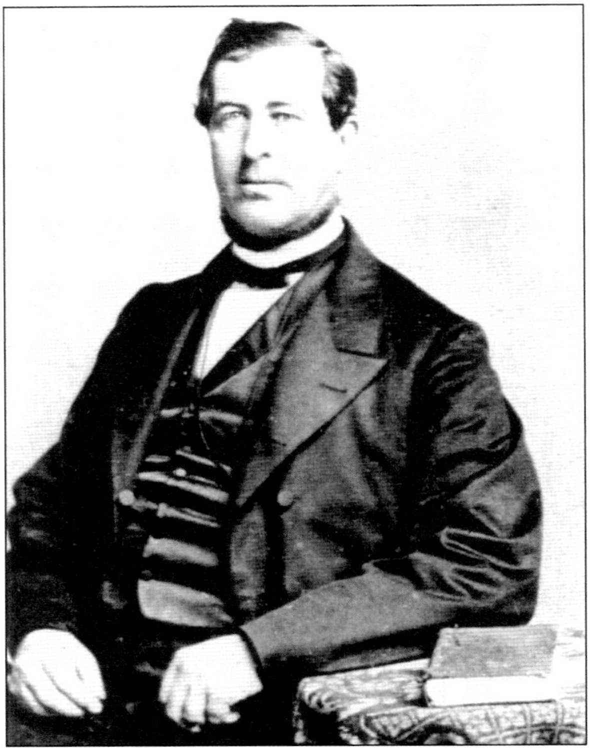

At 34 years old, Daniel J. Morrell became general manager of the floundering Cambria Iron Company in 1855. He navigated Cambria toward profitability, becoming a major player in Johnstown and steel for 30 years. A faithful Quaker, Morrell had a hard-driving toughness that angered some. On the other hand, he took risks, like providing William Kelly space for conducting secret experiments with a converter, that mirrored the Bessemer steelmaking process. Morrell served in Congress, representing steel interests, and thus protected the mills back home. (Courtesy of the Johnstown Area Heritage Association archives.)

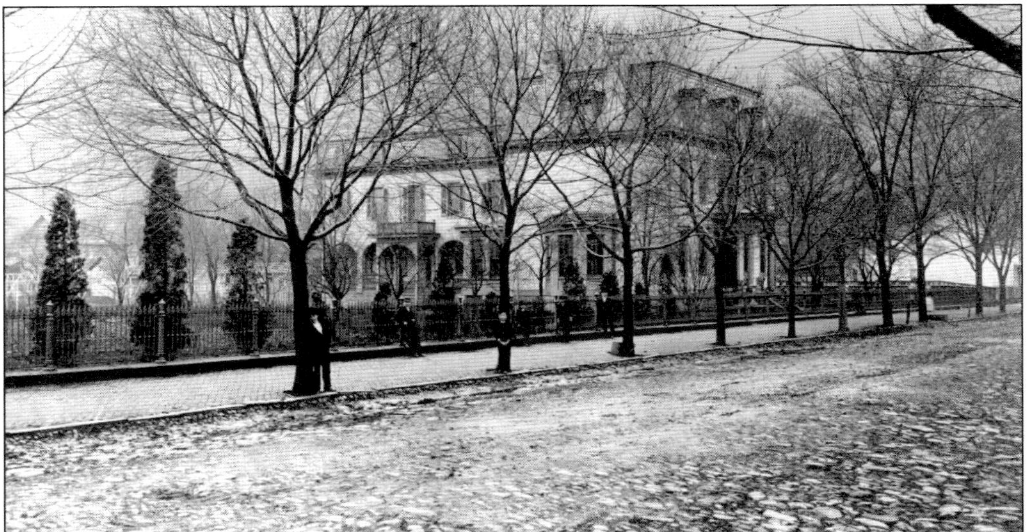

Daniel J. Morrell's home sprawled along lower Main Street on the site of the current public library. Surrounded by an elaborate iron fence and bordered by brick sidewalks, the place certainly befitted a man of his stature. Its mansard rooftop is barely visible behind trees and lush landscaping. Morrell died in 1885, four years before the great flood washed through Johnstown's downtown. He was buried in Sandyvale Cemetery. The Morrell Circle at Grandview Cemetery now serves as a resting place for the family. (Courtesy of the Johnstown Area Heritage Association archives.)

William Kelly invented the Kelly converter *c.* 1855. His discovery allowed steel to be made more economically without damaging the core product's strength or integrity. This process rivaled the Bessemer method of steelmaking founded in England around the same time. (Courtesy of the Johnstown Area Heritage Association archives.)

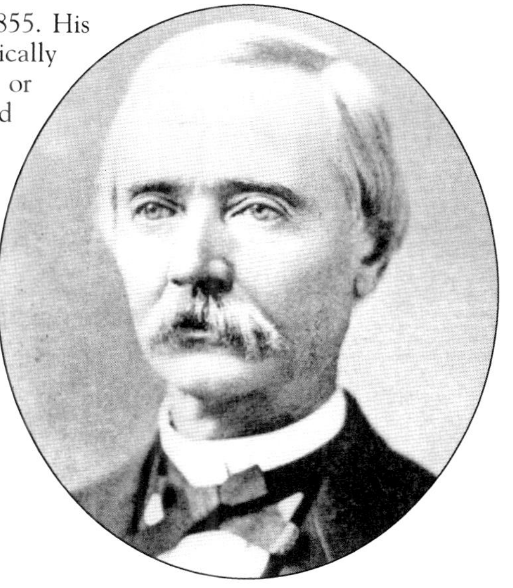

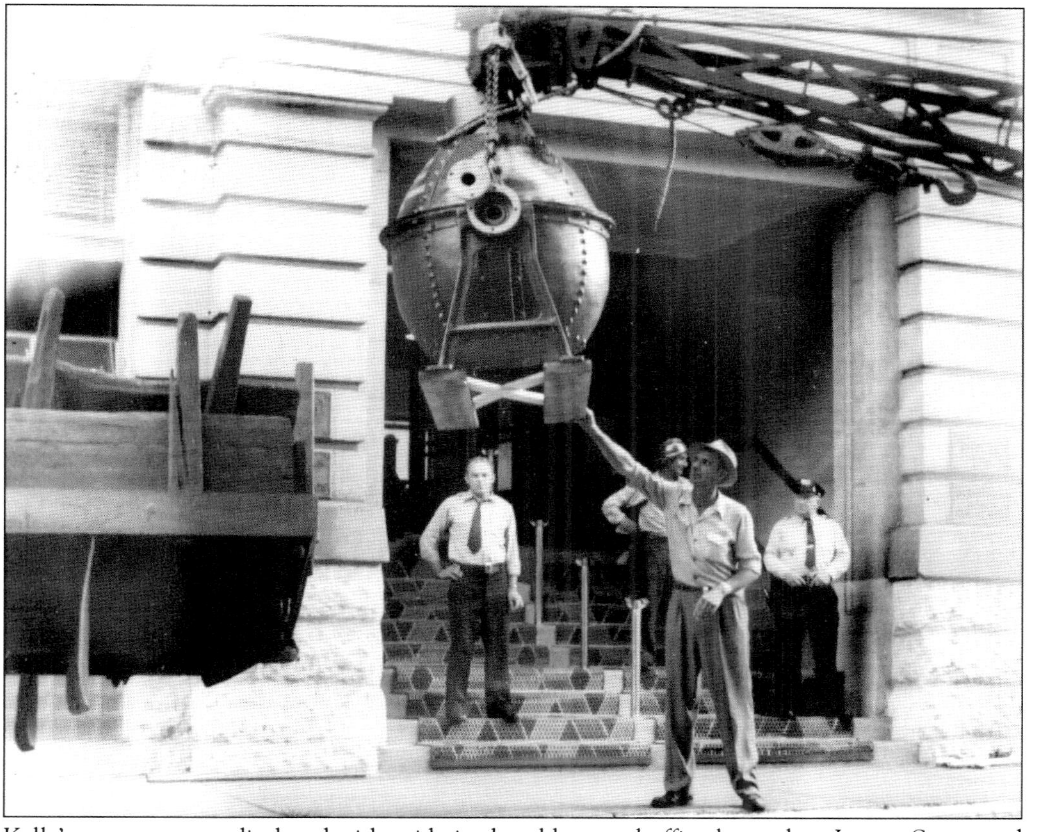

Kelly's converter was displayed with pride in the old general office located on Locust Street and then at the new general office at Walnut Street *c.* 1954. After Bethlehem Steel closed the offices in Johnstown, the converter was moved to the Smithsonian Institution in Washington, D.C. (Courtesy of the Johnstown Area Heritage Association archives.)

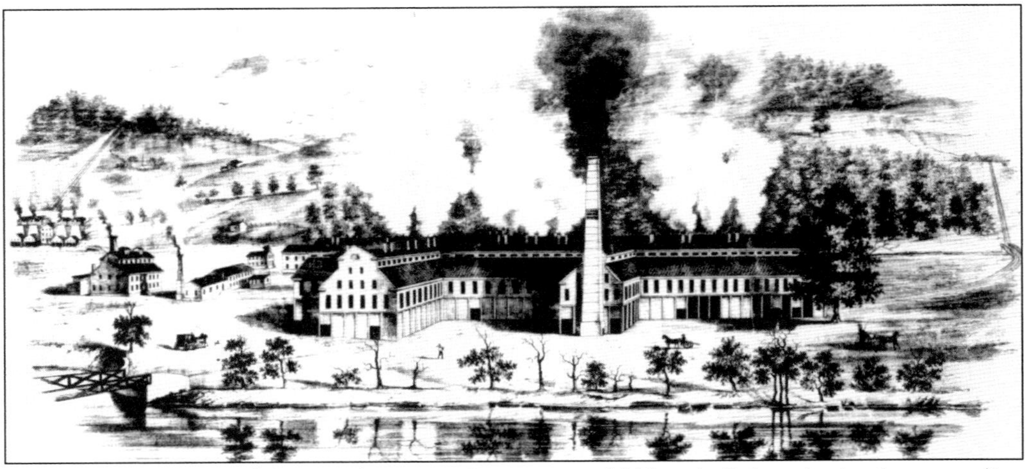

An artist's rendering of the Cambria Iron Company c. 1860 embellishes the land surrounding the mill with groves of healthy pine trees and lush landscaping. Only one stack of the rolling mill appears to spew a black trail of smoke generated by the business of making iron. The truth of life in a steel mill city is far from this idealized image, but no one complained. The bottom line was that Johnstown depended on the mills as much as the mills depended on Johnstown. (Courtesy of the Johnstown Area Heritage Association archives.)

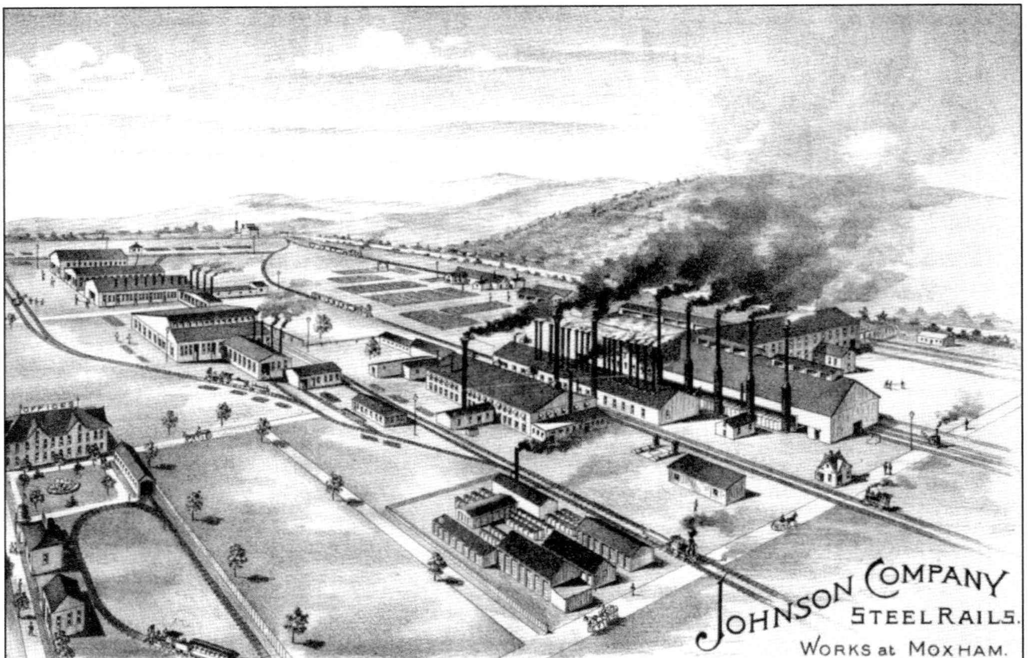

Johnson Steel Street Rail Company was the forerunner of the United States Steel Corporation plant in Moxham. Johnstown's budding reputation for innovation in the steel industry attracted companies like Johnson, which required special adjustments for the manufacture of its products. Management at Cambria Iron Company accepted these challenges, taking on tasks that other nationally known steel producers rejected. (Courtesy of the Johnstown Area Heritage Association archives.)

This closeup of one of Cambria Iron's six blast furnaces c. 1885 provides an insider's view of the 75-foot-high stack. (Courtesy of the Johnstown Area Heritage Association archives.)

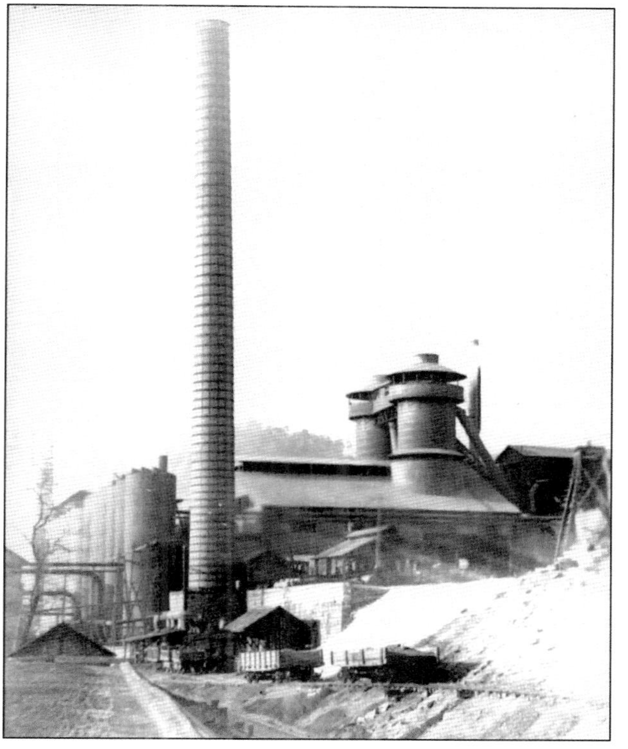

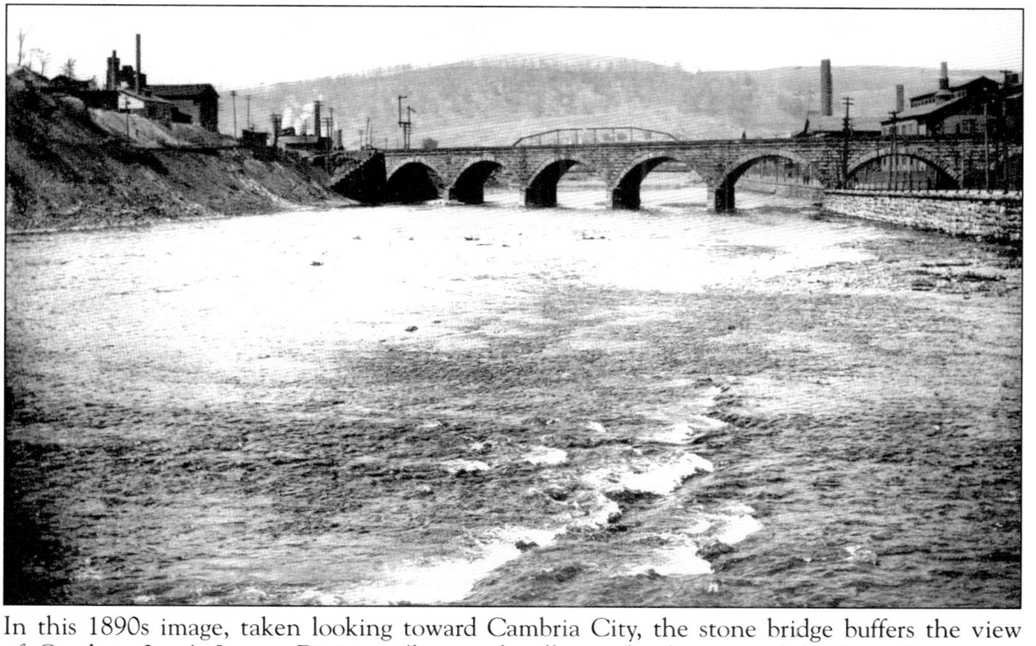

In this 1890s image, taken looking toward Cambria City, the stone bridge buffers the view of Cambria Iron's Lower Division (known locally as the lower works). According to an engineering report, the stones used on this bridge were harvested from a quarry at Mineral Point. One side of the bridge is now covered with concrete. (Courtesy of the Cambria County Historical Society.)

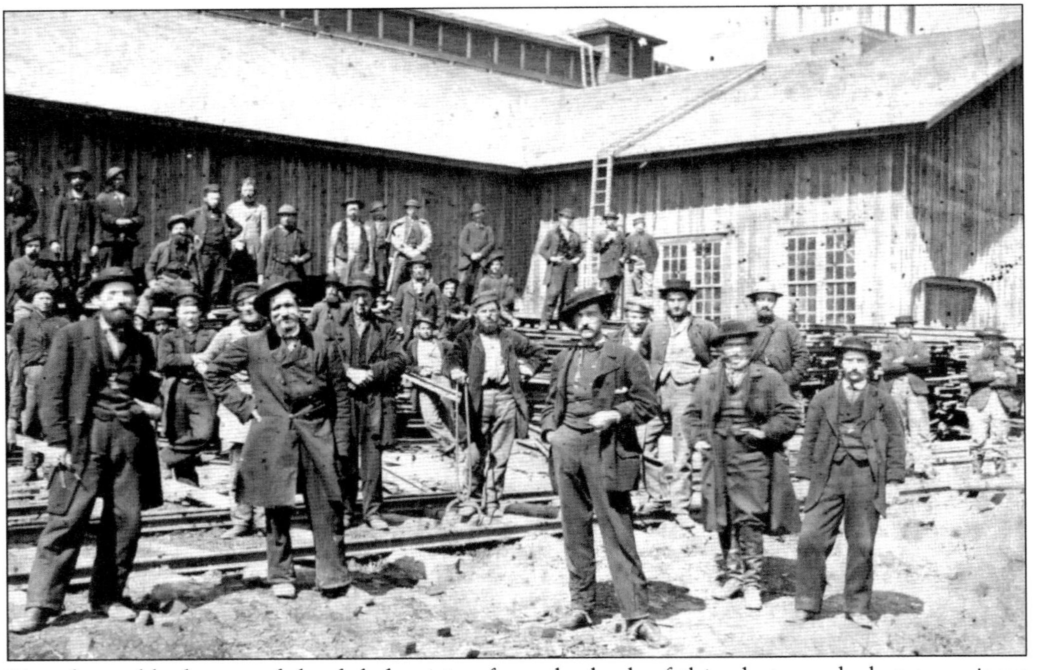

Time has robbed most of the faded writing from the back of this photograph, but two pieces of information are evident. First, this is a crew from the rolling mills in 1864, and second, it is likely that many of these men had returned to their jobs after serving in the Civil War. (Courtesy of the Cambria County Historical Society.)

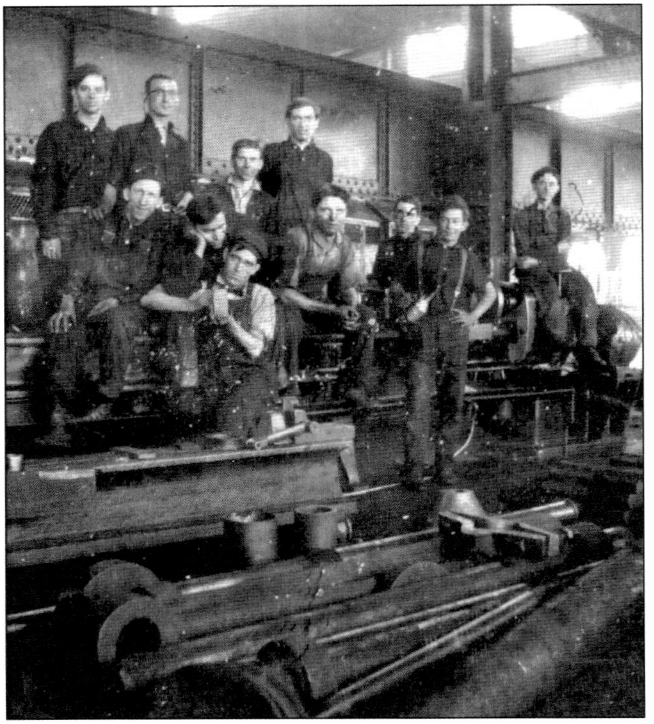

In this 1910 photograph, workers from the second-floor machine shop of the Cambria Steel Company, located near the Cambria City bridge, sit among the tools of their trade. (Courtesy of the Cambria County Historical Society.)

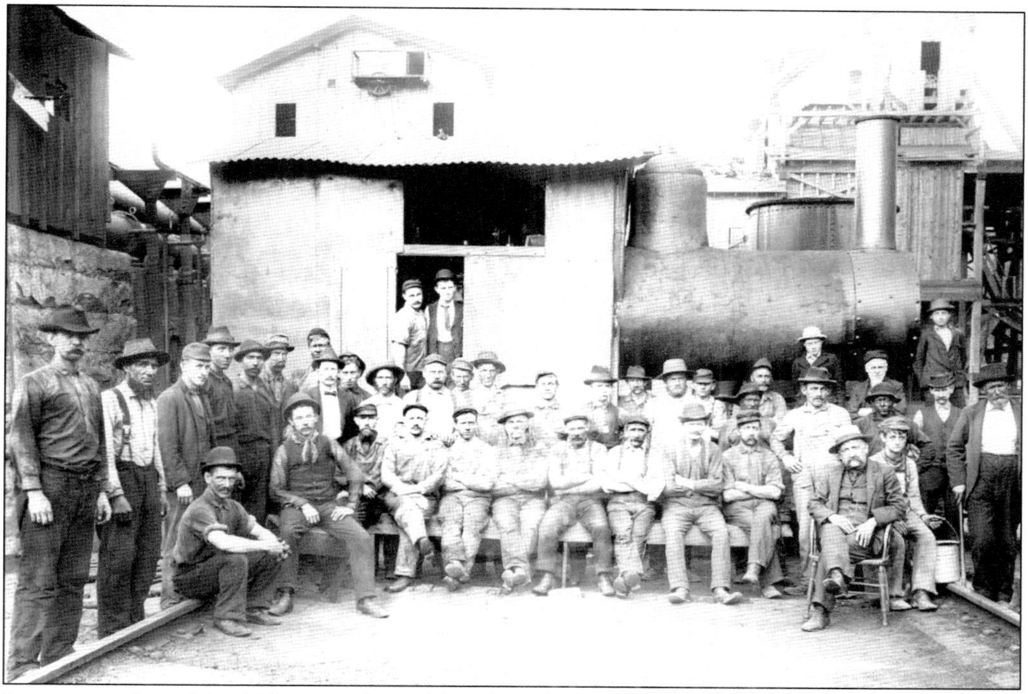

In crews such as this, shift mates formed bonds with one another. The work and camaraderie is apparent as the men stop to pose for a photograph. (Courtesy of the Johnstown Area Heritage Association archives.)

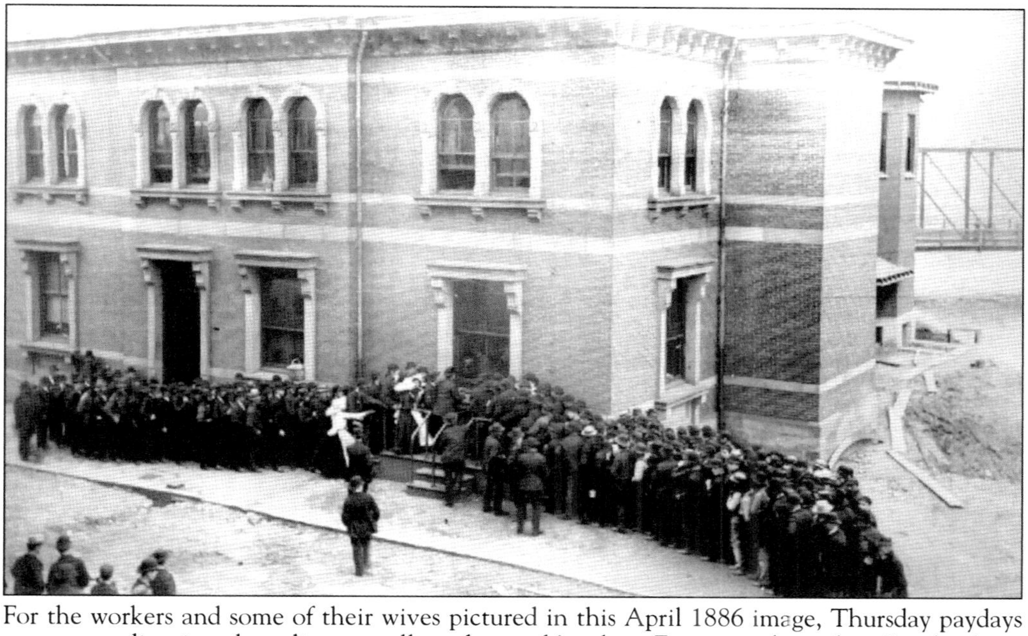

For the workers and some of their wives pictured in this April 1886 image, Thursday paydays meant standing in a long line to collect the week's salary. Everyone dressed in Sunday best. Wives often collected their husband's pay to circumvent a potential binge at a local pub. (Courtesy of the Johnstown Area Heritage Association archives.)

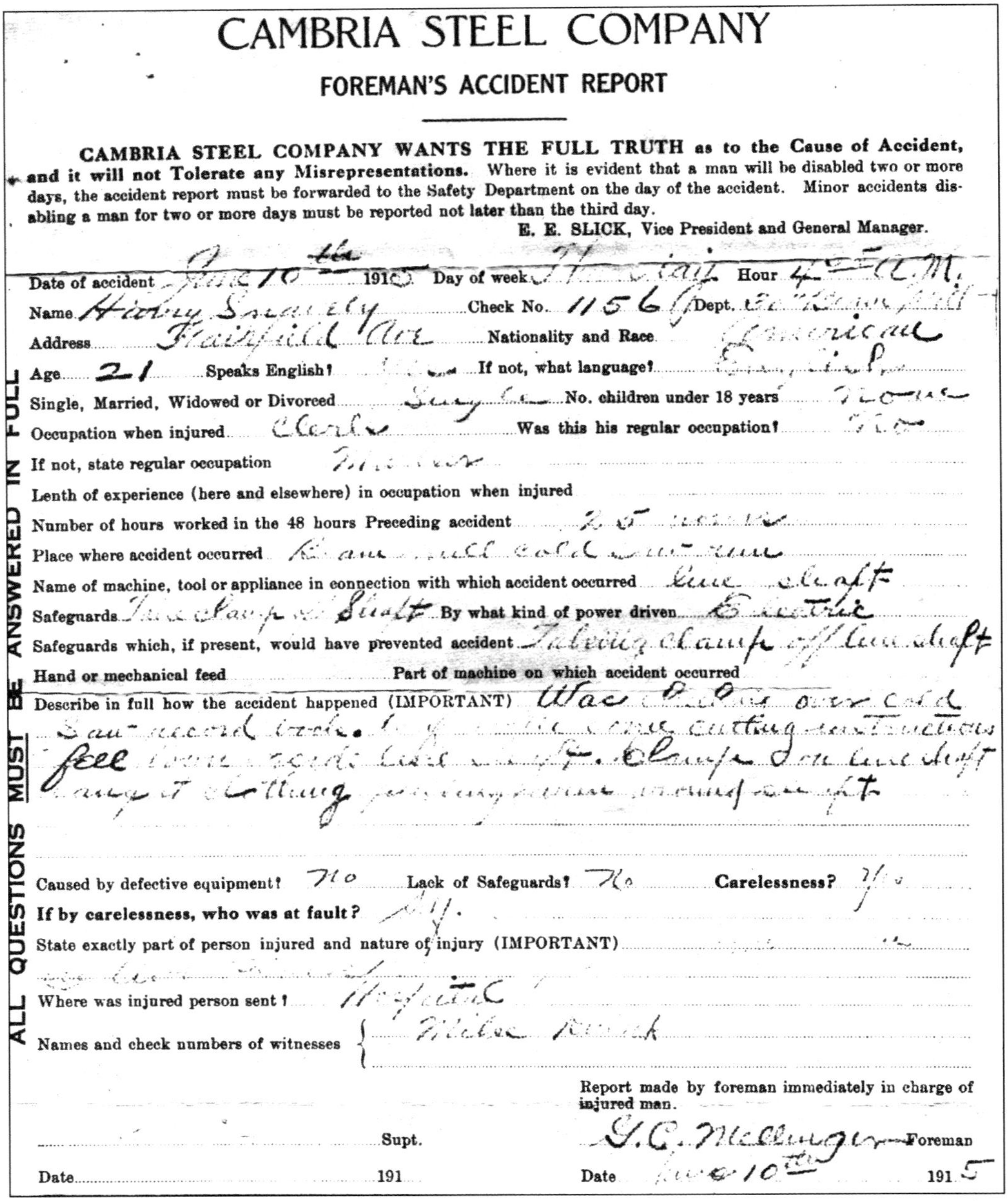

CAMBRIA STEEL COMPANY

FOREMAN'S ACCIDENT REPORT

CAMBRIA STEEL COMPANY WANTS THE FULL TRUTH as to the Cause of Accident, and it will not Tolerate any Misrepresentations. Where it is evident that a man will be disabled two or more days, the accident report must be forwarded to the Safety Department on the day of the accident. Minor accidents disabling a man for two or more days must be reported not later than the third day.

E. E. SLICK, Vice President and General Manager.

ALL QUESTIONS MUST BE ANSWERED IN FULL

Date of accident June 10th 1915 Day of week Thursday Hour 4 A.M.

Name Harry Snavely Check No. 1156 Dept.

Address Fairfield Ave Nationality and Race American

Age 21 Speaks English? If not, what language? English

Single, Married, Widowed or Divorced Single No. children under 18 years None

Occupation when injured Clerk Was this his regular occupation? No

If not, state regular occupation

Lenth of experience (here and elsewhere) in occupation when injured

Number of hours worked in the 48 hours Preceding accident

Place where accident occurred

Name of machine, tool or appliance in connection with which accident occurred

Safeguards By what kind of power driven Electric

Safeguards which, if present, would have prevented accident

Hand or mechanical feed Part of machine on which accident occurred

Describe in full how the accident happened (IMPORTANT)

Caused by defective equipment? No Lack of Safeguards? No Carelessness? Yes

If by carelessness, who was at fault?

State exactly part of person injured and nature of injury (IMPORTANT)

Where was injured person sent? Hospital

Names and check numbers of witnesses

Report made by foreman immediately in charge of injured man.

Supt.

G. C. Mellinger Foreman

Date 191 Date June 10th 1915

Dated June 10, 1915, this faded official accident report from the Cambria Steel Company makes it perfectly clear that the company will "not tolerate any misrepresentations" regarding on-the-job injury. Harry E. Snavely, a 21-year-old worker, must have felt intimidated as his foreman filled out the form indicating that the injury to Snavely's hand was due to his own carelessness. Actually, during his shift as a clerk that day, Snavely noticed a notebook of important data had fallen into a chute and he reached to retrieve it. At that moment, another worker activated a machine that caught Snavely's hand. Snavely was treated at the company hospital. Injured men feared that accidents deemed to be the result of personal carelessness would cost them not only their health but also their job. (Courtesy of Robert Snavely.)

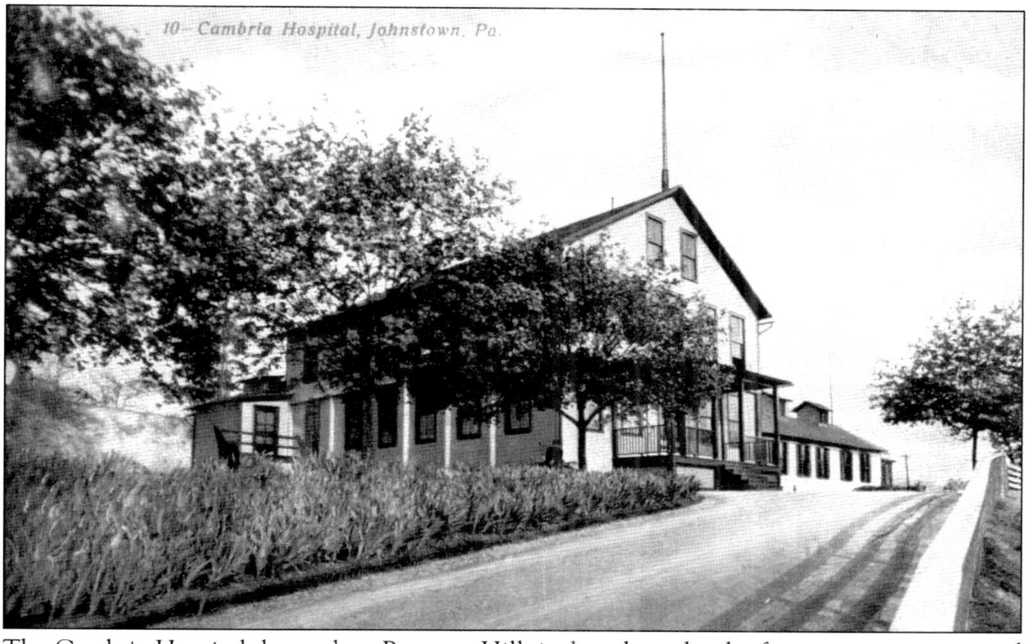

The Cambria Hospital, located on Prospect Hill, is thought to be the first company-sponsored hospital in the nation. Here, Cambria Iron Company employees were treated for a variety of injuries, including broken bones and burns. This was the only hospital in the community until Memorial Hospital was built after the 1889 flood. (Courtesy of the Cambria County Historical Society.)

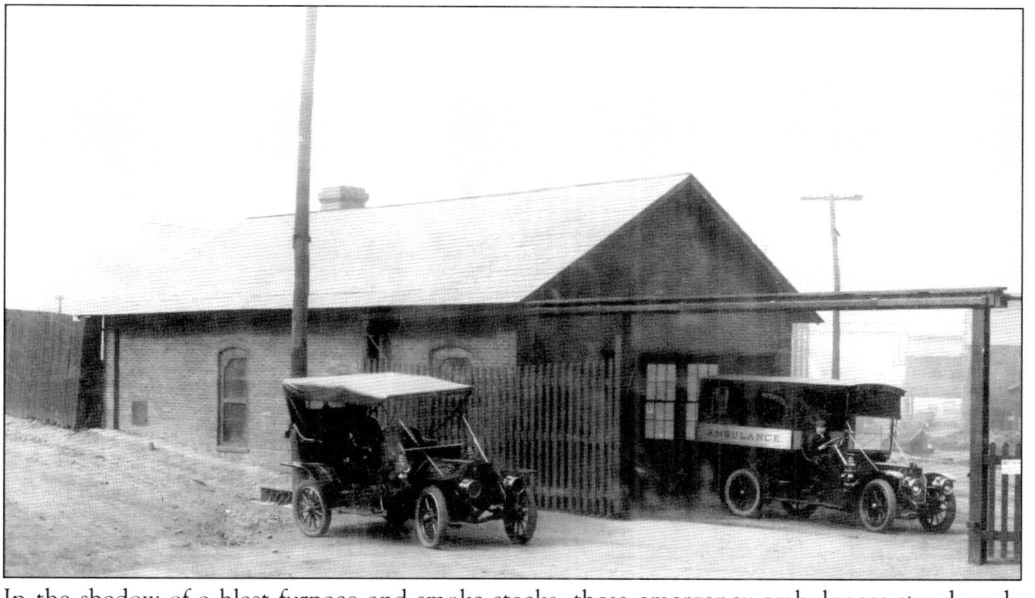

In the shadow of a blast furnace and smoke stacks, these emergency ambulances stand ready to transport injured workers to the hospital in 1911. The vehicles were more formally called Cambria Steel Company safety appliances. Considering the hazardous work, a fast response to an accident call could mean the difference between life and death. (Courtesy of the Johnstown Area Heritage Association archives.)

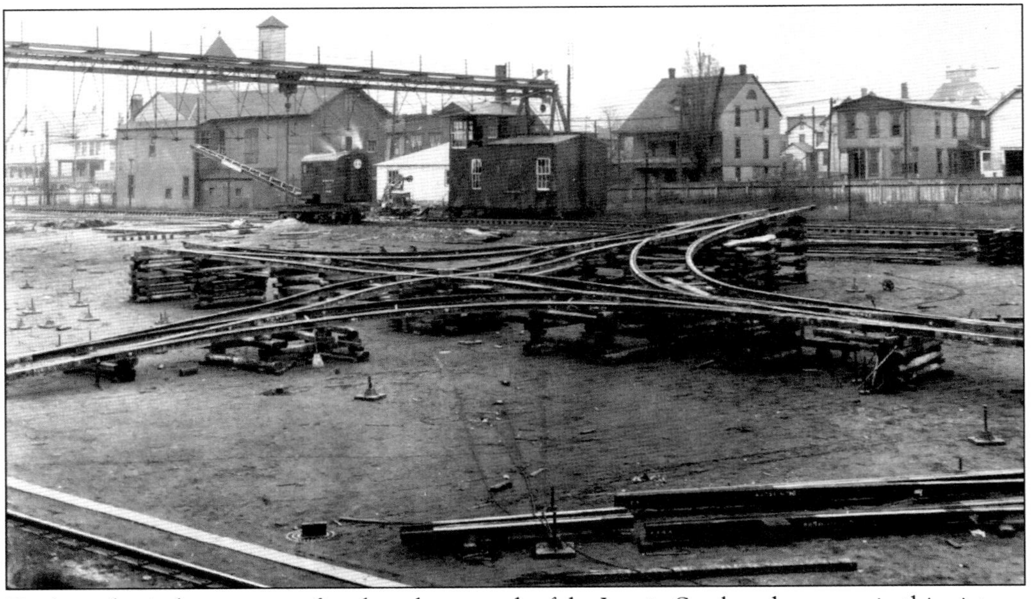

Tracks and switches were test fitted on the grounds of the Lorain Steel yards, as seen in this picture, taken along Central Avenue in the Moxham section of town. (Courtesy of Jeanne D. Buck.)

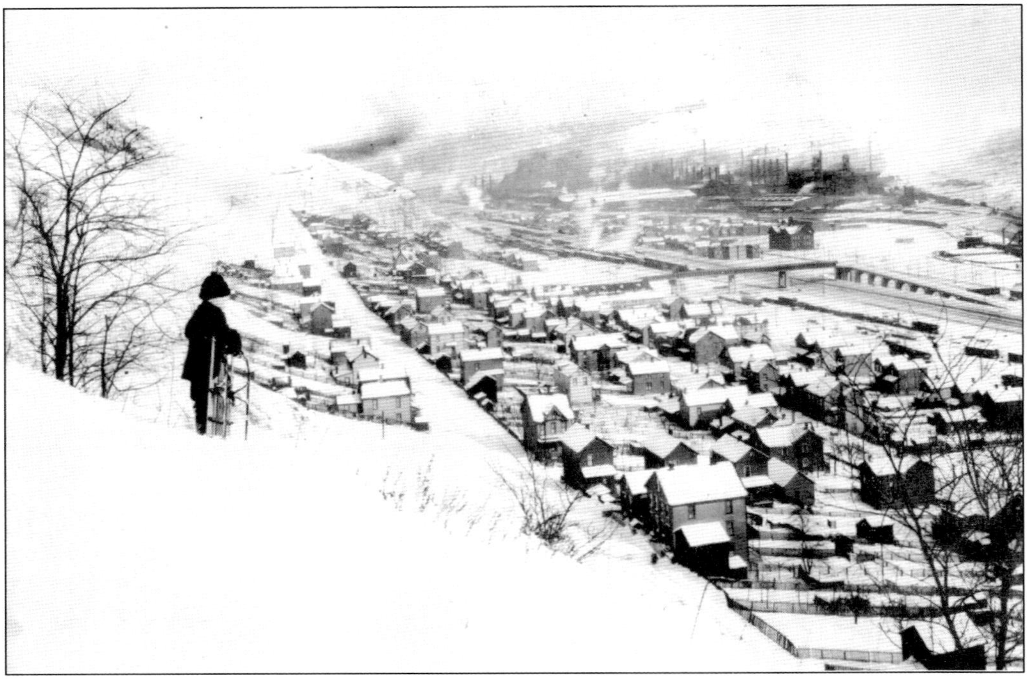

What mother would like to see her child standing on a hilltop with a sled in hand? This daredevil, *c.* 1919, scans the snow-covered roofs of the Woodvale neighborhood, looking toward the steel mills in the distance. The Johnstown Bethlehem Steel Gautier Division held the contract, per purchase order T330, to produce exclusively all sled runners for Flexible Flyers until March 10, 1973. It is a guess as to whether or not this chap tested his Flexible Flyer on the hill that day. (Courtesy of the Johnstown Area Heritage Association archives.)

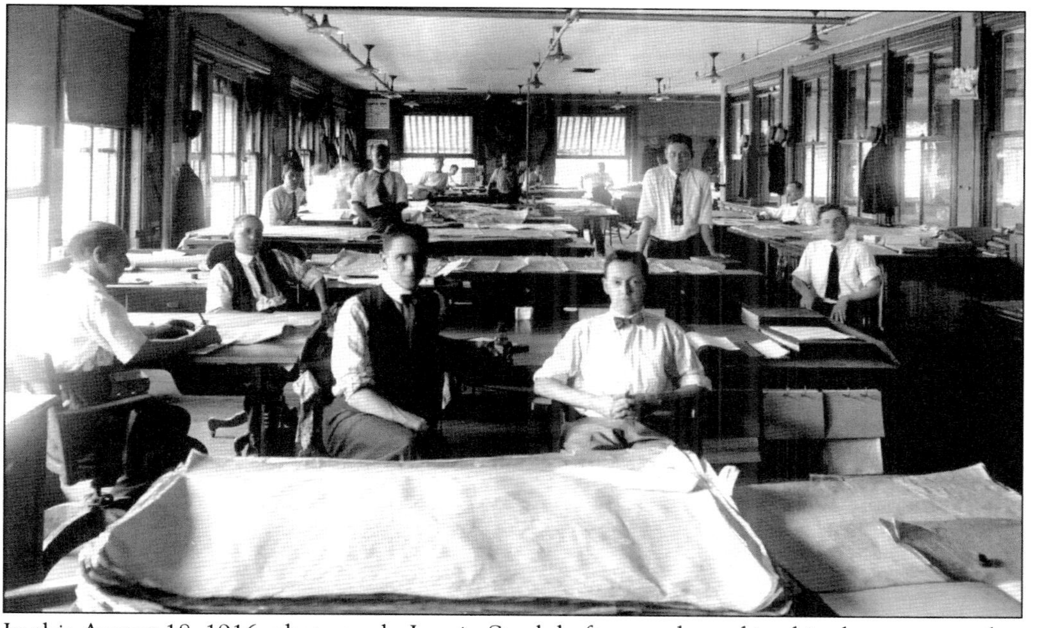

In this August 18, 1916, photograph, Lorain Steel draftsmen, dressed in shirtsleeves to combat the summer heat, appear to be taking a break from their craft. Their workroom seems well ventilated by open windows and brightly lit by overhead lights. The conditions in this office are a far cry from those endured by the workers in the steaming mills who were assigned to construct the projects designed by these young men. (Courtesy of the Johnstown Area Heritage Association archives.)

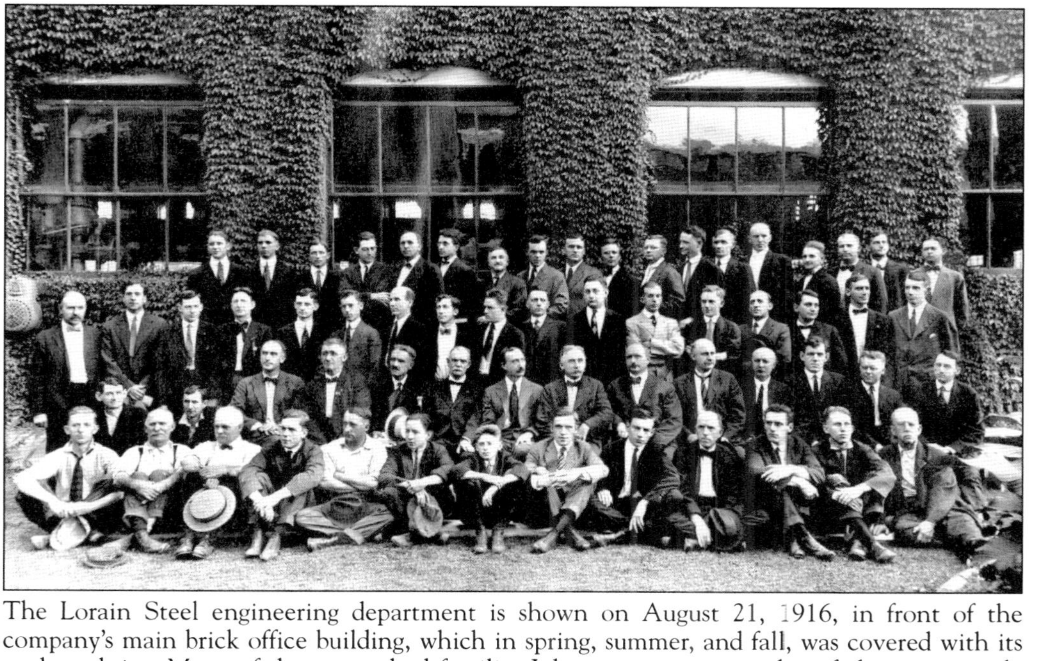

The Lorain Steel engineering department is shown on August 21, 1916, in front of the company's main brick office building, which in spring, summer, and fall, was covered with its trademark ivy. Many of these men had familiar Johnstown names, as their fathers were early pioneers in the area. (Courtesy of Jeanne D. Buck.)

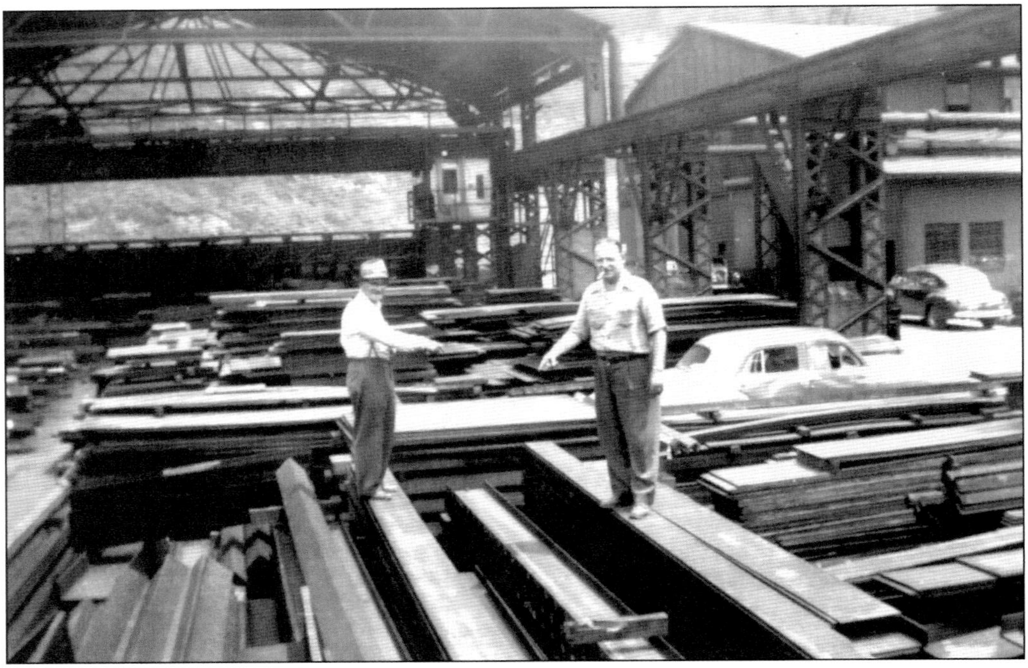

Foremen from the boiler shop and the roof shop inspect beams in the boiler stockyard of Bethlehem Steel in 1959. (Courtesy of Robert Snavely.)

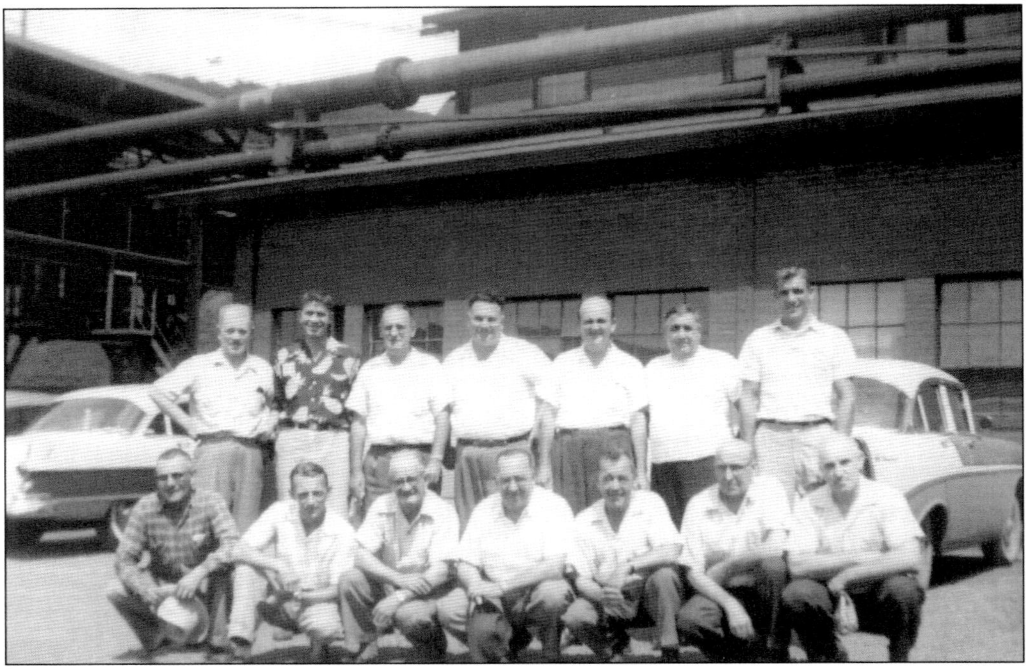

The boiler shop foreman and office clerks of Bethlehem Steel's stockyard pose for a photograph in the 1950s. The faces and clothing are much different from those of workers at the beginning of this chapter. Chances are excellent that these men are second- and third-generation steelworkers, since it was common practice to follow fathers to work in the mill. (Courtesy of Robert Snavely.)

Photographed on May 3, 1927, this idle coal tipple serviced a vital coal vein under Hogback. The Johnstown and Stonycreek Railroad transported coal mined here to the United States Steel plant in Moxham. (Courtesy Jeanne D. Buck.)

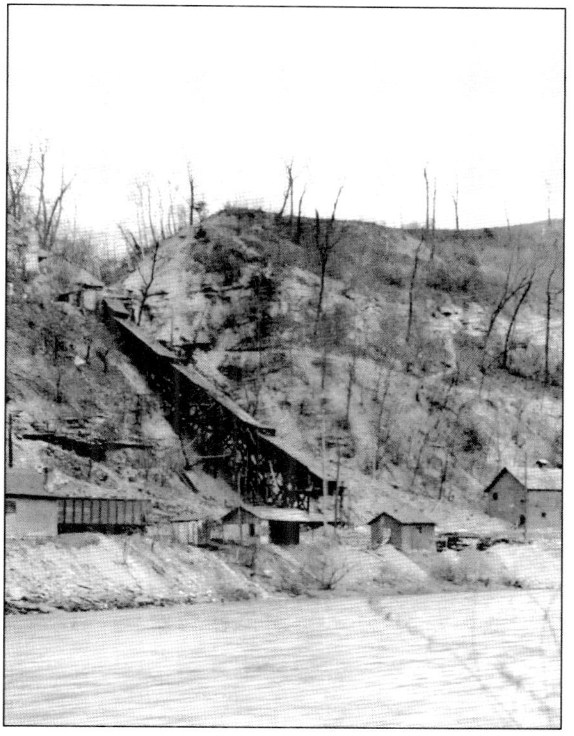

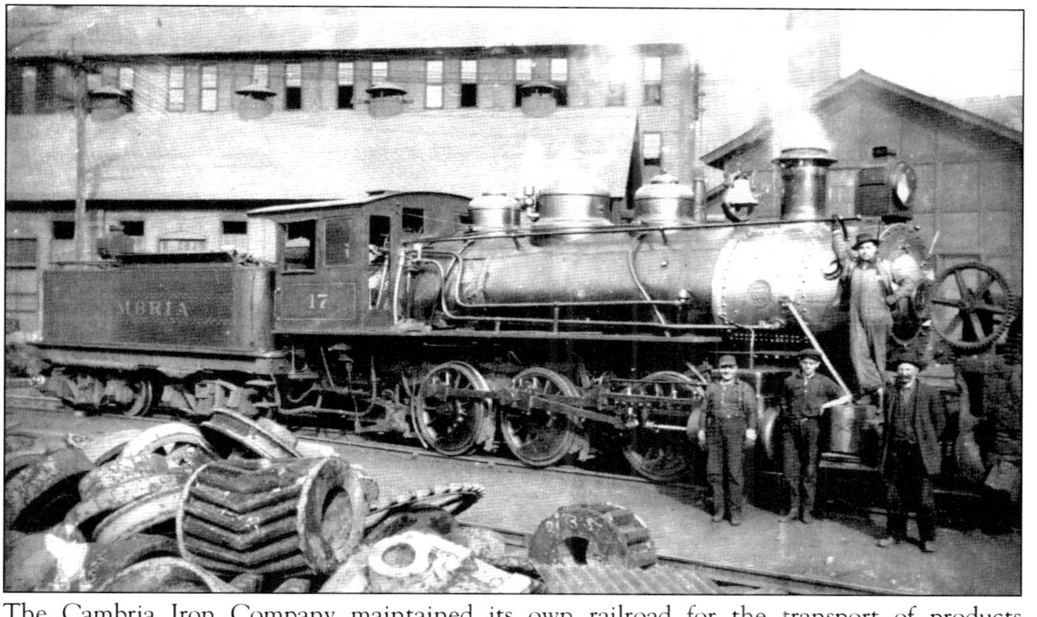

The Cambria Iron Company maintained its own railroad for the transport of products throughout the plant. Here, a crew from the Cambria Railroad poses in front of an engine and tender (coal car) at the Gautier Division. (Courtesy of the Johnstown Area Heritage Association archives.)

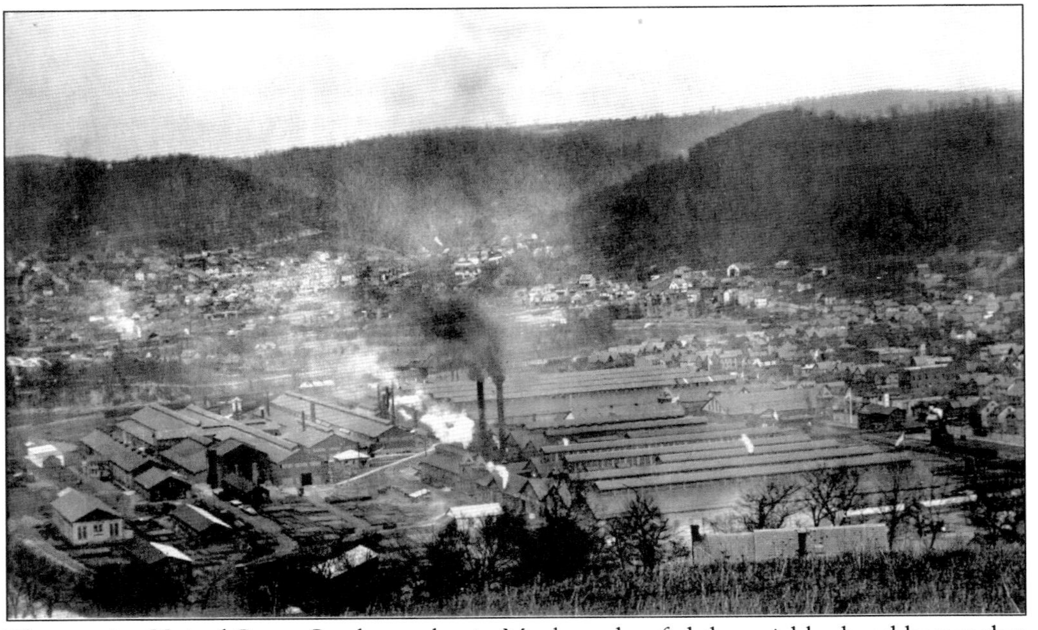

The massive United States Steel complex in Moxham dwarfed the neighborhood homes that surrounded it. Women often started their mornings by sweeping ash from their porches, trying to minimize the tracking of black dust into their homes. (Courtesy of Jeanne D. Buck.)

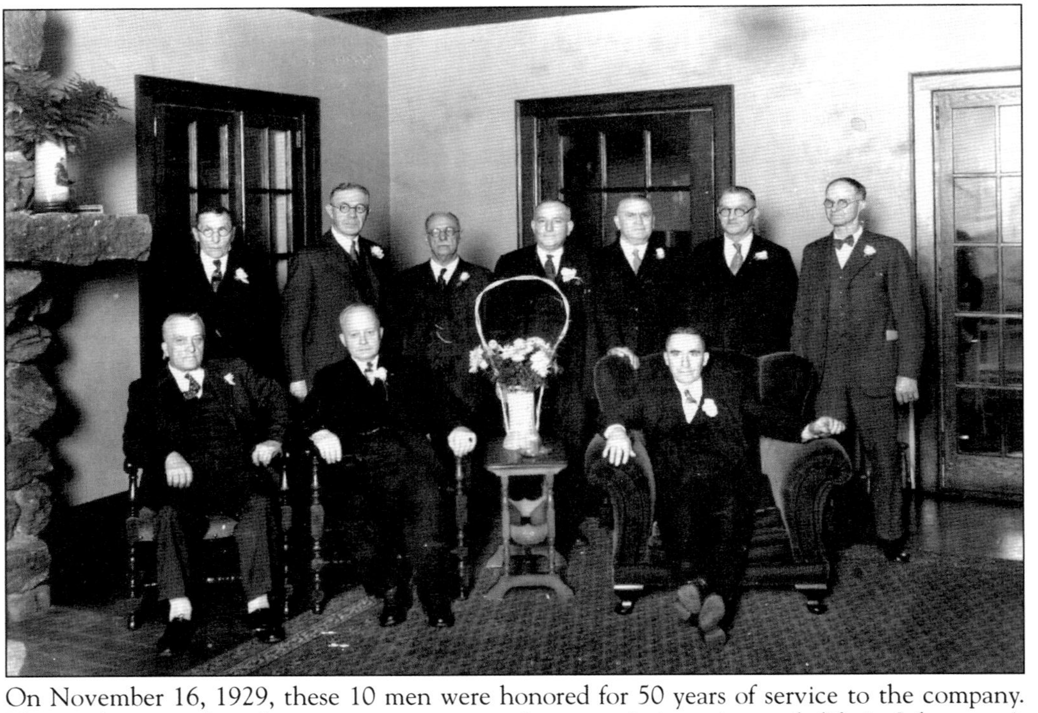

On November 16, 1929, these 10 men were honored for 50 years of service to the company. Those who started working as young men easily spent their entire work life in Johnstown's factories, mills, and coal mines. Becoming a company lifer is no longer a luxury in today's workforce. (Courtesy of the Johnstown Area Heritage Association archives.)

The Lorain Steel Company and Johnstown and Stonycreek Railroad hosted a summer picnic for employees and their families. Besides the usual food, music, and games, this ninth annual outing, in August 1927, featured an amateur vaudeville competition for the employees' children. (Courtesy of the Johnstown Area Heritage Association archives.)

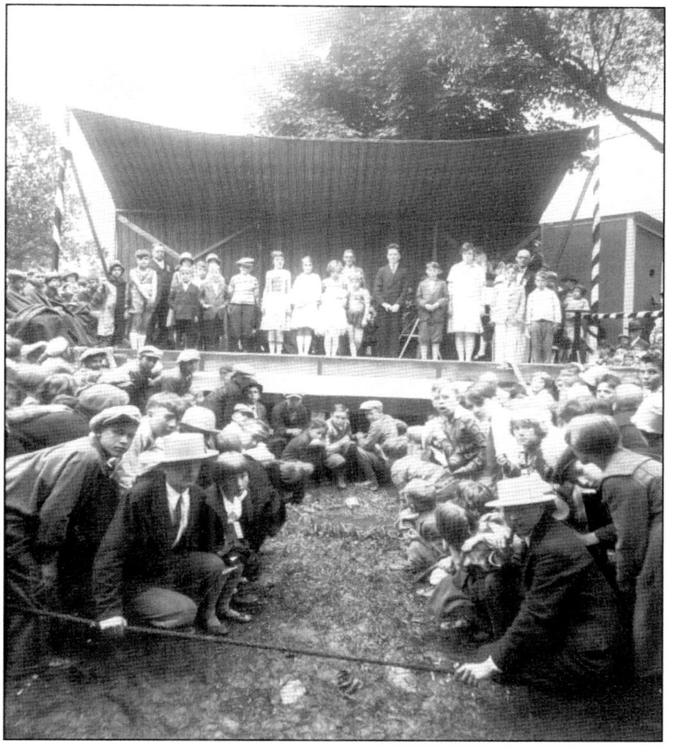

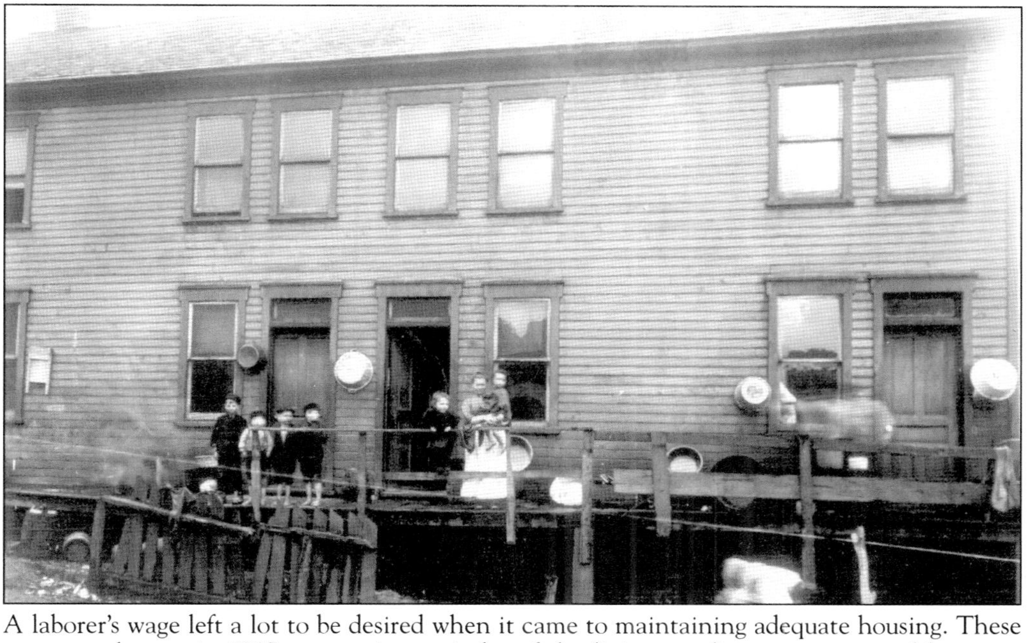

A laborer's wage left a lot to be desired when it came to maintaining adequate housing. These tenement homes in 1907 are a grim reminder of the living conditions experienced by many families in the Johnstown area. Eventually, some companies built neighborhoods of two-family and single-family homes for workers to rent or own. (Courtesy of the Johnstown Area Heritage Association archives.)

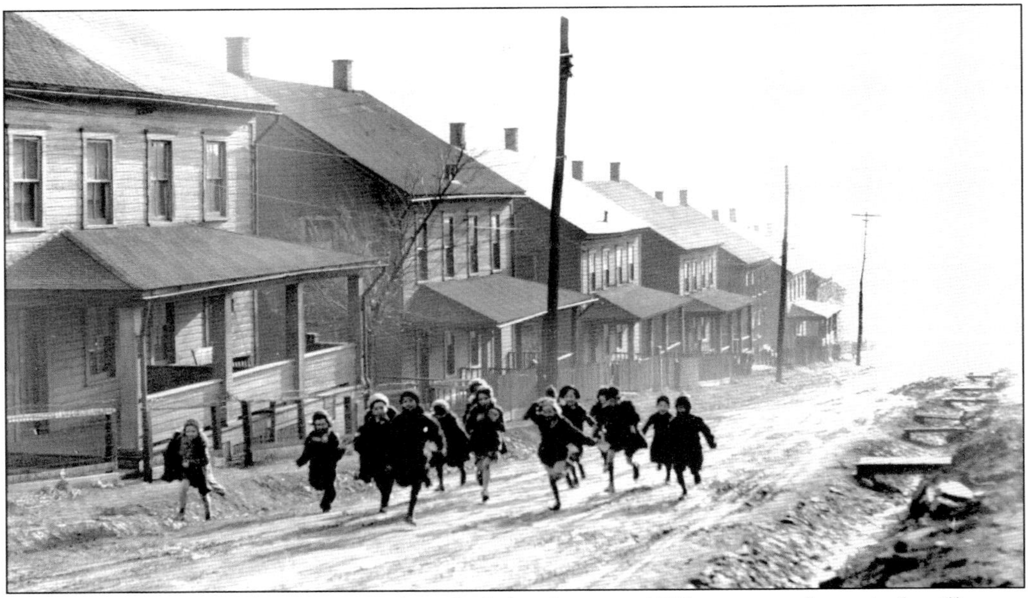

Photographer Frederick W. Ritter identified this January 1938 scene as "a typical mill town street on the hillside along the factories of Johnstown Pennsylvania." Perhaps these children, dashing up a muddy hillside, have just been dismissed from school. Note the wooden planks that serve as sidewalks across the gutters. These duplex residences were often shared by relatives living side by side. The nuclear family was healthy and strong in Johnstown. (Courtesy of the Cambria County Historical Society.)

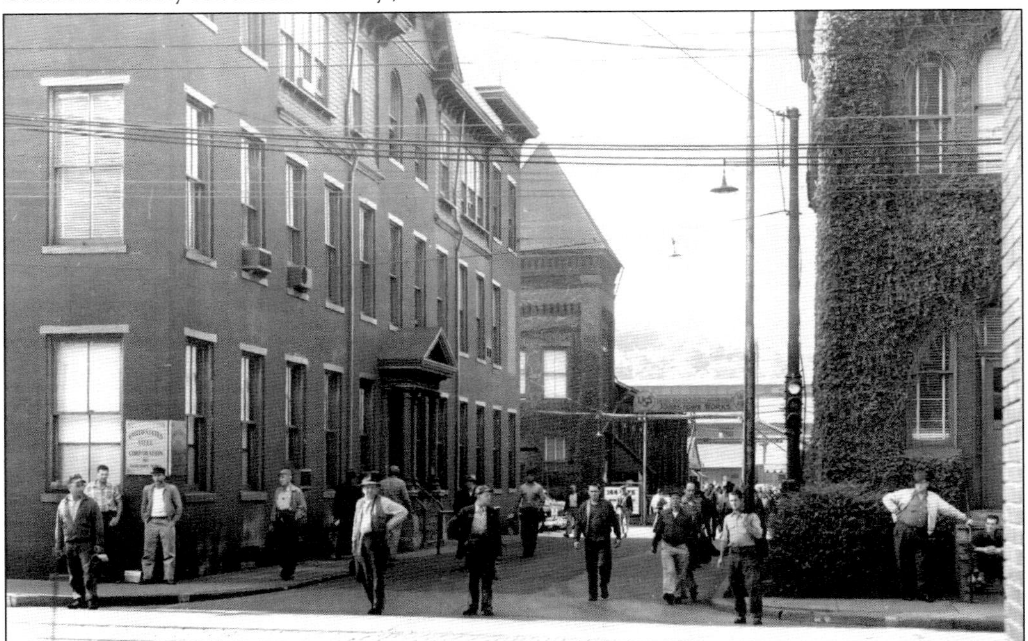

A midday shift change from the United States Steel plant was heralded by a sharp whistle, sending these 1950s workers home for some family time before returning to the heat, noise, and danger of the mill. (Courtesy of Park O. Cover, Cover Studio.)

Three

EDUCATION AND RELIGION

Immigrants came to the new world clinging to their religion. Since they spoke little English and were unaware of American life and culture, the church was the glue that held them together as a community. To entice overseas workers, major steel companies offered immigrants the guarantee of land for their churches. This practice created entire sections of Johnstown, such as Cambria City, built around the towering spires and ringing bells of European-style churches. In the elaborately decorated sanctuary of their church, the immigrants could speak in their native tongue and comfortably practice customs their families had celebrated for generations. Although wages were low and money was tight, many immigrants saved to send their children to parochial school so that the family could maintain its language and a connection to their homeland.

Johnstown's early population prized education, although a high-school education was rare. At the turn of the century, it was common to quit school after completing eighth grade. Joseph Johns had the foresight to create a space in his city plan for educational purposes. The first high school was built on the corner of Napoleon and Market Streets. At the height of steel production, the booming population required that more school buildings be constructed. One-room schoolhouses made way for massive buildings that sometimes resembled cathedrals of learning, sporting tall bell towers and solid brick exteriors.

After the steel industry declined and people relocated, a lack of children and funds to maintain the large, nearly empty buildings meant the closing, combining, and eventual razing of some of Johnstown's most extraordinary monuments to education. Today, a new high school sits in tribute to the town's continued commitment to provide the best education for its children.

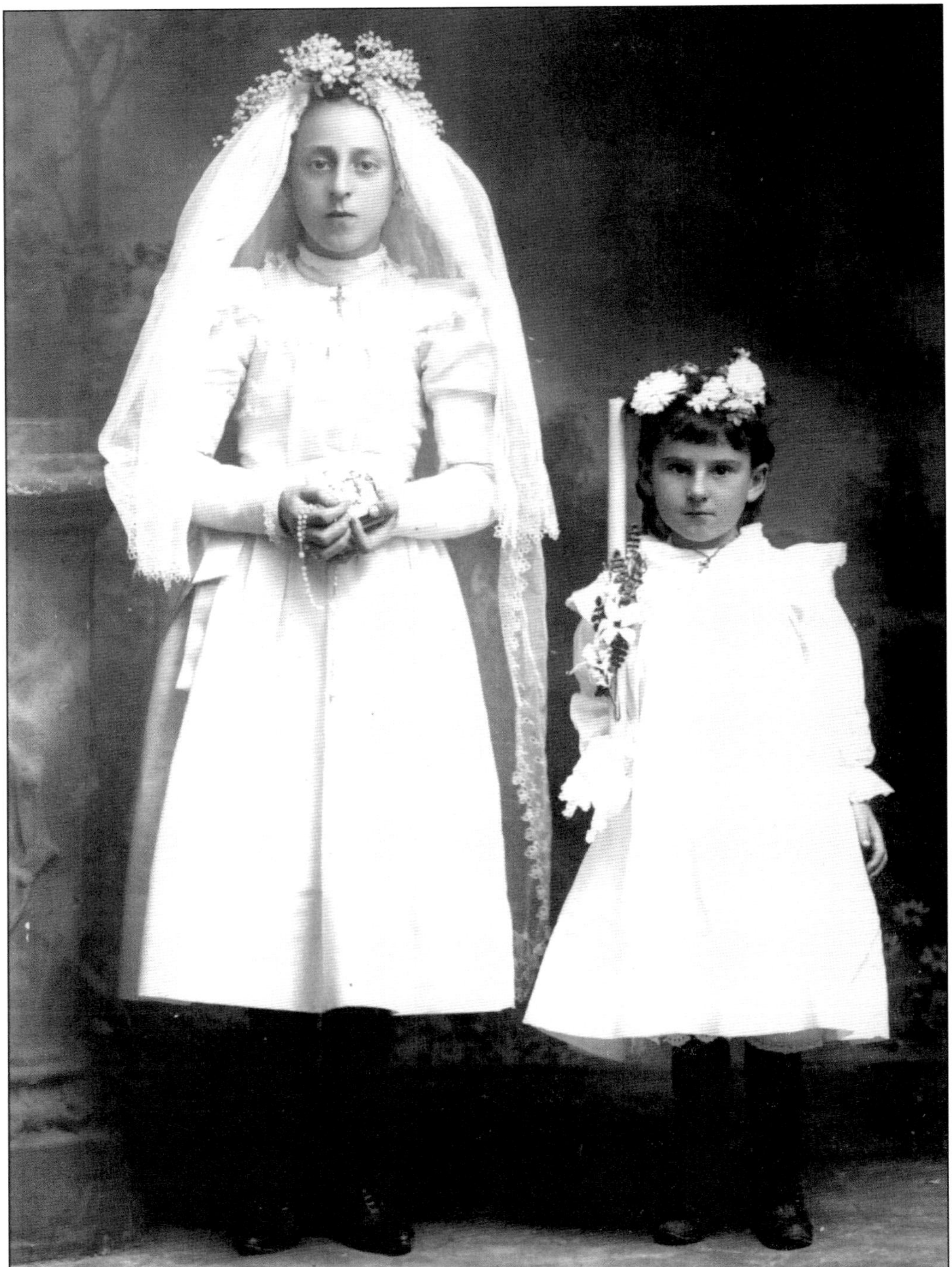

Sacraments of a first Holy Communion or formal confirmation were important holy days of celebration for immigrant families. In this photograph, taken perhaps *c.* 1880, it is obvious from their expressions that these girls understand the solemnity of the moment. (Courtesy of the Johnstown Area Heritage Association archives.)

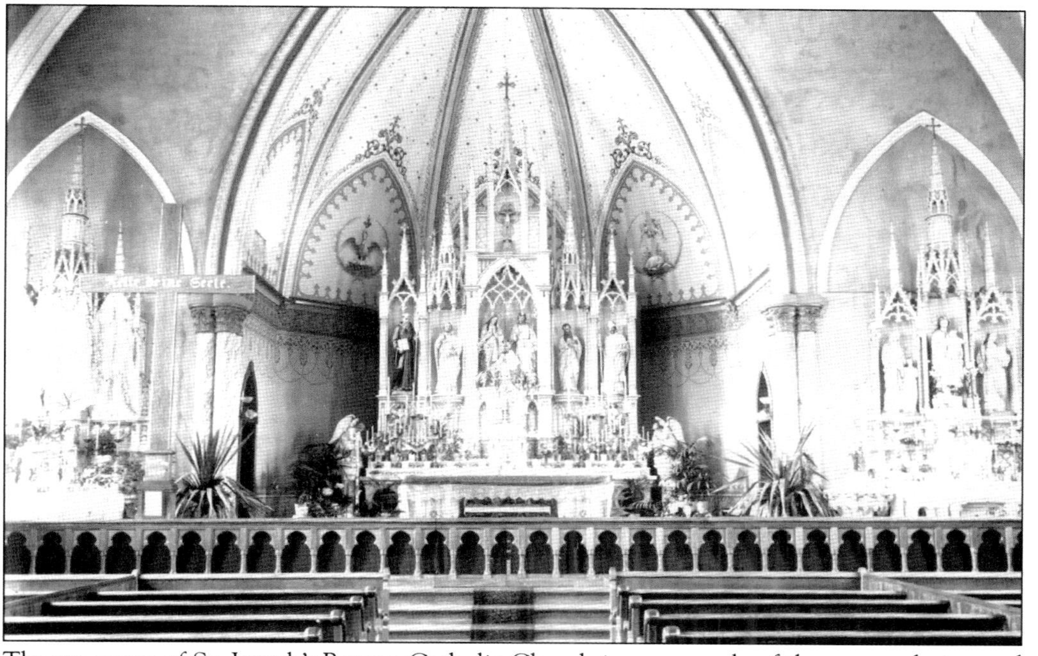

The sanctuary of St. Joseph's Roman Catholic Church is an example of the ornate design and workmanship brought to America by immigrants. The freestanding cross to the left of the altar is inscribed with the date 1897 and the German phrase *Rette deine Seele*, which means "save your soul." Church services were often conducted in the parishioners' native tongue and the Roman Catholic universal language of Latin. (Courtesy of the Johnstown Area Heritage Association archives.)

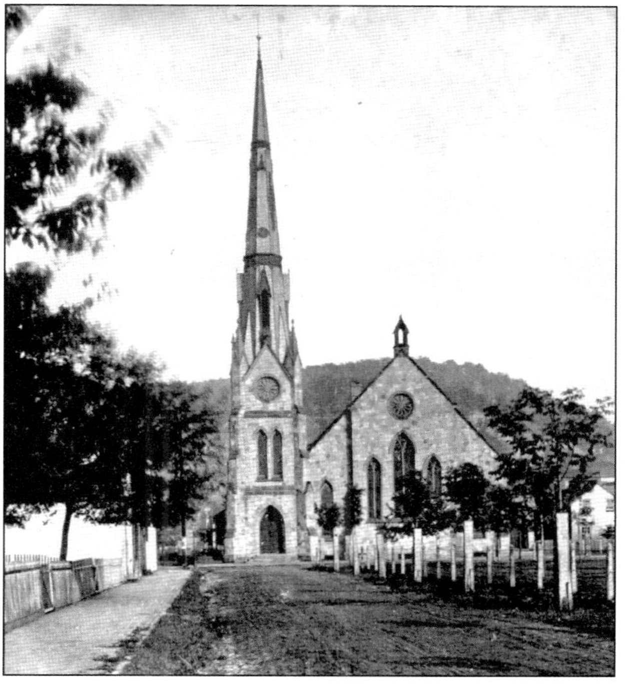

The First Methodist Episcopal Church, on the corner of Franklin and Locust Streets, can claim to have saved lives spiritually and literally. The solid construction allowed it to survive the three major Johnstown floods. Some accounts of survivors of the 1889 flood report that the building created a bottleneck of debris and water that allowed the precious seconds necessary for some citizens to escape the wave that finally enveloped the city. (Courtesy of the Johnstown Area Heritage Association archives.)

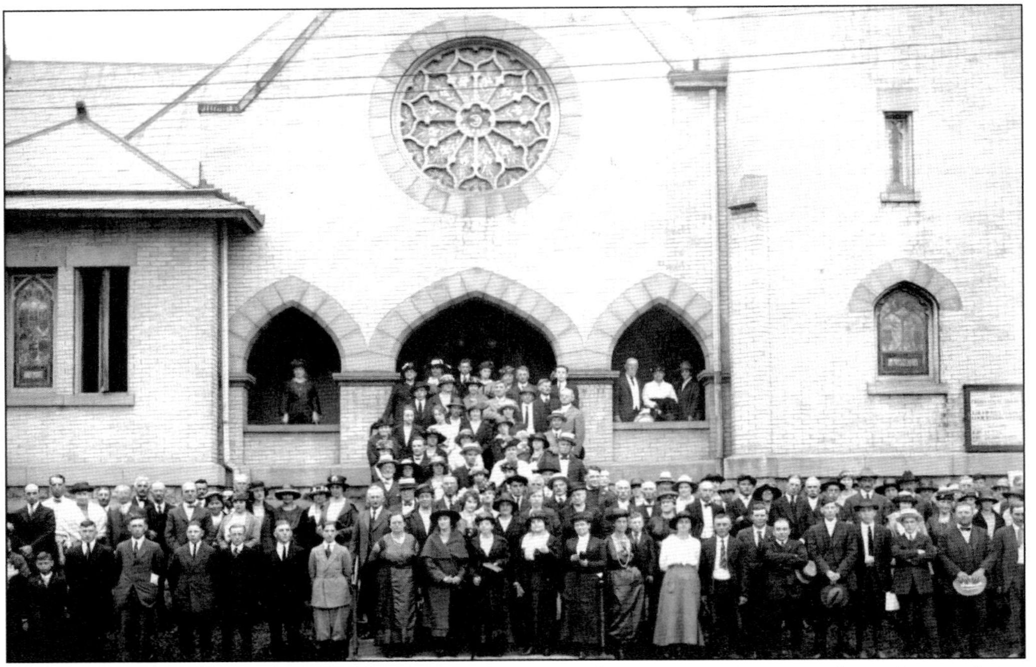

In a twist on modern church directory composites, the congregation stands in front of the First Presbyterian Church for a group photograph c. 1910. Worship services were first held in this church, at 309 Lincoln Street, in 1832. A sign on the front of the building extends an invitation for guests to attend the 9:30 a.m. Bible school and an 11:00 a.m. service on Sunday morning. (Courtesy of the Johnstown Area Heritage Association archives.)

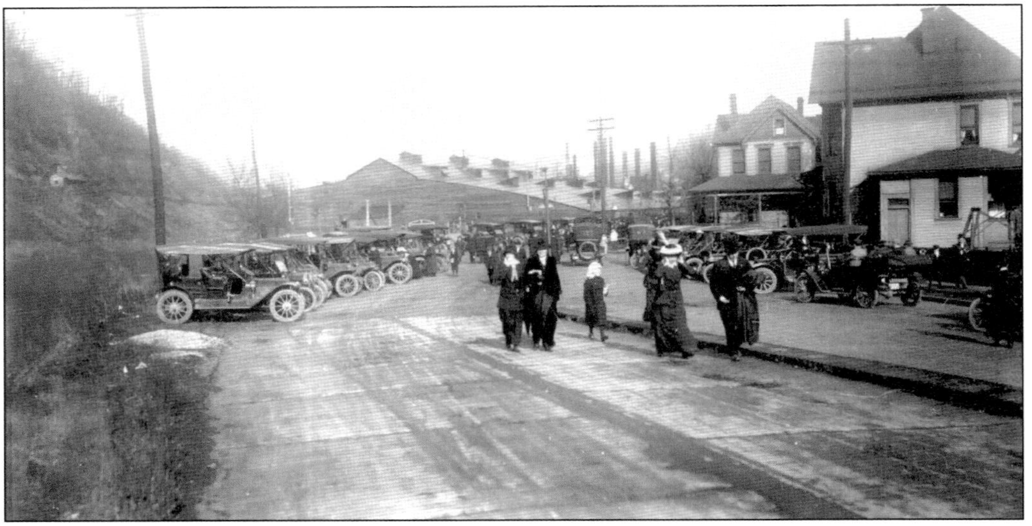

Worshipers step quickly along Johns Street on their way to Billy Sunday's tabernacle services in 1913. Newspapers reported that during Billy Sunday's six weeks in Johnstown, more than 600,000 people sat mesmerized by his evangelical trouncing of alcohol use and other "sins of the flesh." Bill Sunday's campaign is credited with spurring the formation of Johnstown's Young Women's Christian Association (YWCA). (Courtesy of the Johnstown Area Heritage Association archives.)

The Christian Home on Edson Avenue in the Eighth Ward was sponsored by area churches and provided a home atmosphere for orphans. (Courtesy of Jeanne D. Buck.)

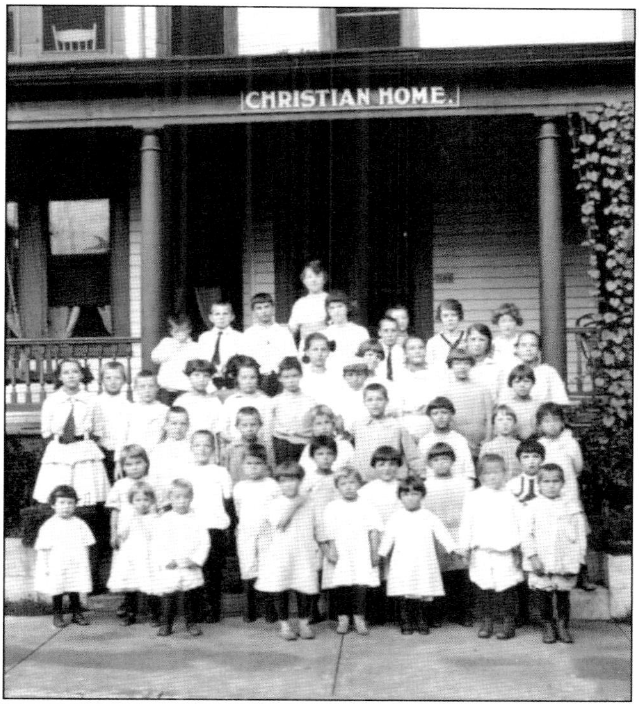

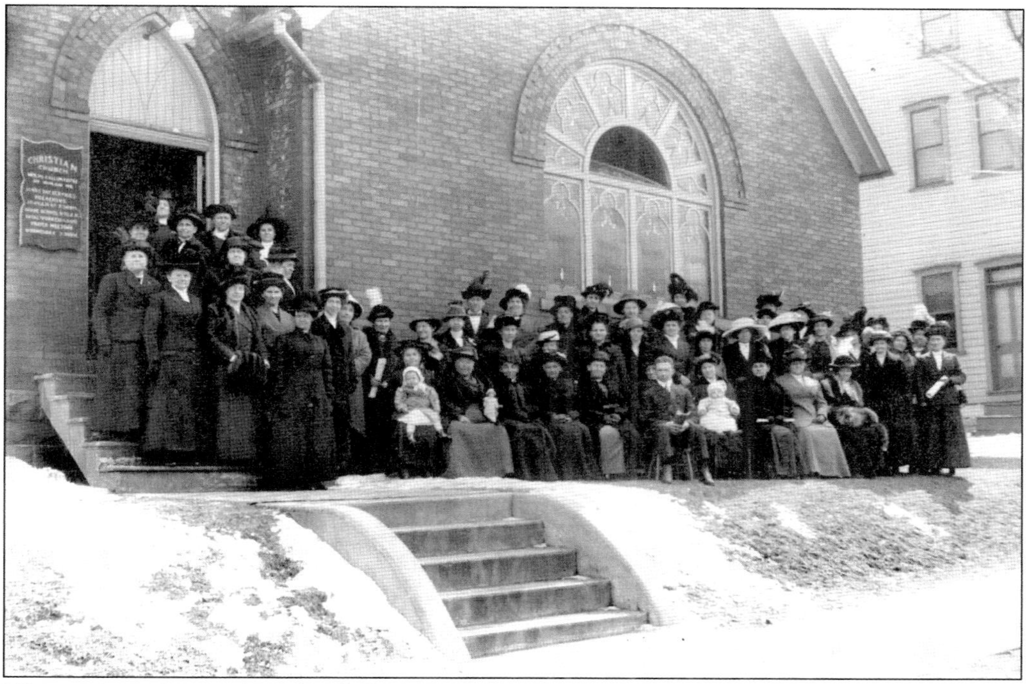

Women from the Sunday school classes of the Moxham Christian Church tolerate the cold and snow c. 1895 in order to record their image for posterity. In later years, this building was ravaged by fire; the congregation rebuilt it in the same location, the corner of Wheat Street and Cypress Avenue. (Courtesy of Jeanne D. Buck.)

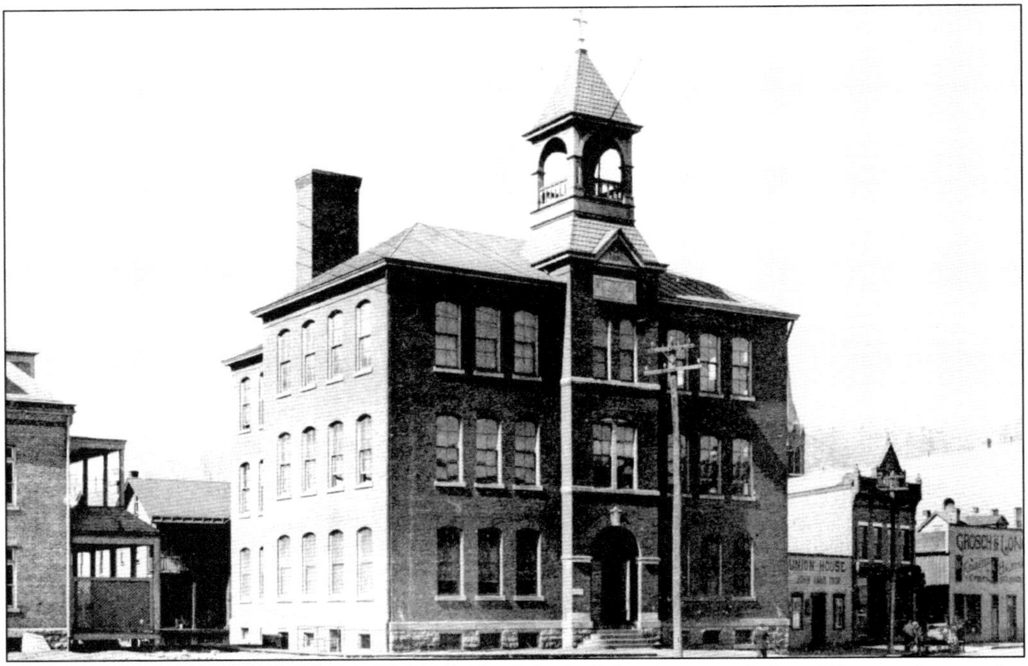

Originally a modest undertaking in 1835, St. John's School expanded rapidly, serving as the parochial school for the children of the St. John Gualbert Cathedral. The cathedral still stands at 117 Clinton Street, but this impressive three-story school building, seen here in 1895, was demolished in the 1960s. (Courtesy of the Cambria County Historical Society.)

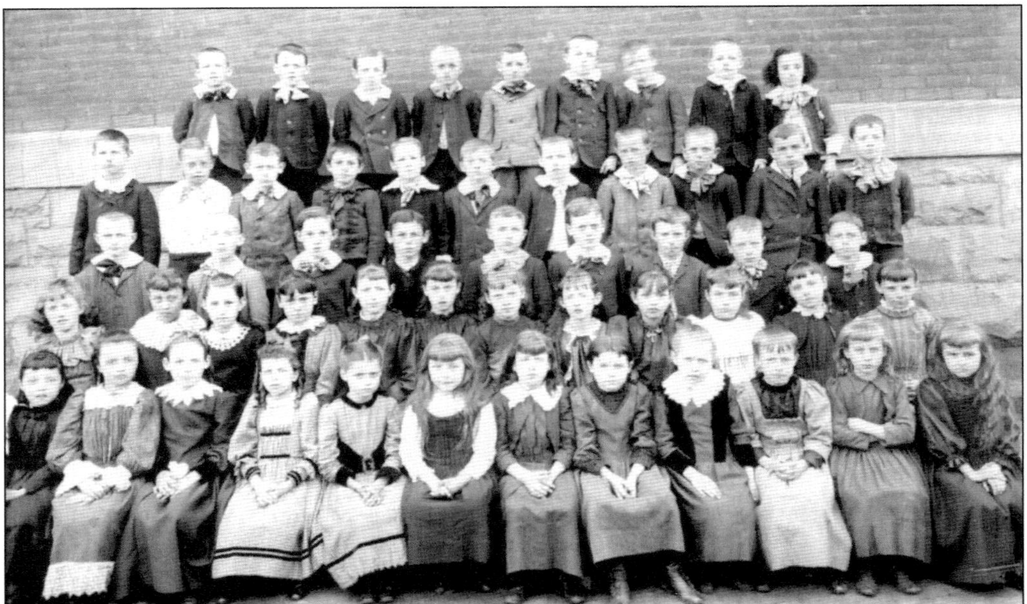

Elementary students from St. John's School break from their studies to sit for a class portrait c. the 1880s. (Courtesy of the Johnstown Area Heritage Association archives.)

St. Casimir School students stand on Power Street in 1929, waiting to march in honor of Polish-born Revolutionary War hero Gen. Casimir Pulaski. The girls' pinafores sport the Polish eagle. The school opened in 1903 and remained independent until the 1960s, when eight parochial schools combined to form West End Catholic. St. Casimir's school building now houses the Johnstown Day-Care and Head Start programs. (Courtesy of the Johnstown Area Heritage Association archives.)

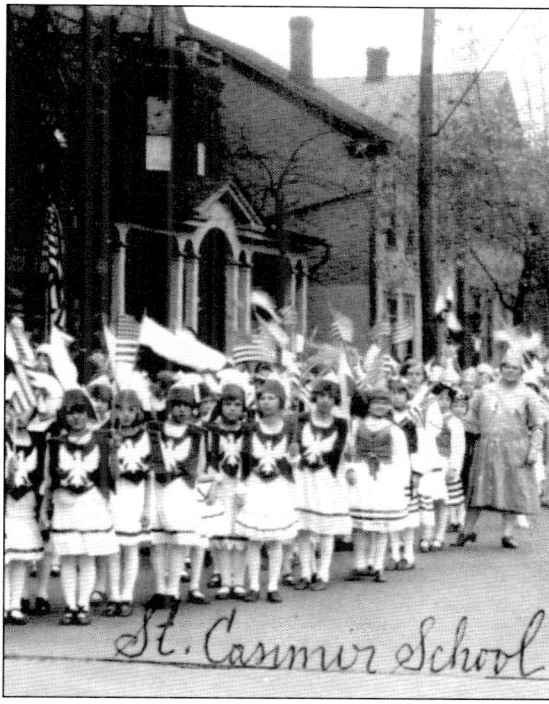

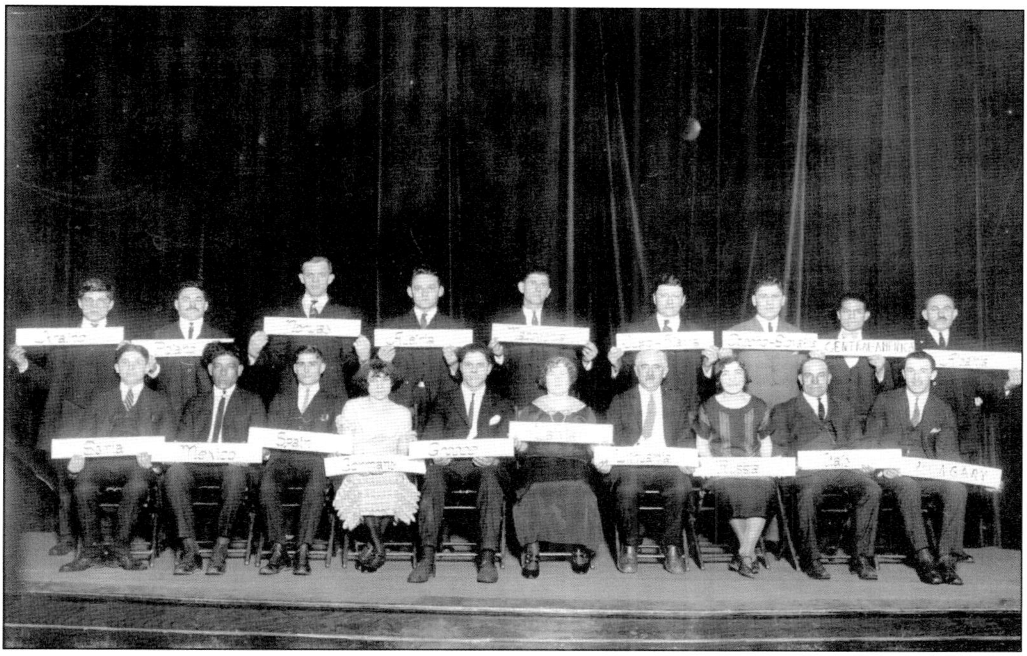

As their children attended parochial school to help them maintain the language and customs of the old country, many parents enrolled in evening Americanization classes in order to learn American culture and earn U.S. citizenship. This 1920 photograph shows the diversity of Johnstown's immigrant population. (Courtesy of the Johnstown Area Heritage Association archives.)

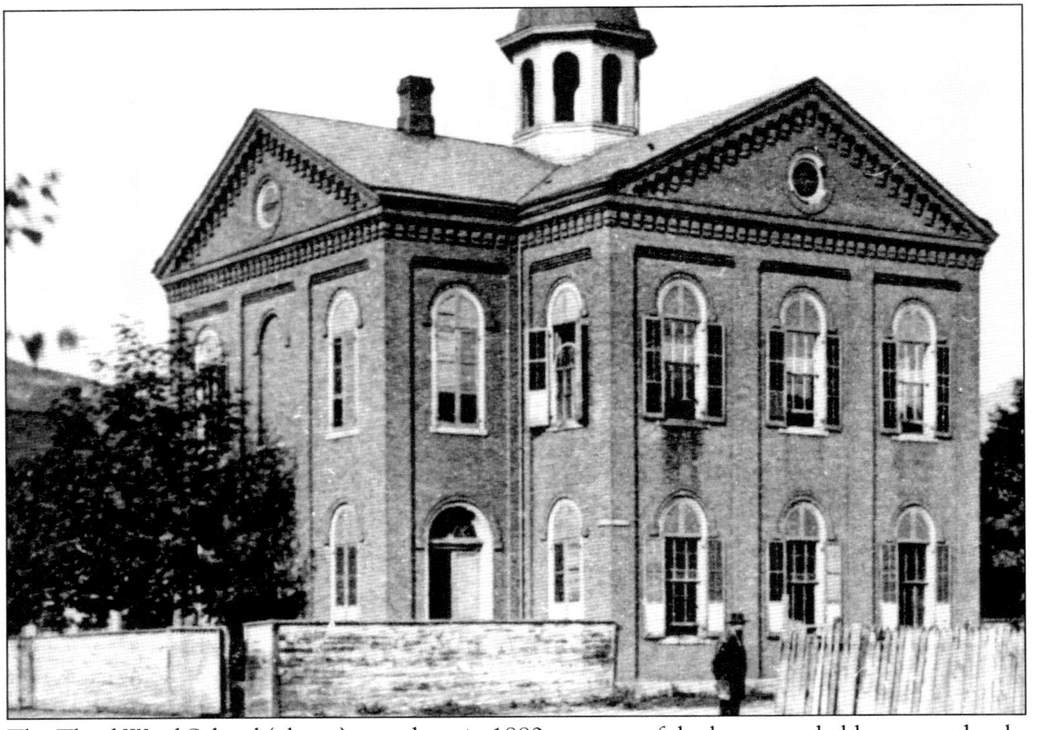

The Third Ward School (above), seen here in 1880, was one of the largest and oldest area schools, as construction on it began before the end of the Civil War. The building was sold to the Baltimore and Ohio Railroad and converted into the railroad's passenger station (below), pictured in 1913. Portions were rebuilt after the building barely survived the 1889 floodwaters. The building was razed in 1936. (Courtesy of the Johnstown Area Heritage Association archives.)

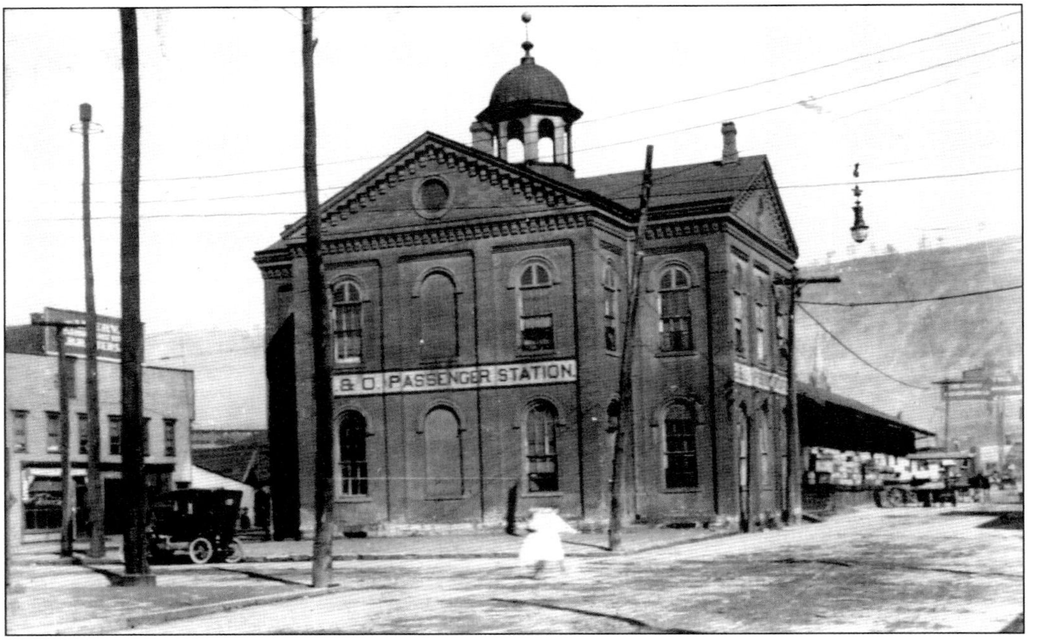

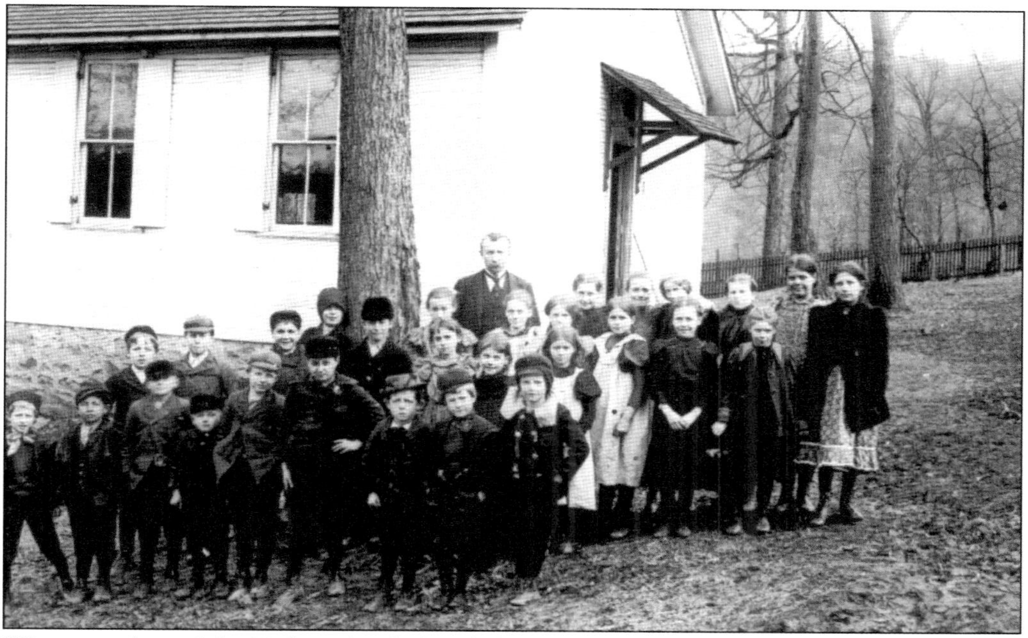

When members of the Vickroy family founded Ferndale, they set aside land at Clay Street and Harlan Avenue for educational purposes. In 1889, this school barely satisfied the needs of the community, considering the large number of children posed in front of the small, one-room schoolhouse. A second story was added to the building in 1895, and the school was used until 1912, when a new large brick school replaced it. (Courtesy of Jeanne D. Buck.)

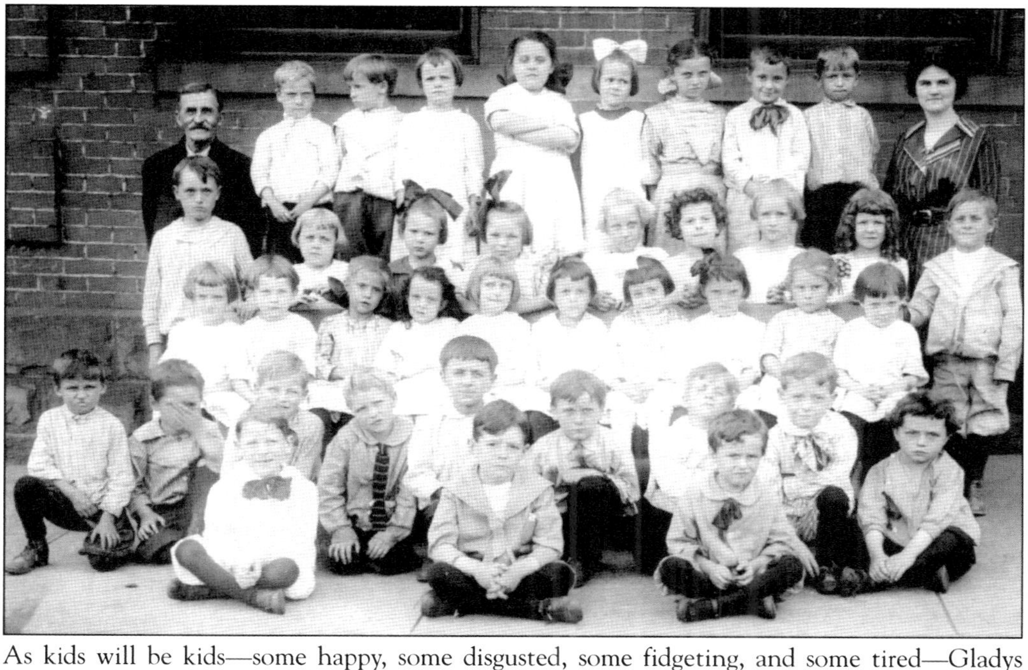

As kids will be kids—some happy, some disgusted, some fidgeting, and some tired—Gladys Evans and her primary students from Conemaugh pose with their principal in front of the school in 1912. (Courtesy of the Cambria County Historical Society.)

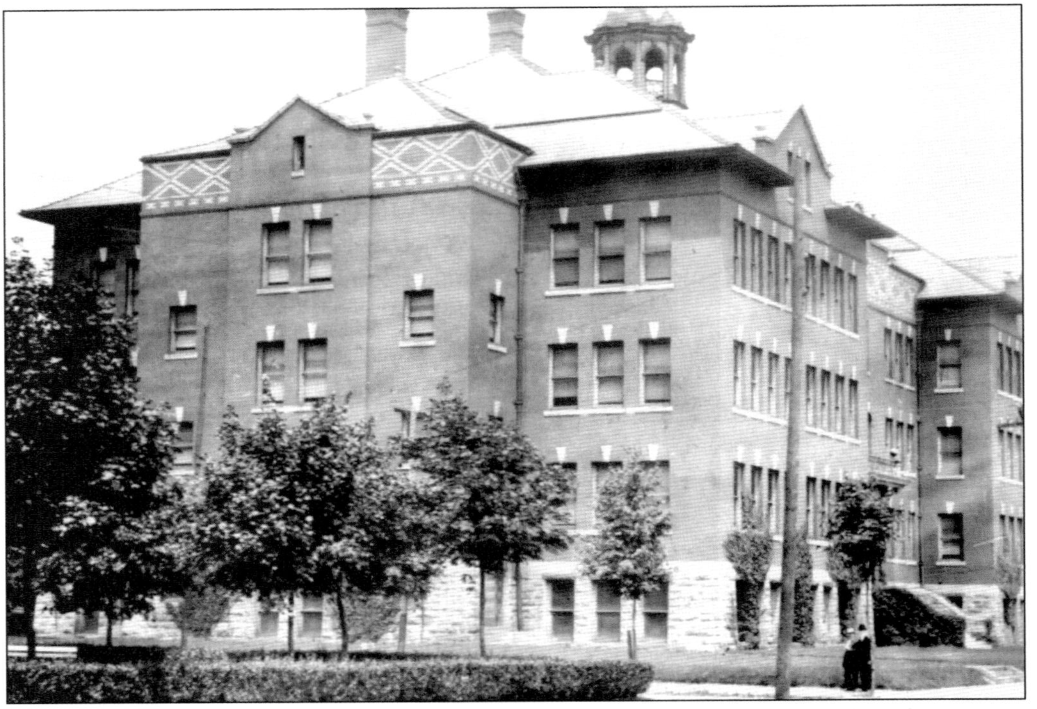

The original Johnstown High School was located on the corner of Napoleon and Market Streets, as was designated by founder Joseph Johns. The impressive brick structure was expanded with additions to accommodate population growth. When a new high school was constructed across the river, this building became Joseph Johns Junior High School. (Courtesy of the Cambria Library System, Johnstown.)

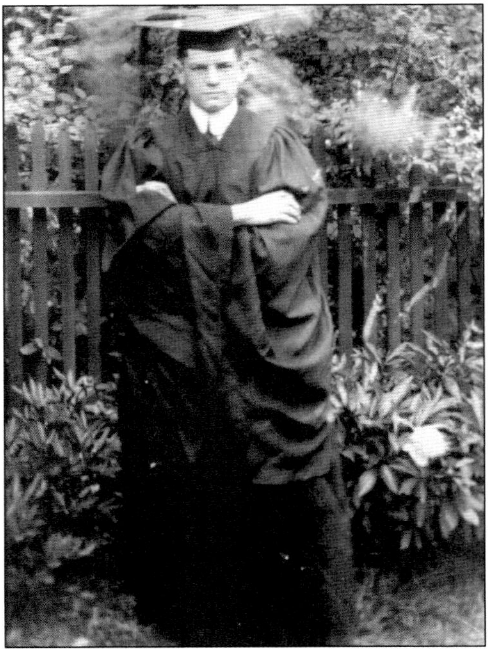

Harry E. Snavely stands educated and prepared for life beyond school in this Johnstown High School graduation photograph taken in 1912. (Courtesy of Robert Snavely.)

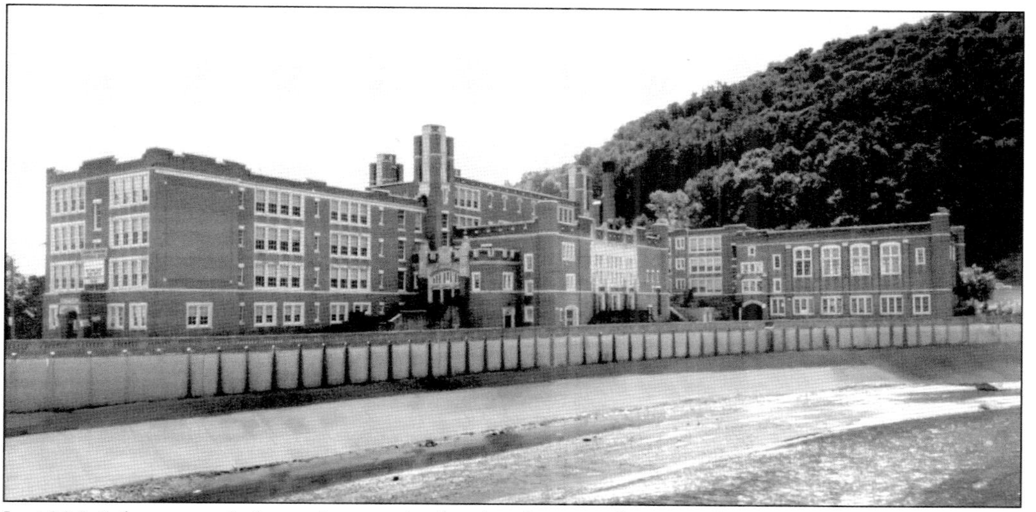

In 1926, Johnstown dedicated a new high school across the river from the former high school. Besides providing extra classrooms, the school featured a large auditorium and gymnasium. In 1985, with maintenance becoming prohibitive and the student population shrinking, the building was razed. Bricks from the exterior were sold to sentimental graduates. (Courtesy of Jim Cover Jr.)

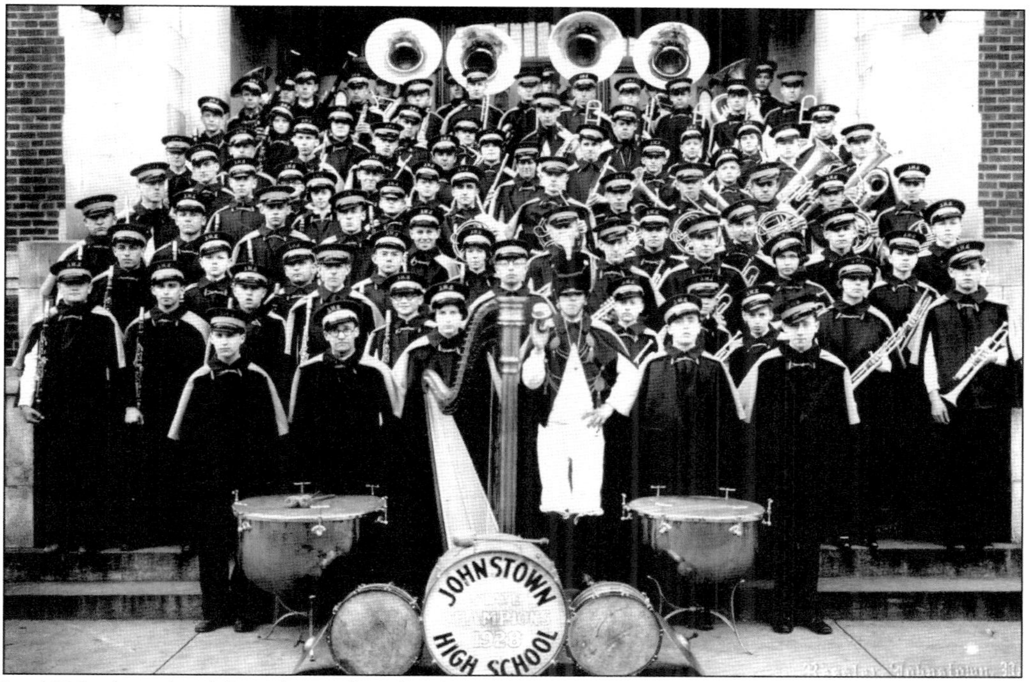

In 1922, the school board voted to fund a marching band, but it was not until the new high school opened that the band was formed. Initially, members wore school-purchased capes with their own black slacks and white shirts. By 1928, the marching Trojans earned their first state championship title. A marching band with a harp and timpani must have impressed the judges. The members received official military-style uniforms in 1930. (Courtesy the Johnstown High School band archives, Ressler - Johnstown, PA.)

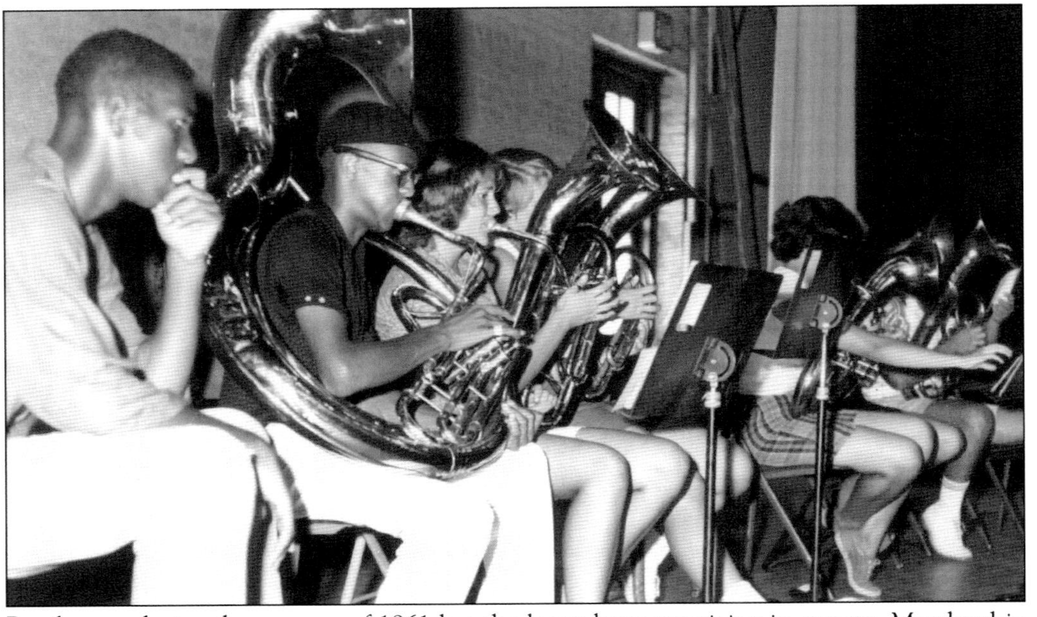

Band camp during the summer of 1961 has the lower brass practicing in earnest. Membership continued to grow well into the 1960s and 1970s. However, by the 1980s, the decline in school population affected all school activities. The marching Trojan band may be smaller now, but the quality of its performances and the dedication of its members has not waned. (Courtesy the Johnstown High School band archives.)

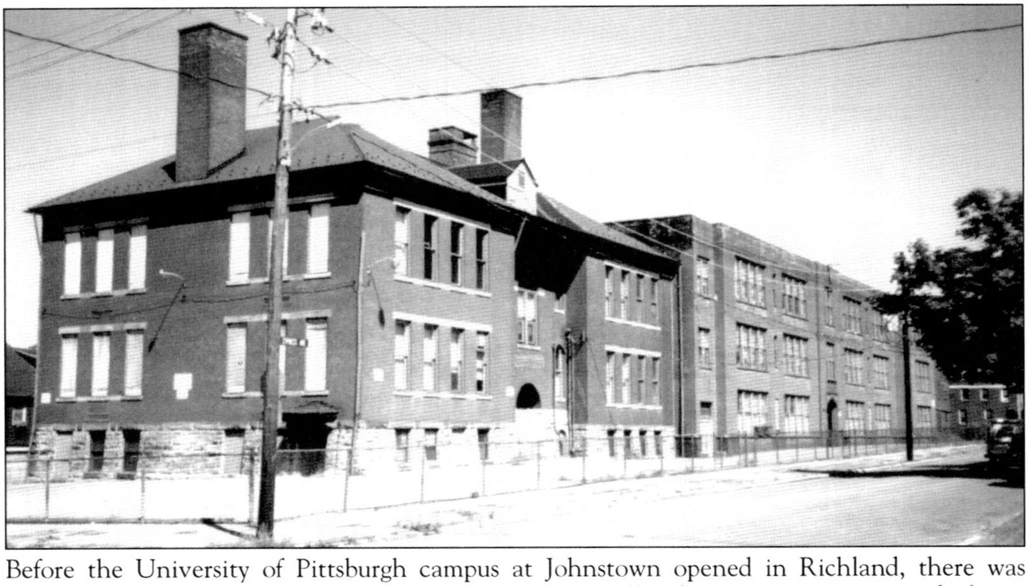

Before the University of Pittsburgh campus at Johnstown opened in Richland, there was the Johnstown Center, University of Pittsburgh. Initially, the university convened classes at Johnstown High School. As the program grew and more classrooms were needed, the university converted the empty Cypress Street Elementary School in Moxham into classrooms in which students worked toward undergraduate degrees in engineering and other specialties. Some students affectionately called the facility, pictured here, Cypress Tech. This building was demolished *c.* 2000. (Author's collection.)

Johnstown's Sixth Ward School looks more like a cathedral than a house of education. When economic downturns created a smaller population, buildings that incurred high heating bills and repair costs were closed and students were shuttled to other schools. (Courtesy of the Cambria County Historical Society.)

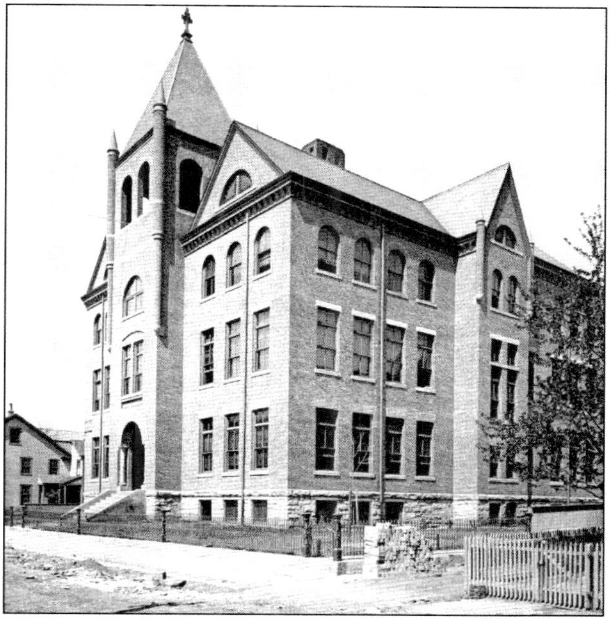

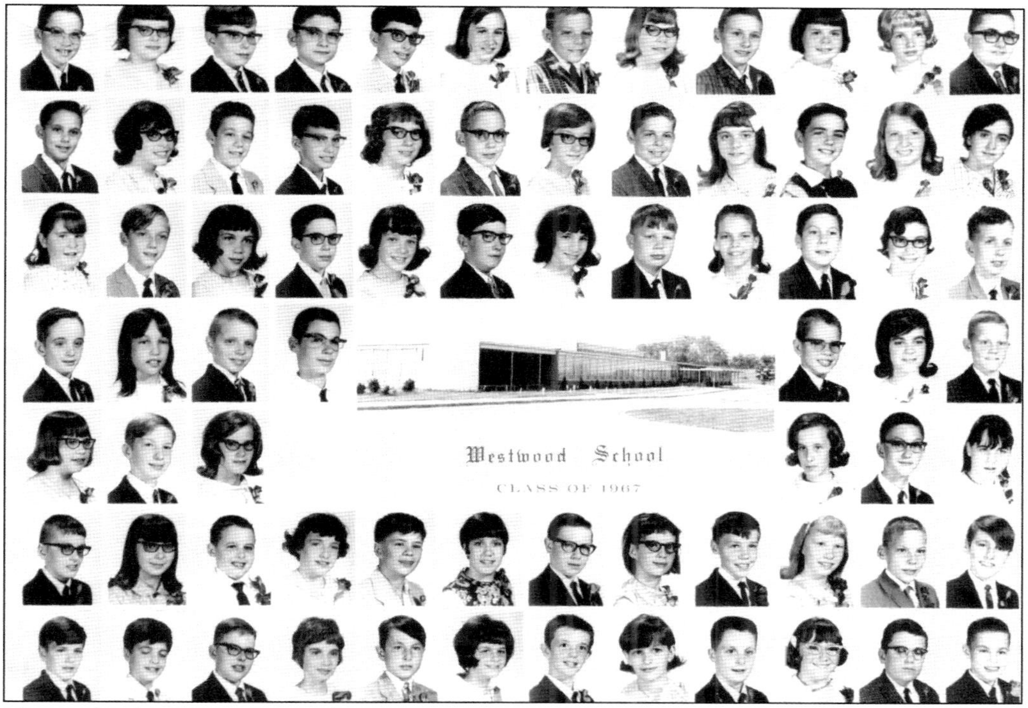

This is the first class to complete kindergarten through sixth grade at Westwood Elementary School. Compared to the Sixth Ward School above, Westwood featured sprawling 1960s architecture. Students enjoyed hot cafeteria lunches, bright classrooms, and a stage for plays. In 1991, Westwood was renamed West Side School and the new gym became the temporary home court for Johnstown High School games. To date, this was the last elementary school built in greater Johnstown. (Courtesy of Jim Cover Jr.)

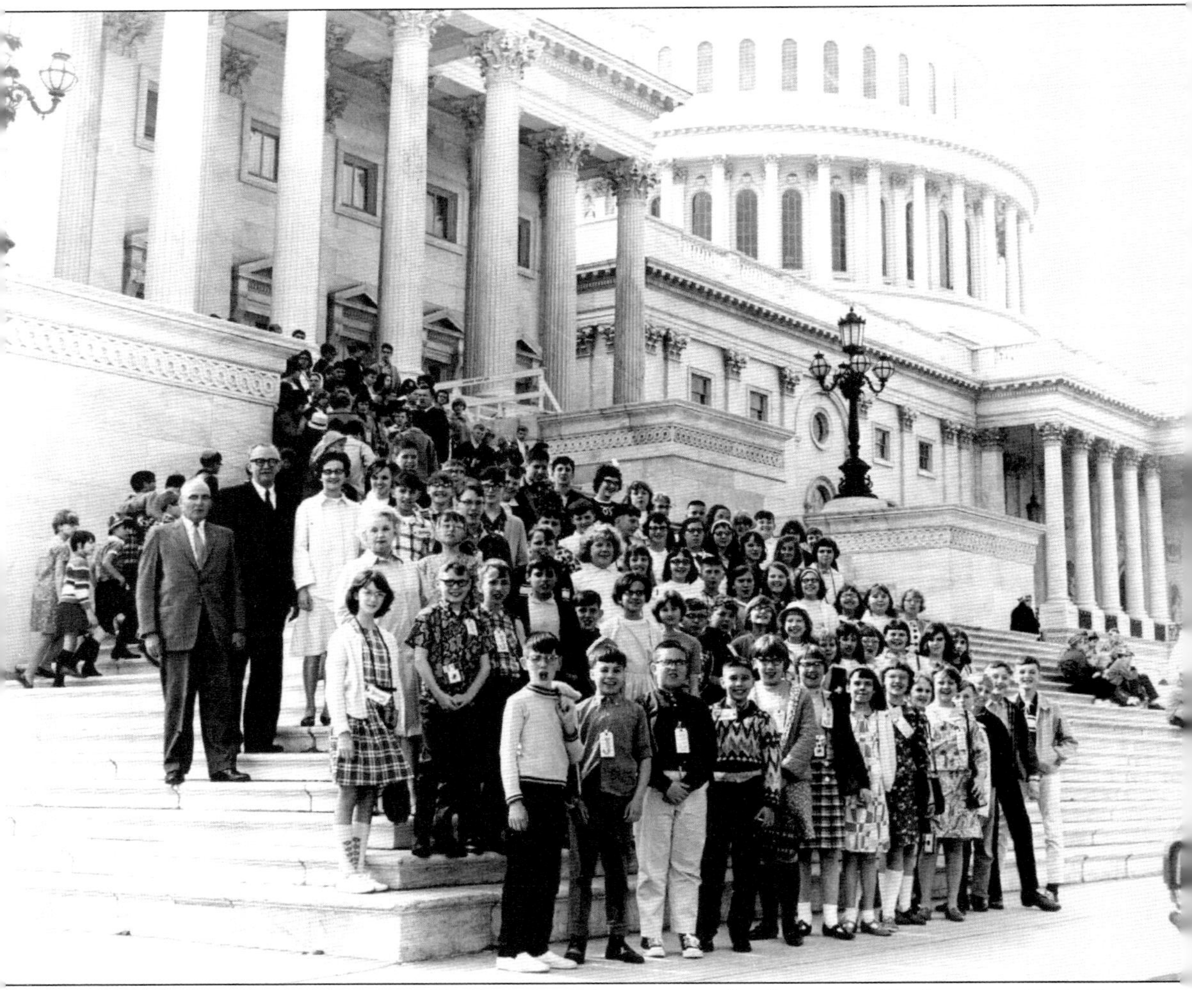

In 1965, students from various Johnstown elementary schools visited Washington, D.C. For many of them, this was their first trip outside of Pennsylvania. One of the highlights of the field trip was the opportunity to meet Congressman John P. Saylor, second from the left on the steps of the Capitol. John Phillips Saylor was born on a farm outside of Johnstown in 1908. After earning a law degree, he worked at his father's firm until joining the U.S. Navy to serve in World War II. Later, with his election to the House of Representatives in 1949, Saylor became a champion for environmental issues, particularly the protection of national waterways. He was instrumental in the passage of the National Wild and Scenic Rivers Act, signed on October 2, 1968, by Pres. Lyndon Johnson. This bill earned him the nickname "Mr. Conservation." Saylor served as a congressman for 24 years until his death in 1973. (Author's collection.)

Four

SURVIVING DISASTER

Time and time again, the world has witnessed examples of the strength of Johnstown's people. Surviving three major floods, massive fires, and numerous calamities on a grand scale, Johnstown residents have repeatedly united to overcome adversity and rebuild the community.

After the 1889 flood, workers quickly cleared debris so that steel manufacture could resume and much needed paychecks be earned again. Donations sent to the city were spent on a modern hospital. Even before all of the bodies were recovered, construction of the world's steepest inclined plane began just months after the flood.

Clara Barton became a part of Johnstown's history when she arrived to coordinate relief in 1889. More than 2,200 people were killed, scores were injured and missing, and families were separated during the cruel rush of water that pounded Johnstown. Virtually everyone in town lost their home and livelihood. Many consider this recovery effort the first true test for Barton and her fledgling American Red Cross. The recovery became a template for future national disasters, but it could not have worked as well as it did without the participation of the entire community.

Johnstown rallied around Pres. Franklin D. Roosevelt as he toured the city after the St. Patrick's Day flood in 1936, anticipating his announcement of a flood protection project. For 41 years, the title Flood Free City graced some signs on downtown streets. The signs seemed surreal when floodwaters rose again in 1977.

Grandview Cemetery opened in 1885 with the intention of serving the growing population. The cemetery became the site of one of the most powerful images of the 1889 flood and now contains the graves of those lost in each of the three floods.

Every generation living in Johnstown since 1889 has experienced a flood. Yet, Johnstown stands firm, proving that, if tested, hearts can be as strong as steel.

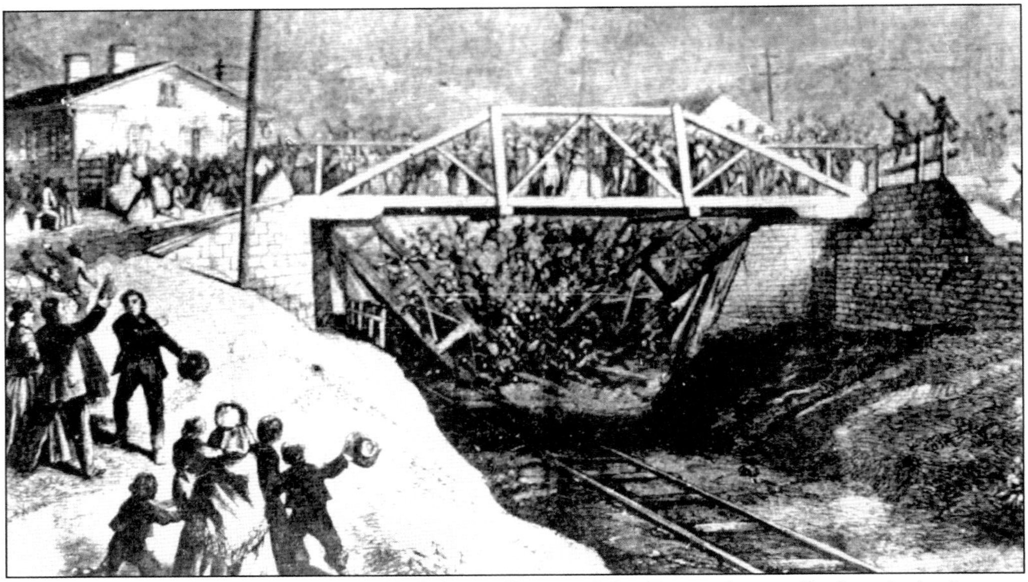

Historian Henry Wilson Storey called the collapse of the Pennsylvania Railroad platform at the Cambria Steel Company on September 14, 1866, "the first great disaster in Johnstown." Some 2,000 people greeted the 11:00 a.m. train, which was carrying Pres. Andrew Johnson, Lt. Gen. Ulysses S. Grant, and Adm. David G. Farragut. The train moved forward, allowing the enthusiastic crowd passage to a closer platform. Without warning, the floor fell and, according to Storey, "persons sank from sight as though the earth had opened." Newspaper accounts at the time reported that 7 people died and 387 sustained injuries. (Courtesy of the Johnstown Area Heritage Association archives.)

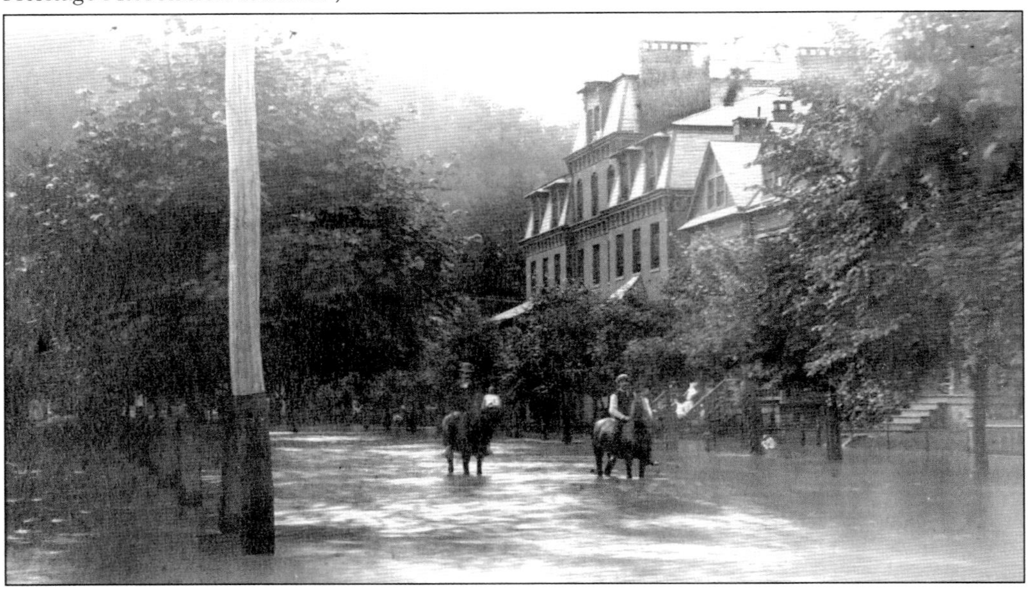

Flooding was always a concern for residents located in the valley near the confluence of the two rivers. It was not unusual to suffer spring flooding, as shown in this 1887 photograph, taken two years before the 1889 flood. Two brave men navigate the high waters on Main Street by horse rather than boat. (Courtesy of the Johnstown Area Heritage Association archives.)

Despite the heavy rain, residents celebrated on May 31, 1889, Memorial Day, with a morning parade and service at the Union Cemetery. When Lake Conemaugh surged from its pen at 3:15 p.m., residents were already moving personal belongings to their second floor or attic. Several individuals tried to warn Johnstown of the impending disaster. Railroad engineer John Hess pulled long on the train whistle and navigated his engine backwards into town. Those within earshot recognized the danger signaled by the unrelenting train whistle. (Courtesy of the Johnstown Area Heritage Association archives.)

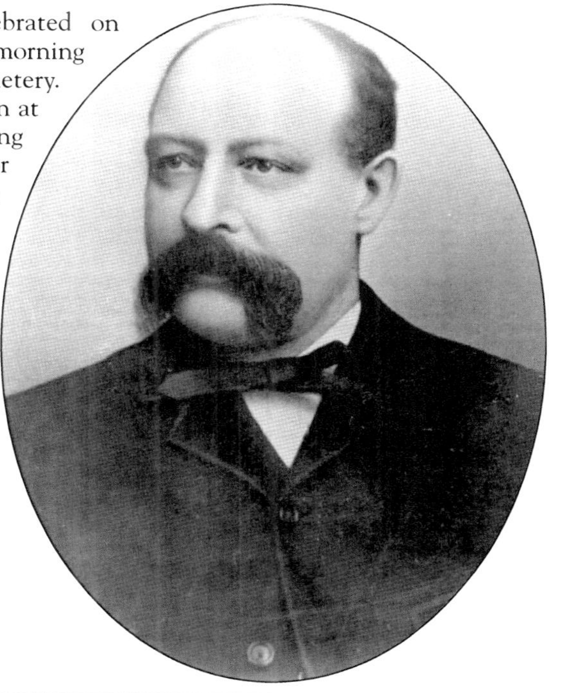

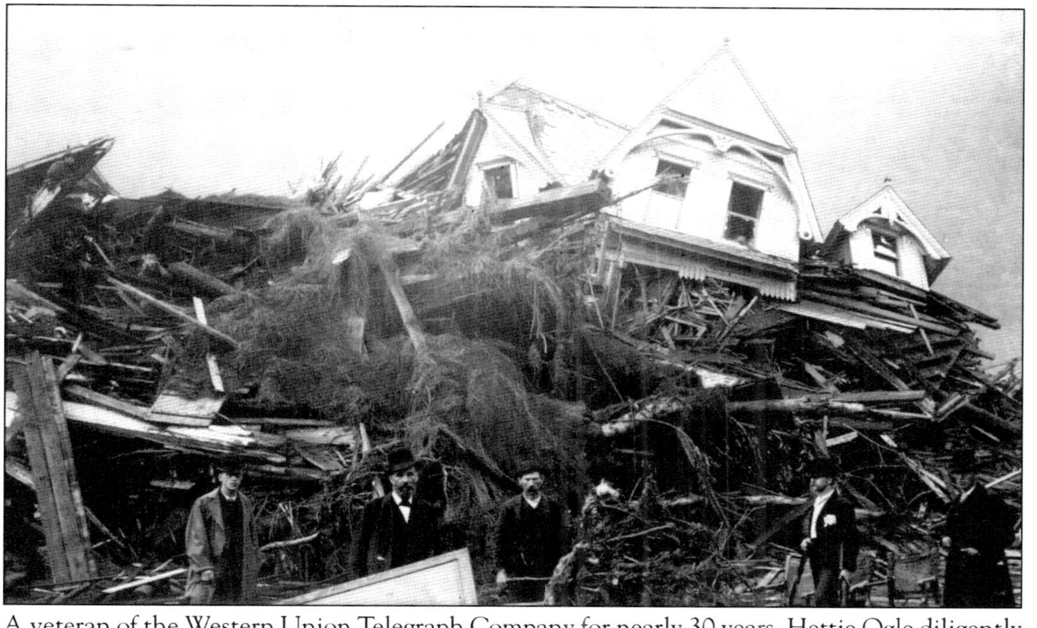

A veteran of the Western Union Telegraph Company for nearly 30 years, Hettie Ogle diligently kept vigil near her equipment, which she and her daughter, Minnie, moved to the second floor. She conveyed the dam's condition to the Pittsburgh office and signed off, knowing that the rising water would disable her lines. Pittsburgh now knew of the potential catastrophe. Undoubtedly, the two women were unprepared for the wave that smashed the Western Union Telegraph building shown here. Hettie Ogle and Minnie were never knowingly recovered or identified. (Courtesy of the Cambria County Historical Society.)

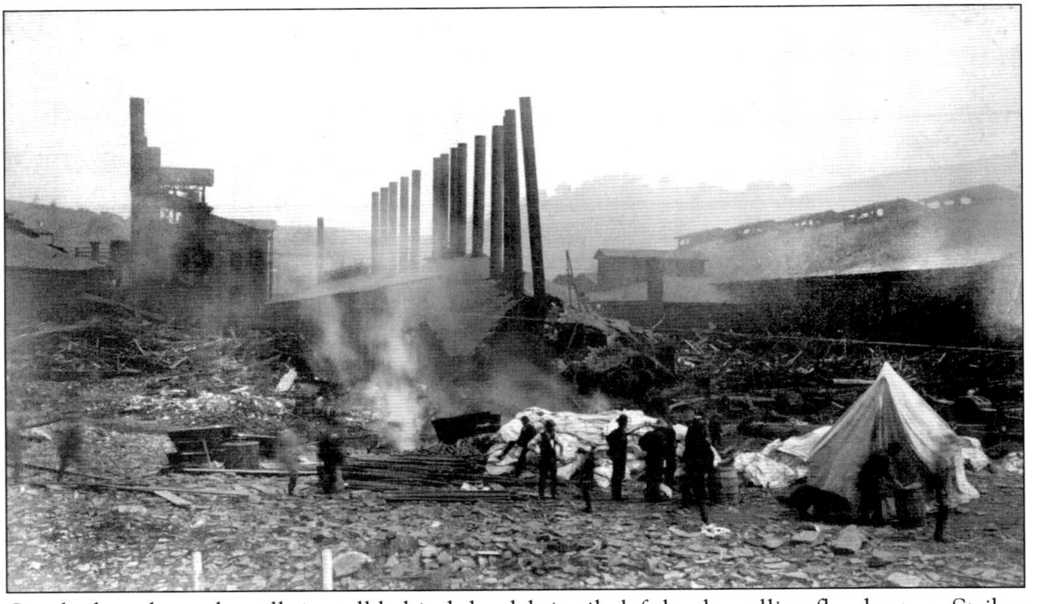

Crooked smokestacks still rise tall behind the debris pile left by the rolling floodwaters. Strikes by workers and threats of work stoppages never closed this plant. It was not until the water came pounding into Cambria Iron that the mills stopped. Work ceased for only a short time, as men, still dazed from the trauma of their losses, cleared the mills enough to begin production. (Courtesy of the Cambria County Historical Society.)

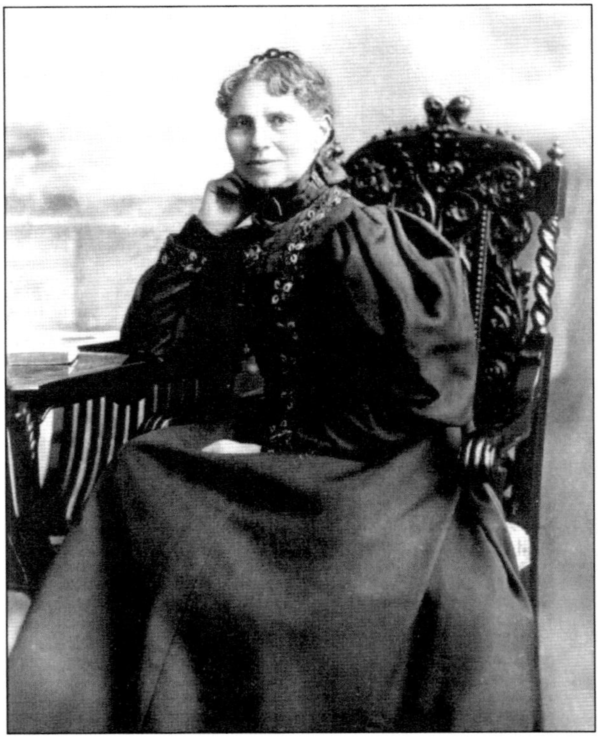

Clara Barton founded the American Red Cross in May 1881. This tiny woman faced a daunting task after the 1889 flood, as more than 2,200 perished and thousands of survivors were homeless and without income. She made Johnstown her home for more than four months, distributed over $200,000 worth of supplies, coordinated the building of temporary shelters and hospitals, and fed thousands. (Courtesy of the Johnstown Area Heritage Association archives, with permission of the Clara Barton National Historic Site, National Park Service.)

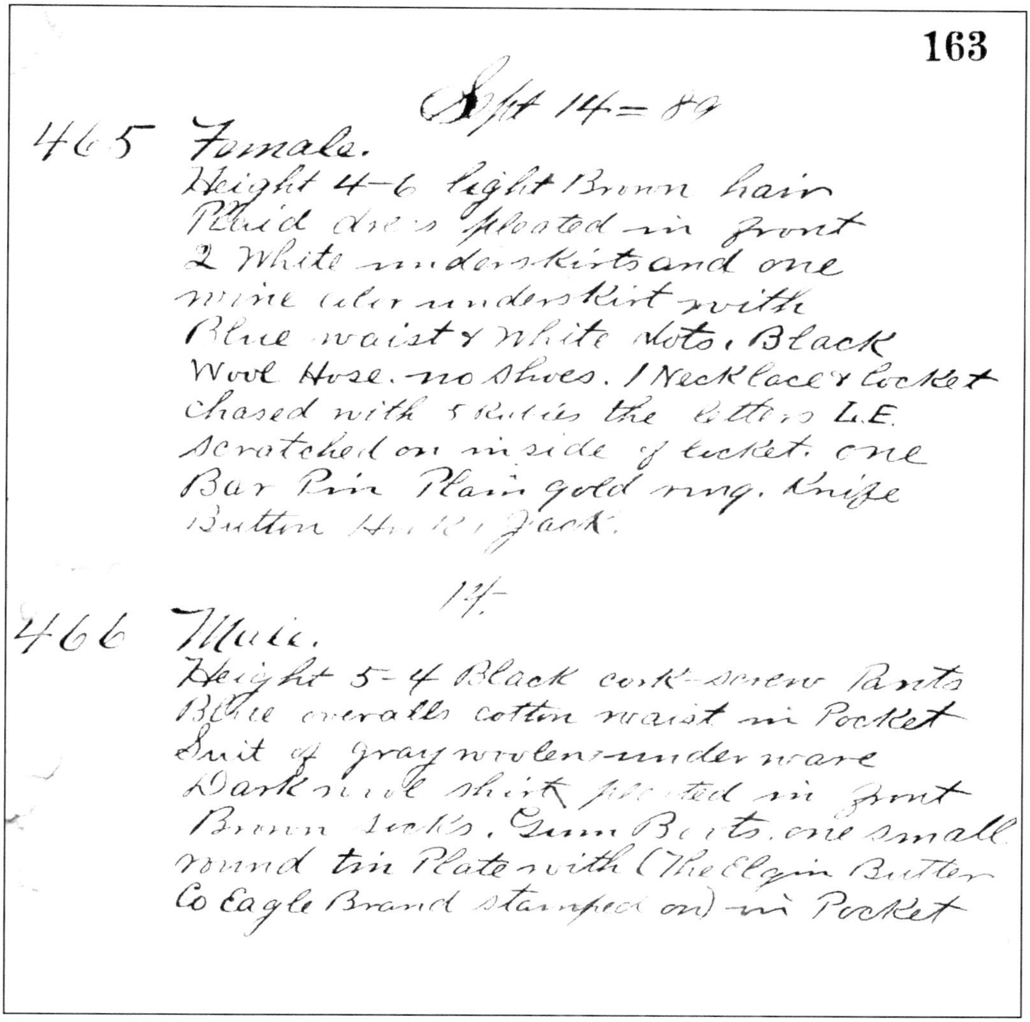

163

Sept 14=89

465 Female.
Height 4-6 light Brown hair
Plaid dress pleated in front
2 White underskirts and one
wine color underskirt with
Blue waist & white dots. Black
Wool Hose. no shoes. 1 Necklace & locket
chased with 5 Rubies the letters L.E.
scratched on inside of locket. one
Bar Pin Plain gold ring. Knife
Button Hook, Jack.

14.

466 Male.
Height 5-4 Black cork-screw Pants
Blue overalls cotton waist in Pocket
Suit of gray woolen underware
Dark wool shirt pleated in front
Brown socks. Gum Boots. one small
round tin Plate with (The Elgin Butter
Co Eagle Brand stamped on) in Pocket

This original Henderson Funeral Home document shows part of page 163 from a mortuary book recording bodies found three and a half months after the 1889 flood. The faded copy reads as follows:

Sept 14=89

465 Female. Height 4-6 light Brown hair Plaid dress pleated in front 2 white underskirts and one wine color underskirt with Blue waist & white dots. Black Wool Hose. no shoes. 1 Necklace & locket chased with 5 Rubies the letters L. E. scratched on inside of locket. one Bar Pin Plain gold ring. Knife Button Hook, Jack.

14.

466 Male. Height 5-4 Black cork-screw Pants Blue overalls cotton waist in Pocket Suit of gray woolen underware Dark wool shirt pleated in front Brown socks. Gum Boots. one small round tin Plate with (the Elgin Butter Co Eagle Brand stamped on) in Pocket.

Without DNA testing, those searching for lost family members depended on these detailed handwritten notes. (Courtesy of Gary Henderson, Henderson Funeral Home.)

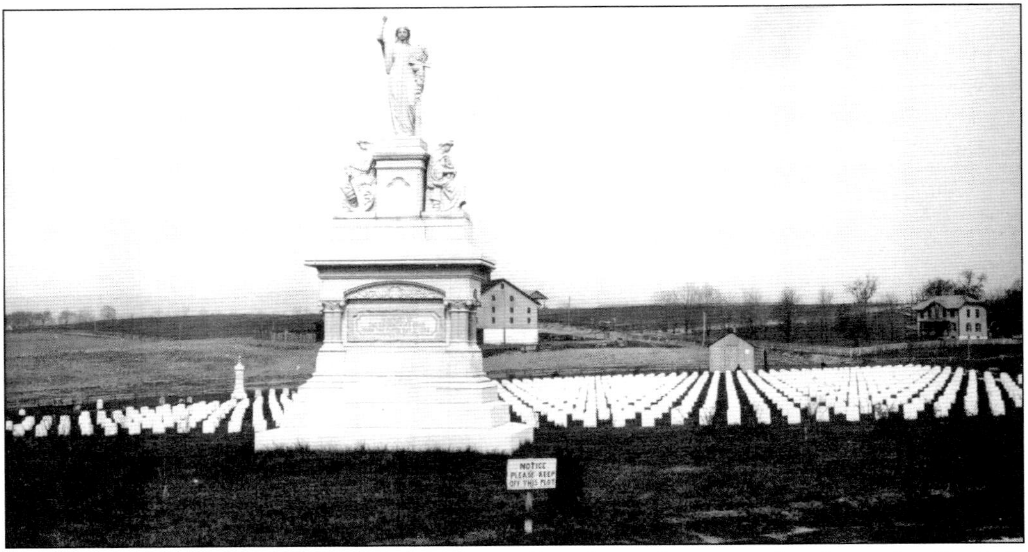

This early photograph of the Unknown Plot at Grandview Cemetery also shows the Cambria Iron Company barns that housed livestock. A small sign in the foreground gives visitors notice to "Please keep off the Plot." The impressive Monument of Tranquility represents Faith, Hope, and Charity with the words "In Memory of the unidentified dead from the Flood, May 31, 1889." Hope is the figure standing on the center pedestal. More than 10,000 people nationwide attended the dedication of the Unknown Plot on May 31, 1892. (Courtesy of the Cambria County Historical Society.)

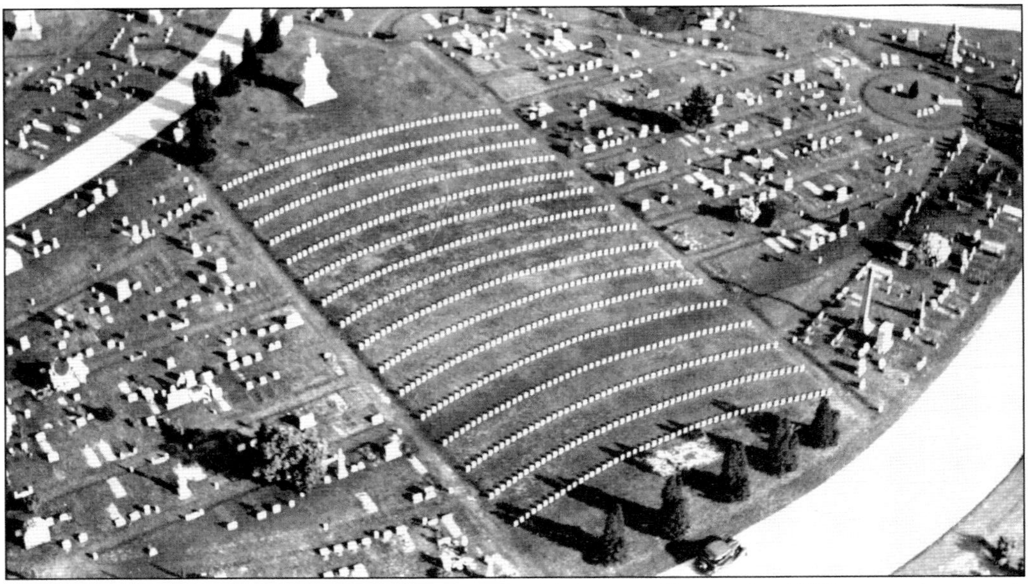

An overhead view of the 777 headstones in the Unknown Plot c. the 1920s provides a stark reminder of the loss of life. Several markers do not sit on graves but were added to fill out the final design. Located high on a hill in Grandview, the Unknown Plot is protected from flooding and camouflaged by trees and, thus, cannot be seen from the valley below—reportedly one of the criteria used for selecting this cemetery site. (Courtesy of the Johnstown Area Heritage Association archives.)

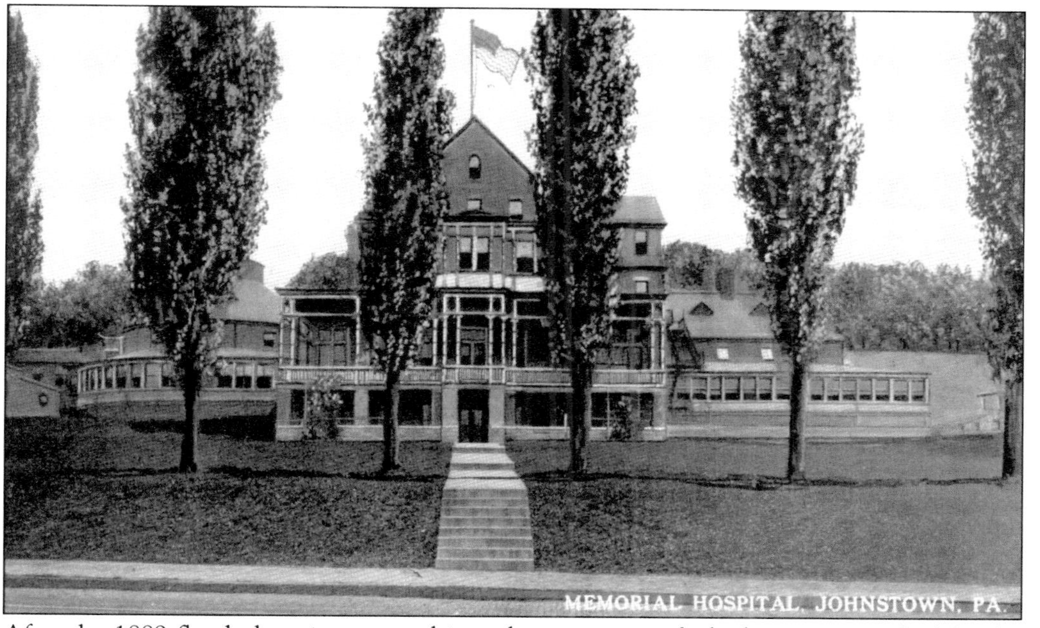

After the 1889 flood, donations poured into the city, some of which were earmarked for the construction of a modern hospital. The Conemaugh Valley Memorial Hospital Association was formed on November 8, 1889, and by February 4, 1892, Memorial Hospital had dedicated its first buildings along Franklin Street. This postcard depicts the hospital as it appeared c. 1910. (Author's collection.)

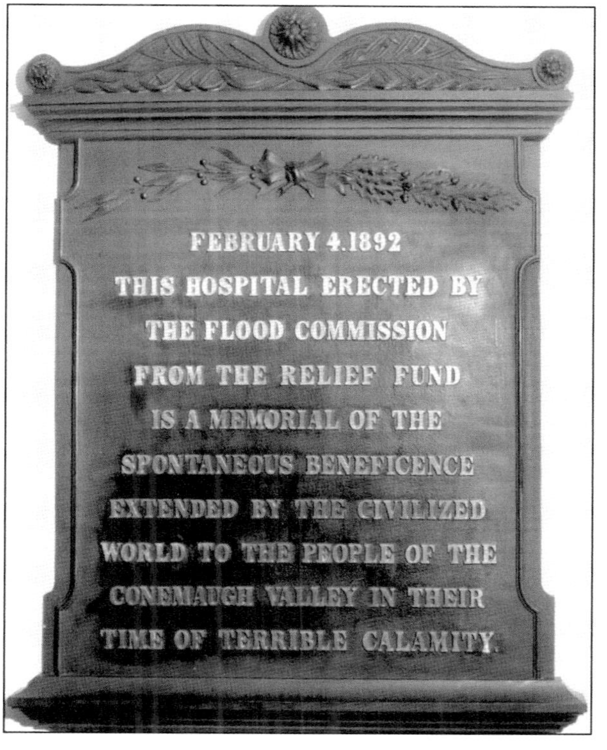

Two bronze plaques presented at the dedication read as follows: "February 4, 1892 this hospital erected by the flood commission from the relief fund is a memorial of the spontaneous beneficence extended by the civilized world to the people of the Conemaugh Valley in their time of terrible calamity." During a recent renovation, these plaques were carefully removed from the hospital exterior and placed inside the lobby to protect them from weather damage. (Courtesy of the Johnstown Area Heritage Association archives.)

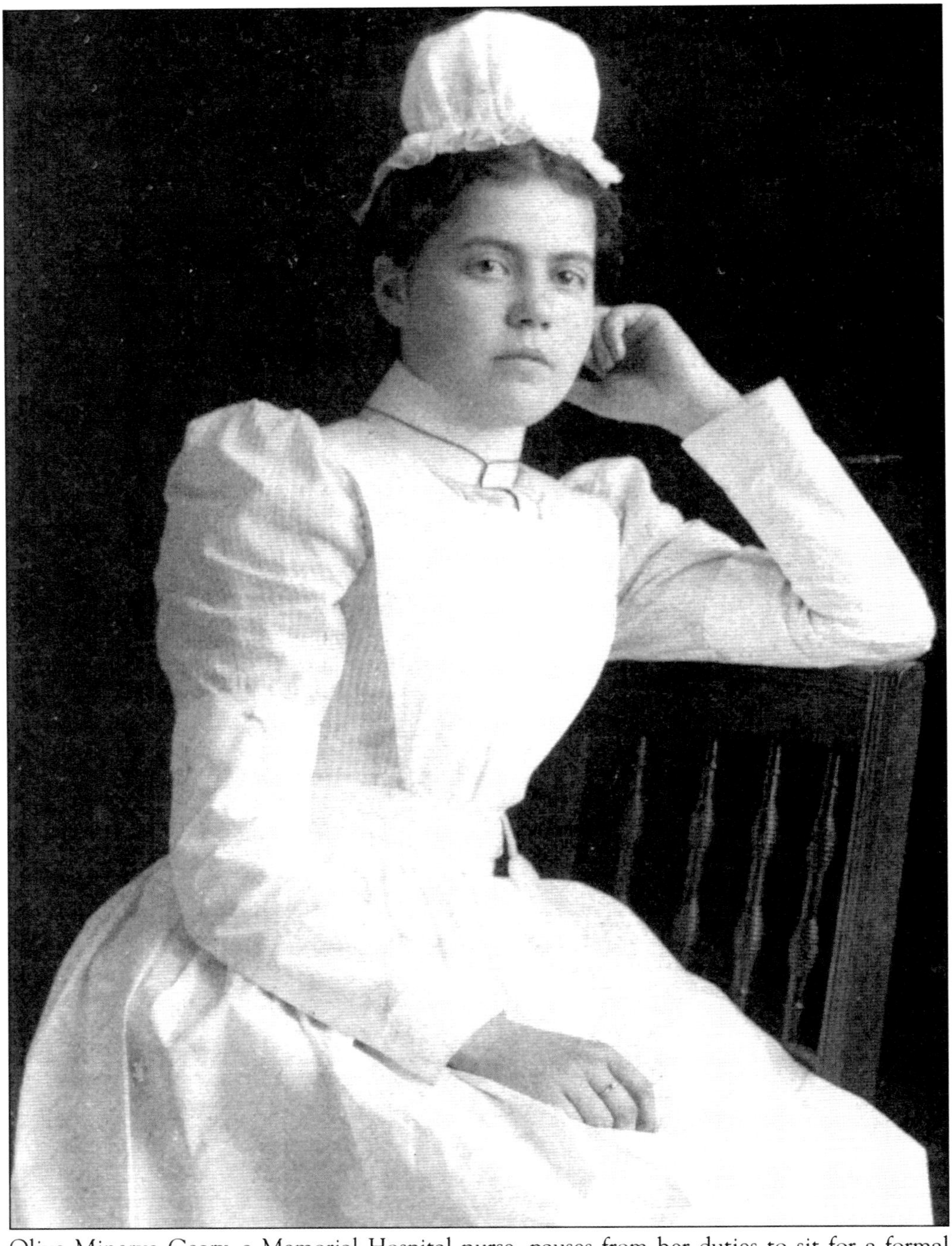

Olive Minerva Geary, a Memorial Hospital nurse, pauses from her duties to sit for a formal portrait in July 1904. Her official uniform features pinstriped mutton sleeves and bodice and white, crisply ironed lower sleeves and pinafore. A nurse's most prized possession, the cap earned upon graduation, sits delicately upon her head. Geary, known affectionately as Aunt Moon to her family, is also believed to have worked in the Cambria Iron Company's infirmary during her career. (Author's collection.)

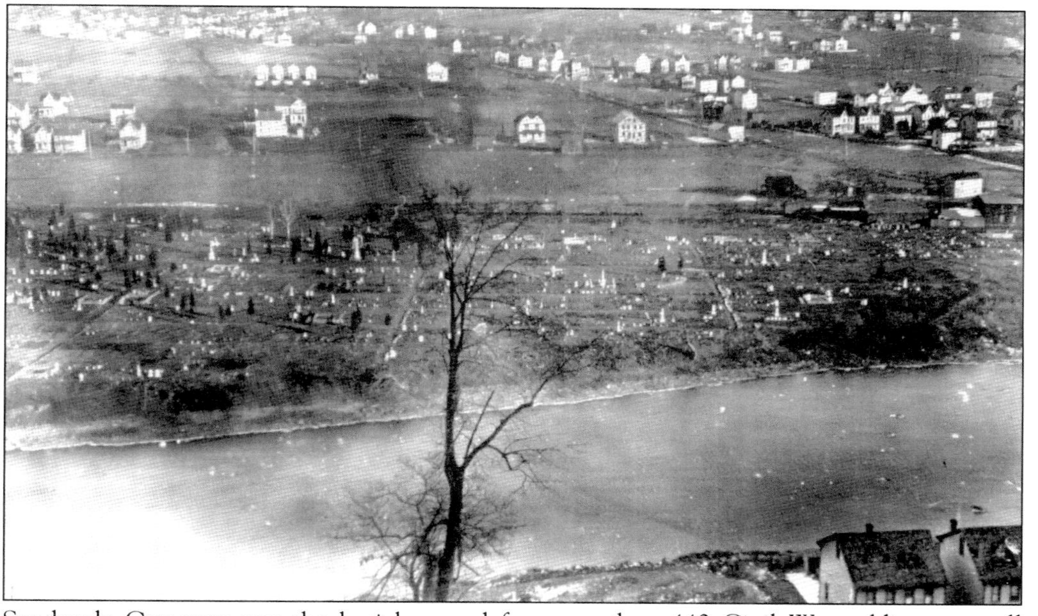

Sandyvale Cemetery was the burial ground for more than 440 Civil War soldiers, as well as Johnstown residents, until the flood washed the graves away. This 1900 photograph demonstrates the determination of the community to continue on, as, just 11 years after the flood, homes can been seen in the foreground, built defiantly right next to the river again. (Courtesy of the Johnstown Area Heritage Association archives.)

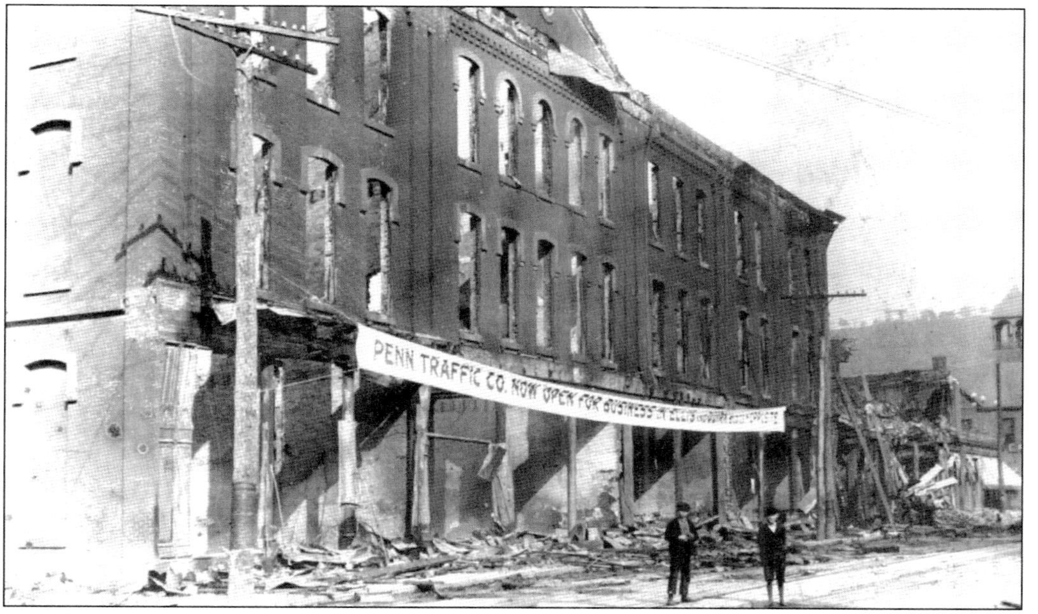

Fire alarms blasted on August 28, 1905, but nothing could save the Penn Traffic store. With damage to the building estimated at $500,000, the owners pushed to reopen, and by October 1905, a banner was stretched across the ruined store, alerting customers, "Penn Traffic Co now open for business in Ellis and Quinn Building opposite." (Courtesy of the Johnstown Area Heritage Association archives.)

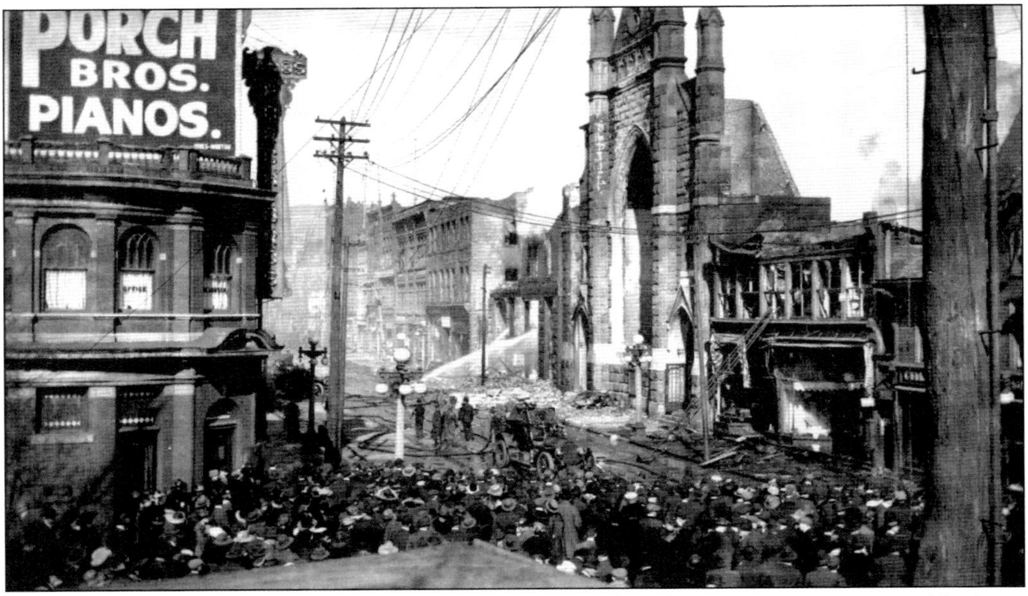

A crowd gathers to watch firefighters take on a blaze that threatens an entire city block on November 17, 1918. Equipment was often no match for the speed of the fires that engulfed sections of Johnstown. Years before, in March 1906, fire struck an entire corner of upper Main Street, destroying Swank Hardware, Henderson Furniture Company, and the Fisher Building. (Courtesy of the Johnstown Area Heritage Association archives.)

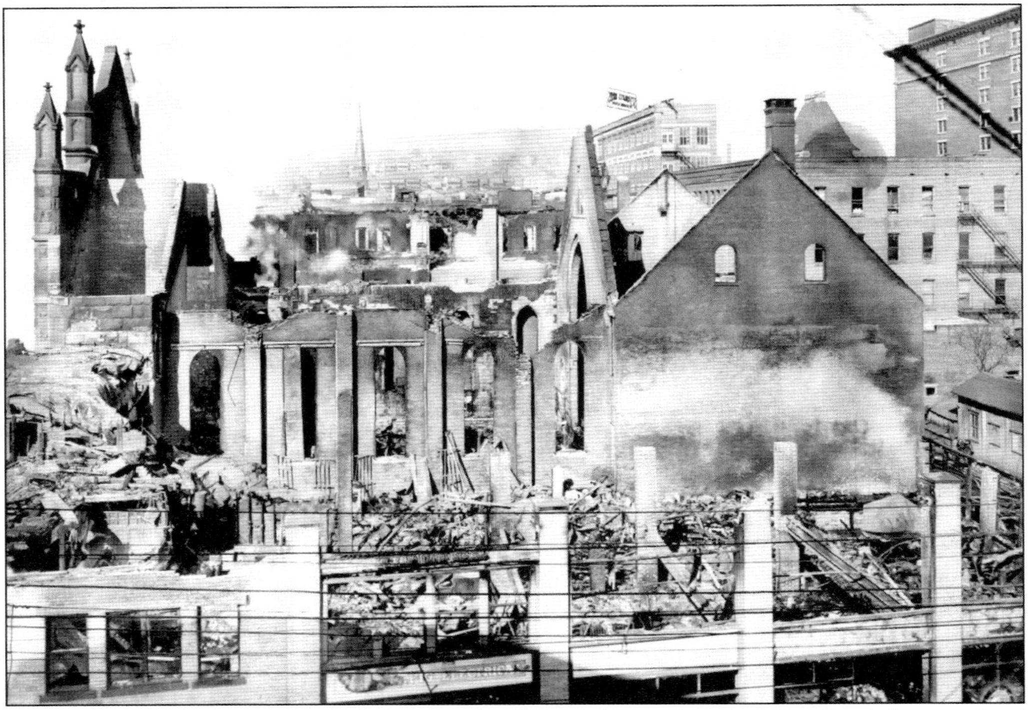
A church sanctuary is exposed after the roof collapsed during the 1918 fire that left one side of a city block smoldering. (Courtesy of the Johnstown Area Heritage Association archives.)

The need for a well-equipped firefighting organization became evident to civic leader Powell Stackhouse when he witnessed the inferno at Frazier's Corner at Main and Franklin Streets on January 13, 1867. The bucket brigades and hand pump were no match for the roaring flames. Stackhouse spearheaded the formation of the Assistance Fire Company No. 1 and procured an Amoskeag engine and horse carriages. The Assistance firehouse, built in 1892, is seen in this c. 1894 photograph. (Courtesy of the Cambria County Historical Society.)

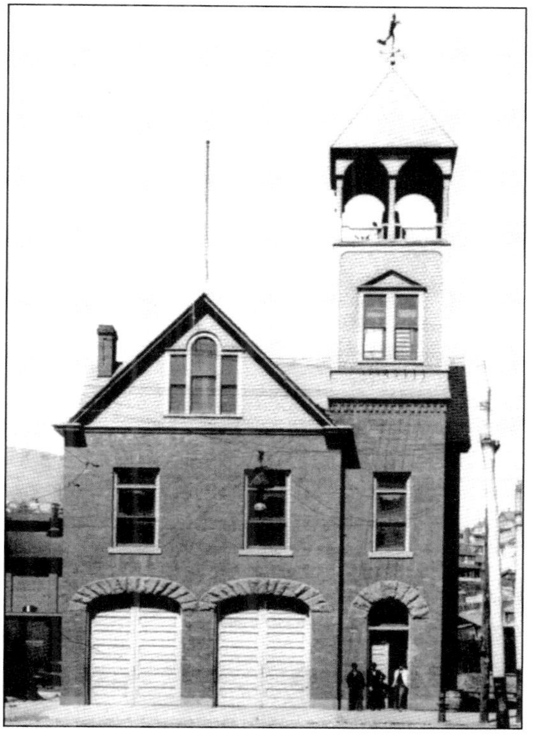

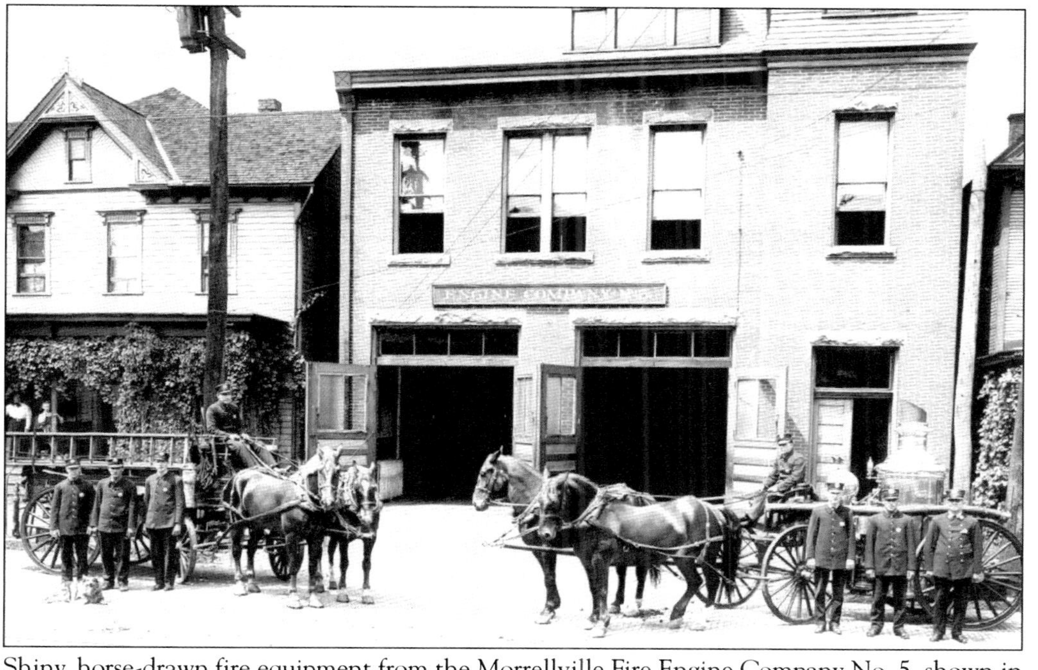

Shiny, horse-drawn fire equipment from the Morrellville Fire Engine Company No. 5, shown in 1915, was always ready for the ringing of the emergency bell. The company first organized on February 18, 1890, and later consolidated with the Empire Fire Company, boosting membership to 45 volunteer firemen. (Courtesy of the Johnstown Area Heritage Association archives.)

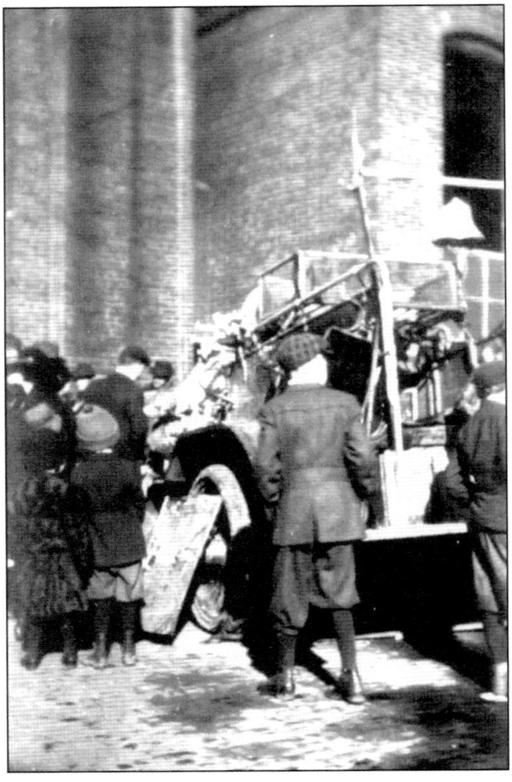

Citizens of Moxham crowd around to inspect the newest fire engine delivered to the neighborhood station in 1915. Moxham's fire company charter was approved on April 14, 1890, and membership exceeded 120 volunteers. (Courtesy of Robert Snavely.)

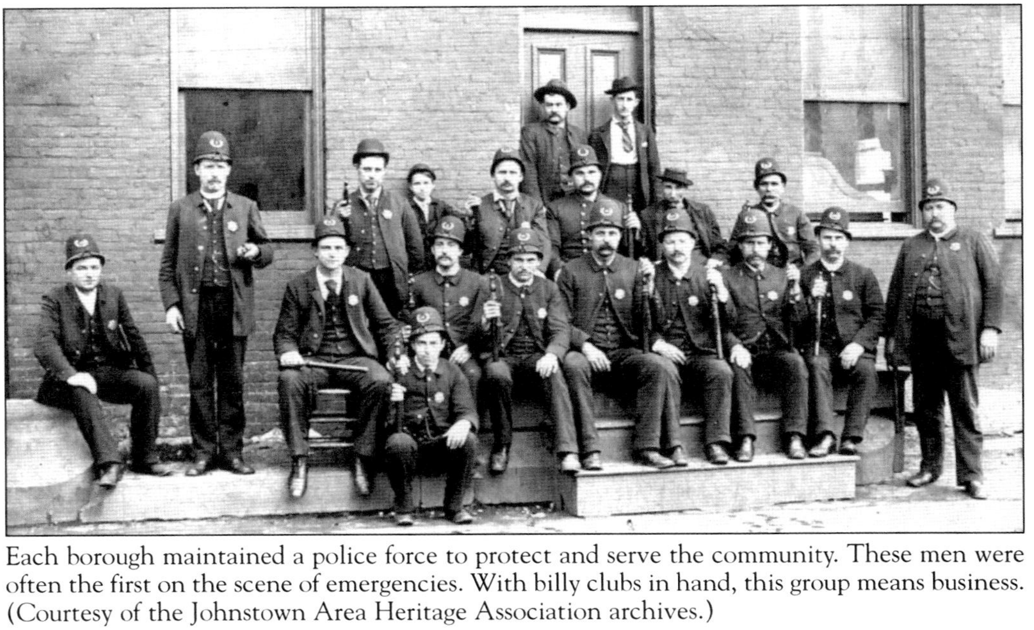

Each borough maintained a police force to protect and serve the community. These men were often the first on the scene of emergencies. With billy clubs in hand, this group means business. (Courtesy of the Johnstown Area Heritage Association archives.)

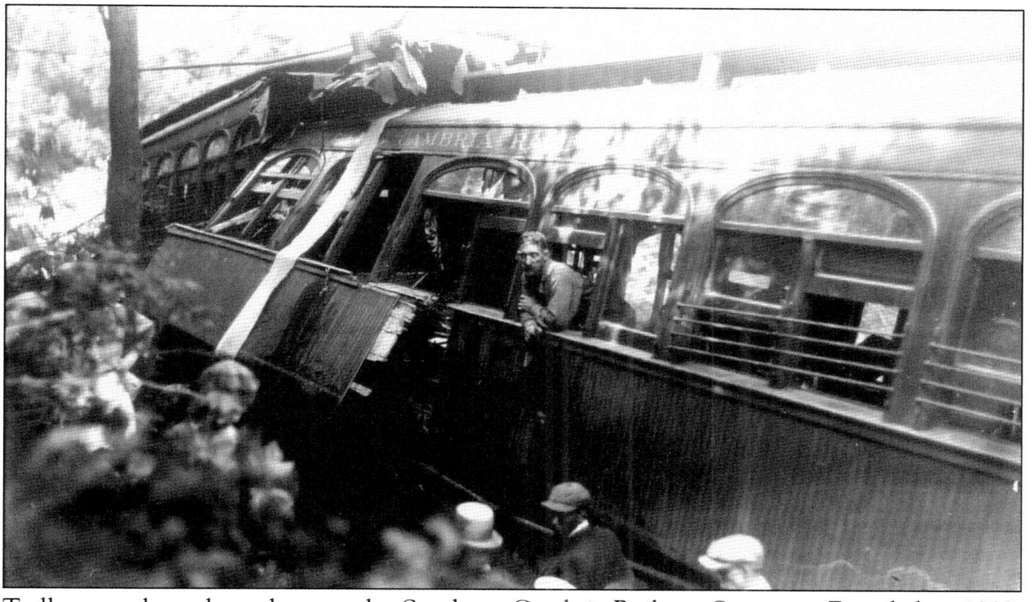

Trolley travel was hazardous on the Southern Cambria Railway Company. Founded in 1882, Southern Cambria serviced nearly 75,000 residents in routes from Johnstown to South Fork and Ebensburg. Head-on collisions due to poor maintenance and a confusing track layout plagued the line. This accident, on August 12, 1916, is just one of the fatal disasters. Tragically, 27 members of families, on their way to summer reunions, were killed when this trolley smashed into another. The Southern Cambria ceased operation c. 1928. (Courtesy of the Johnstown Area Heritage Association archives.)

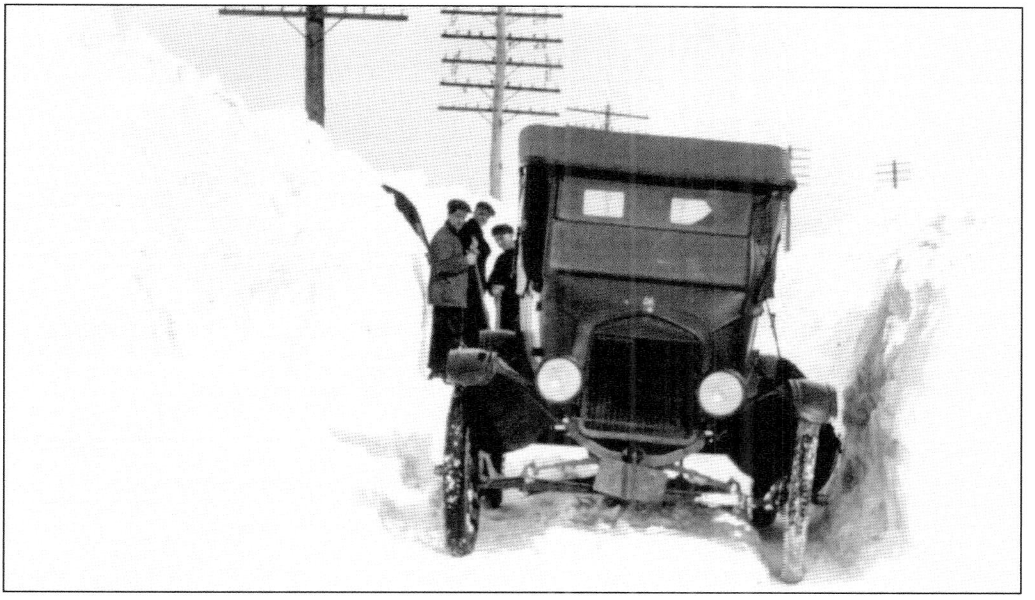

Snowbanks higher than a car were part of a record-breaking snowfall that provided the recipe for another massive flood. Unseasonably warm temperatures and a merciless rainfall thawed a snowpack that translated into 17 feet of water in downtown Johnstown on St. Patrick's Day, March 17, 1936. (Courtesy of the Johnstown Area Heritage Association archives.)

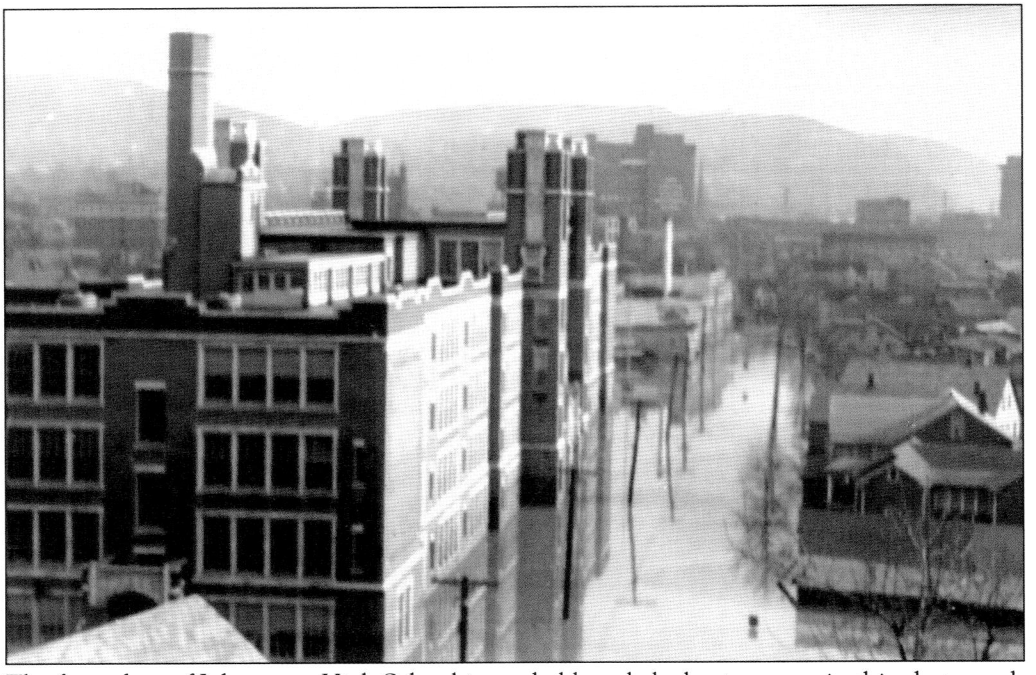

The front door of Johnstown High School is reachable only by boat, as seen in this photograph taken at high-flood stage on St. Patrick's Day 1936. (Courtesy of the Johnstown Area Heritage Association archives.)

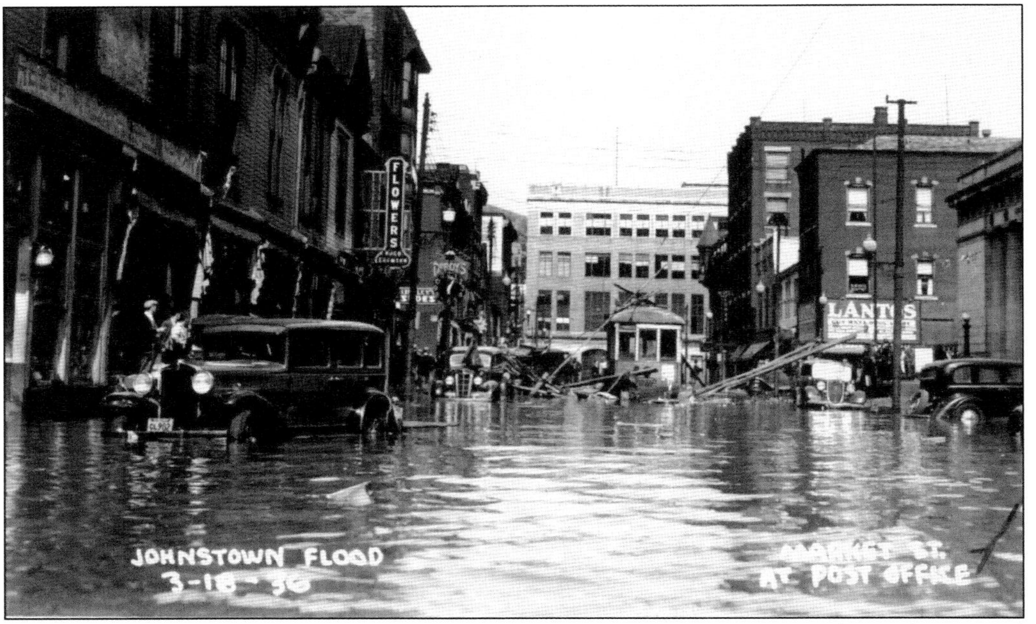

As the water begins to recede, abandoned cars and even a trolley sit among downed wires and debris on Market Street. This March 17, 1936, view looks toward the public safety building. (Courtesy of Jeanne D. Buck.)

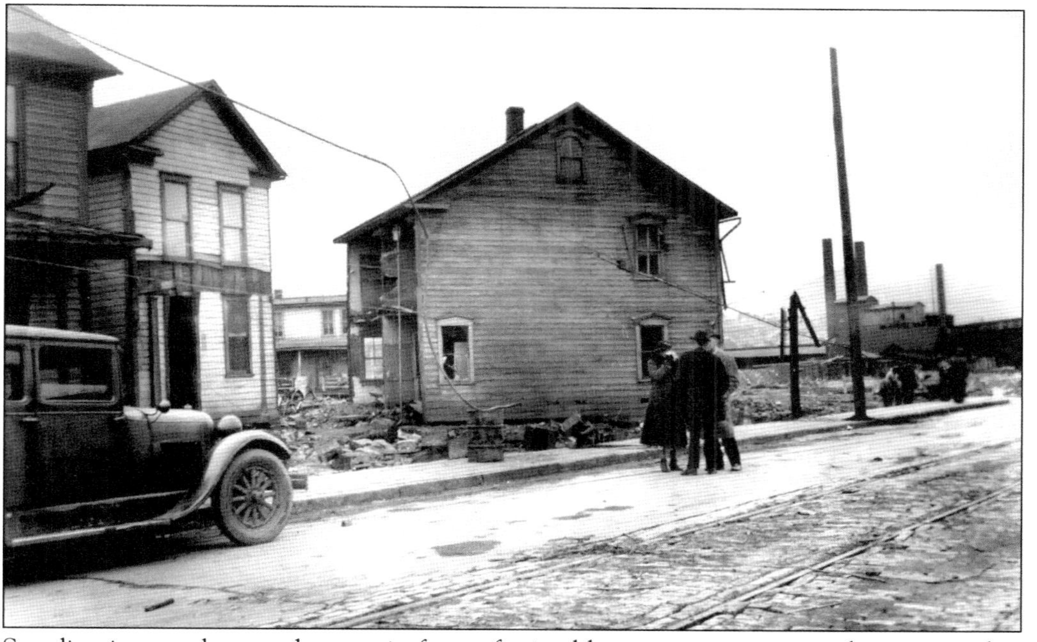

Standing in a mud-covered streets in front of ruined homes, a woman wipes her tears with a white hanky while talking with two men, probably feeling the same sort of loss experienced by flood victims in 1889. The 1936 flood took more than two dozen lives and destroyed over $40 million worth of property. (Courtesy of the Johnstown Area Heritage Association archives.)

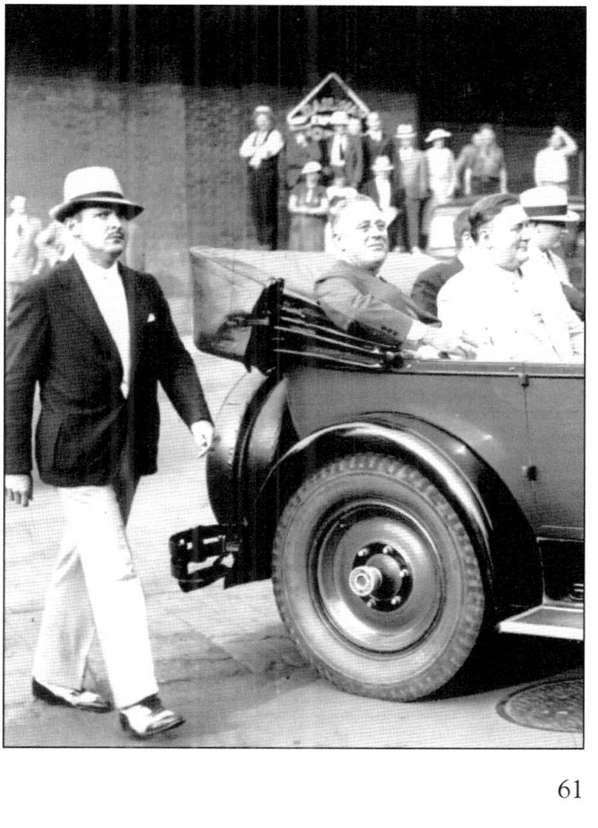

Surrounded by security guards and hopeful residents, Pres. Franklin D. Roosevelt rides with Johnstown's Mayor Daniel Shields to survey the damage caused by the 1936 flood. This visit pushed Congress to authorize the building of extensive flood controls to protect Johnstown from future flooding. The work was completed in 1943, and Johnstown was designated the Flood Free City. The improvements and the title held until 1977, when Johnstown suffered another massive flood. (Courtesy of the Johnstown Area Heritage Association archives.)

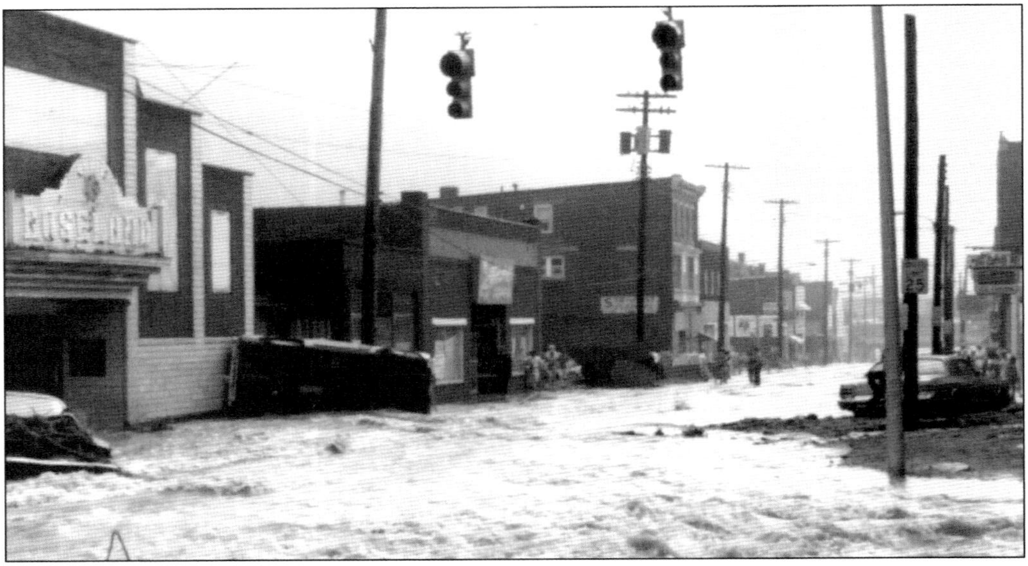

The rain began on July 19, 1977, and continued throughout the night, dumping nearly 12 inches of rain in 10 hours on the sleeping city. By morning, residents were without electricity and battery-powered radios relayed the voice of Pres. Jimmy Carter making the proclamation that Johnstown was again a flood disaster area. Fairfield Avenue was a churning river in front of the Roseland Roller Rink on July 20, 1977. (Courtesy of the Johnstown Area Heritage Association archives.)

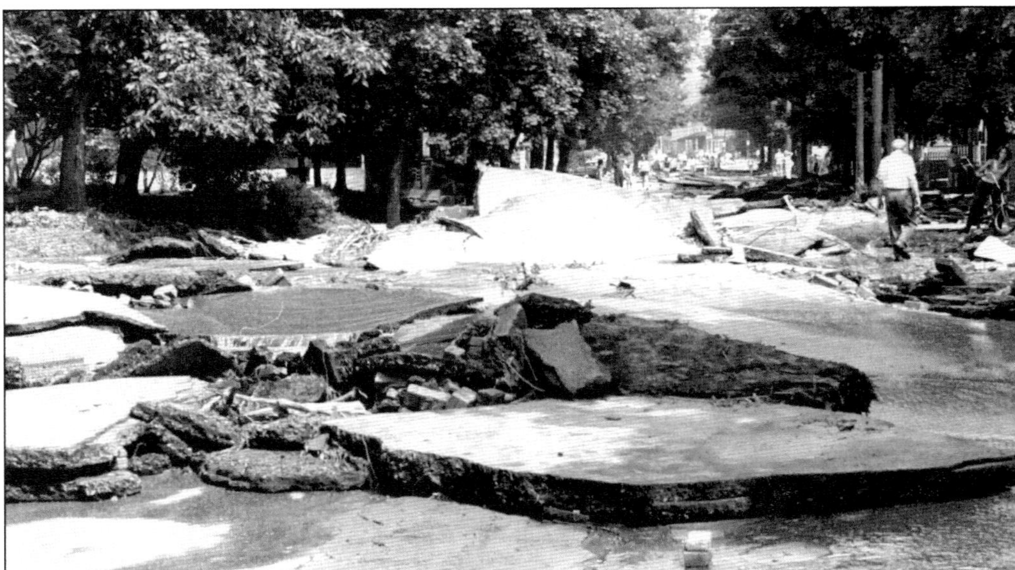

In the 1977 flood, 85 people died and Johnstown sustained projected damages of $300 million. With the economy in dire straits, many businesses like stalwart Penn Traffic decided to close and residents considered moving away. This photograph, taken on Ohio Street and looking east from Russell Avenue, shows the power of the water that buckled concrete and broke pieces of the street into large chunks. (Courtesy of the Johnstown Area Heritage Association archives and the *Tribune-Democrat*.)

Five

RED, WHITE, AND BLUE

Someone once said, "Give Johnstown an opportunity to celebrate and they'll schedule a parade!" Johnstown residents have gathered in front of flag-draped downtown buildings to say "good-bye" and "welcome home." Local marching bands, big and small, have always been a large part of the celebrations. When the nation marked the end of World War I, more steelworkers marched down Johnstown's streets than any other group.

Over and over, Johnstown men and women have heeded the call, sacrificing life and lifestyle to support the country and its military. Two hometown heroes made the national papers in World War II. U.S. Marine Sgt. Michael Strank was immortalized during the flag raising at Iwo Jima, and Lt. Col. Boyd "Buzz" Wagner became America's first air ace of the war. Many Johnstown homes had the familiar blue, silver, and gold star banners in their front windows.

Because Johnstown was a steel town, the call to arms was always especially personal. Men worked double shifts, and when one of their team was called to serve, others took on extra work to cover his position. There was great pride in the mills, and workers gladly outproduced rival city Pittsburgh.

During the Vietnam War, students at Garfield Junior High School were inspired by the visit of a young U.S. Marine named John Murtha. They collected funds for the creation of a monument to stand in front of the school that would bear the names of soldiers lost in Vietnam.

Before the 1936 flood, a statue in Central Park honored veterans of the Civil War. Unfortunately, it did not fair well during the flood, and after many years, Johnstown residents and organizations gathered funds to provide another statue for the pedestal that stands along Main Street. On November 11, 2000, a bronze statue honoring the 54th Pennsylvania Volunteer Infantry was dedicated in Central Park. In conflict or peace, Johnstown proudly shows its colors.

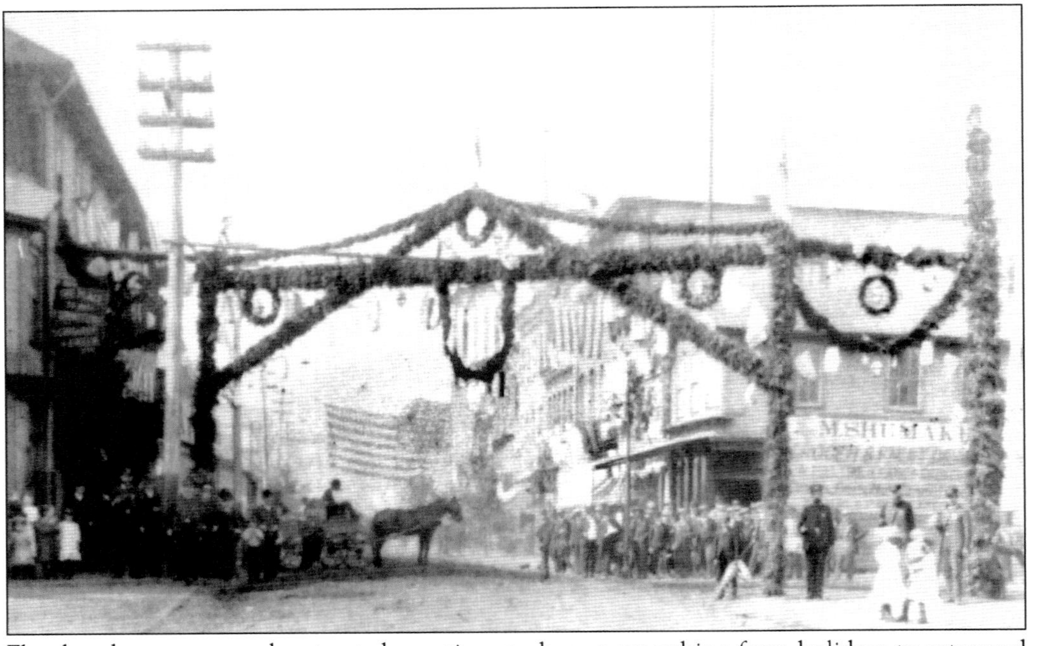

Floral arches were popular street decorations to honor everything from holidays to esteemed visitors. This custom was notably used at the time of Pres. Abraham Lincoln's assassination, as each town along the route of his funeral train created a floral arch to express its grief for the fallen president. This image shows a horse-drawn carriage passing beneath a floral arch on Main Street *c*. the 1880s. (Courtesy of the Johnstown Area Heritage Association archives.)

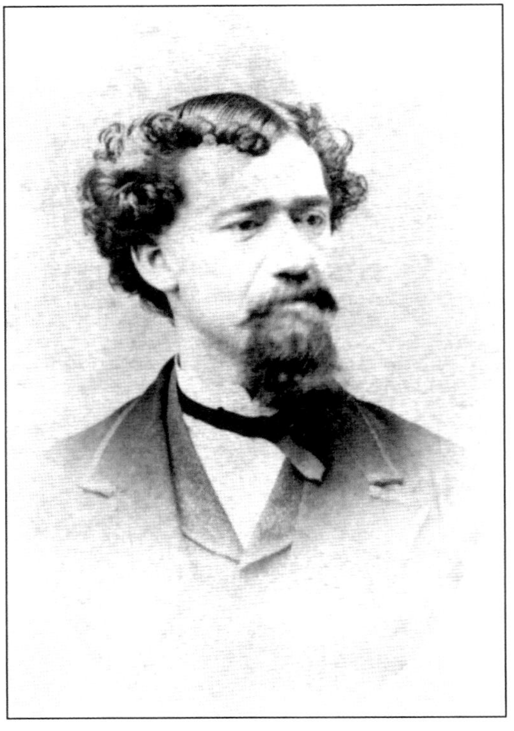

Union Civil War veteran Johnston Glass West enlisted at age 17. He suffered wounds and stints at Libby Prison and Bell Island. After a prisoner exchange, he could have gone home. Instead, he fought at Fredericksburg and Chancellorsville before losing a leg at Gettysburg. Only a short rest later, he headed to Washington to serve in the quartermaster general's department. After he finally settled back in Ferndale with his wife, Mary (Vickroy), West held many political positions. In 1896, he became Ferndale's first elected burgess. (Courtesy of the Ferndale Historical Society.)

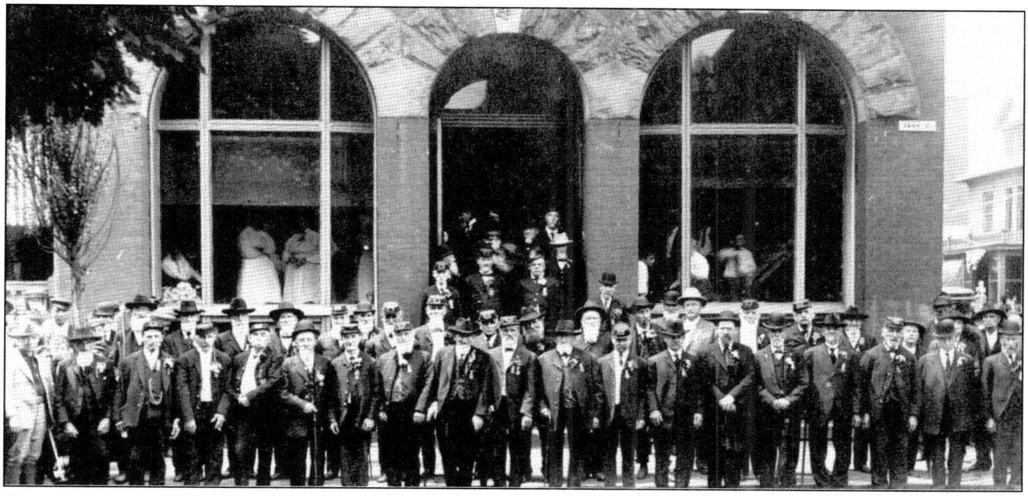

True survivors of war and disaster, these Civil War veterans stand in front of the Park Avenue building of the Grand Army of the Republic (GAR) on May 31, 1909, the 20th anniversary of the 1889 flood. This was the second GAR building, as the first was destroyed in the 1889 flood. (Courtesy of the Johnstown Area Heritage Association archives.)

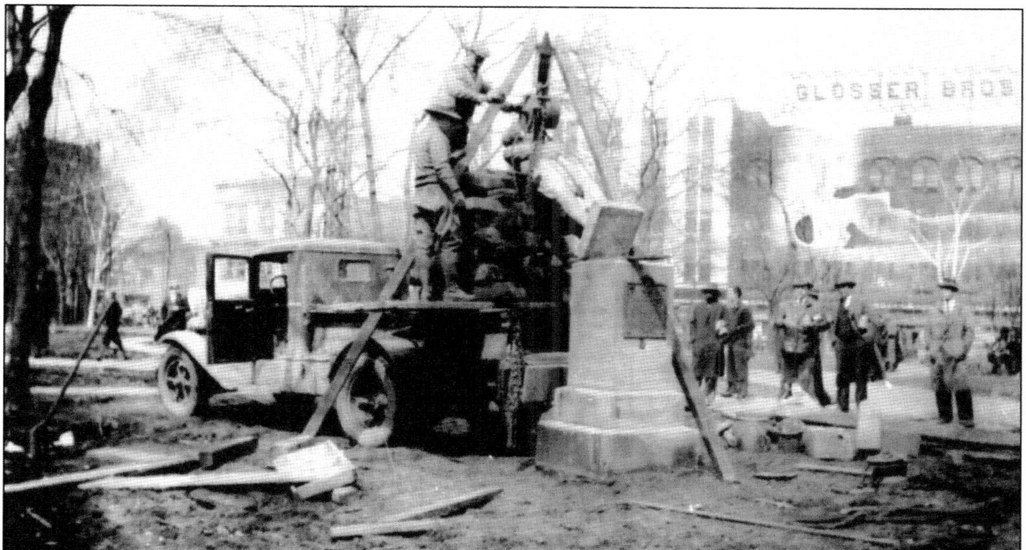

Workmen attempt to position a statue honoring Civil War veterans onto its pedestal in Central Park. This statue was damaged in the 1936 flood and finally stored at the Point Stadium, where it remained without funds for repair. On November 11, 2000, a new statue was installed in Central Park, designed and created by sculptor Gary Casteel. The figure is based on the likeness of Pvt. John Hissong, Company A, 54th Pennsylvania Volunteer Infantry. (Courtesy of the Johnstown Area Heritage Association archives.)

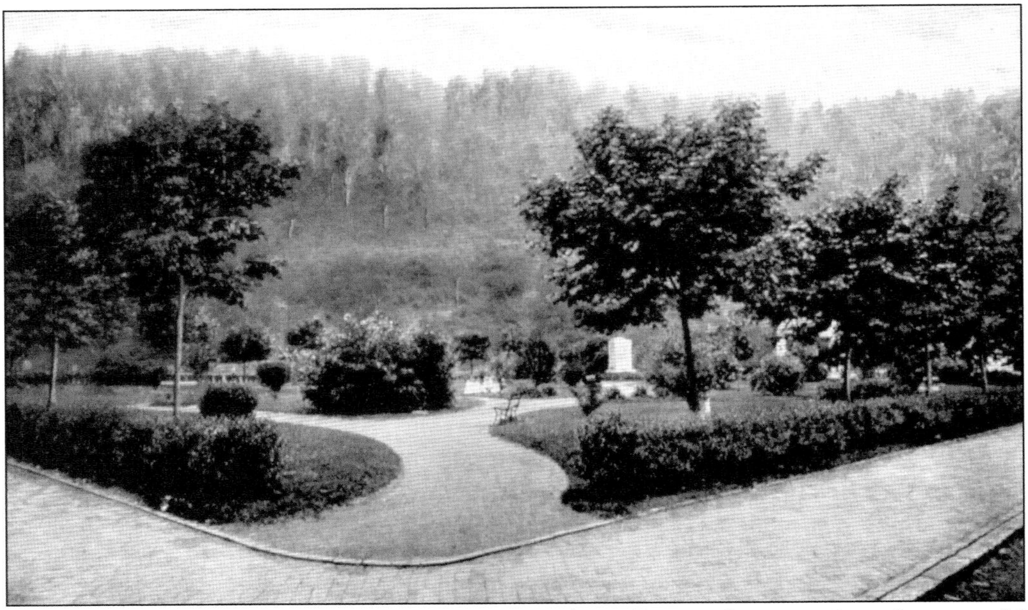

This postcard of the Union Cemetery, on Napoleon Street, shows a place for peaceful contemplation. Joseph Johns designated the land for use as a community cemetery. After the 1889 flood, it was renamed Union Park. (Courtesy of the Cambria County Historical Society.)

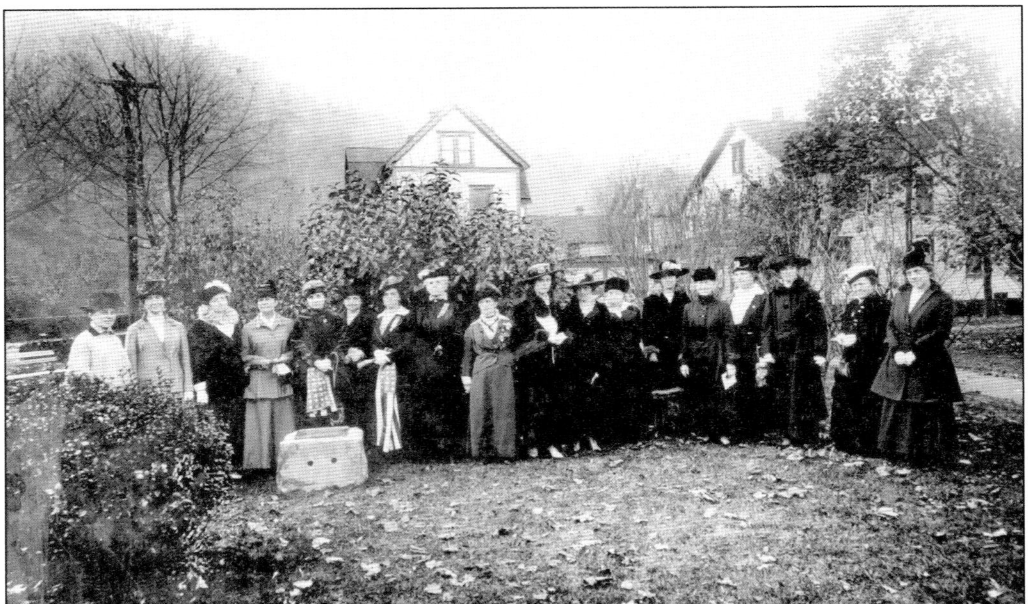

Women of the Daughters of the American Revolution (DAR) dedicate memorials for two Revolutionary War soldiers, George Lucas and Samuel Cole, in an 1898 ceremony at the Union Cemetery. The markers are actually sleepers removed from the defunct Allegheny Portage Railroad. They were relocated to the DAR plot in Grandview Cemetery in 1949 to make way for the construction of the War Memorial Arena. (Courtesy of the Cambria County Historical Society, photograph by J. W. Fletcher.)

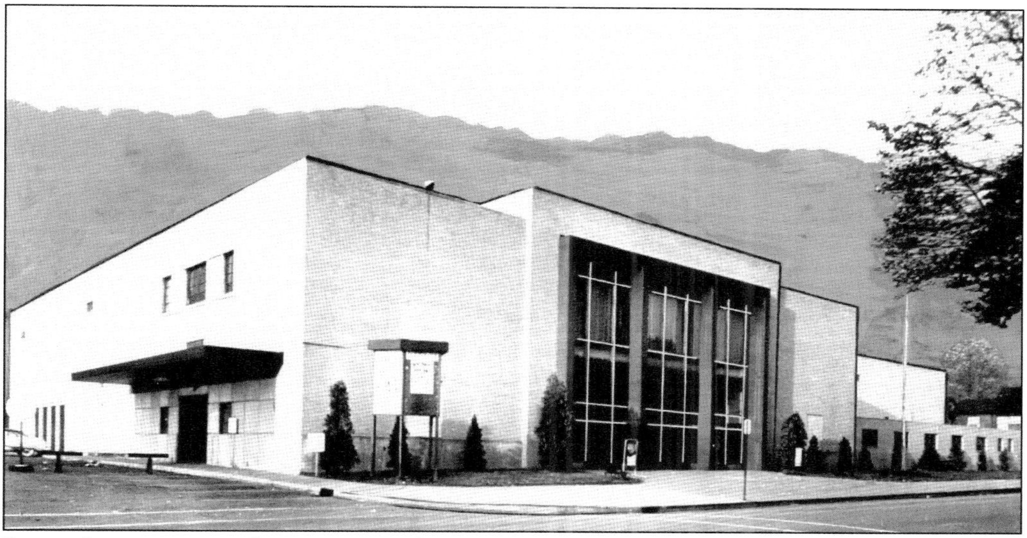

Pictured as it appeared on opening day in 1950, Johnstown's War Memorial Arena stands on Napoleon Street on the land formerly used as the Union Cemetery. Remains discovered during preconstruction were removed to other resting places. (Courtesy of the Cambria County Historical Society and the *Tribune-Democrat*.)

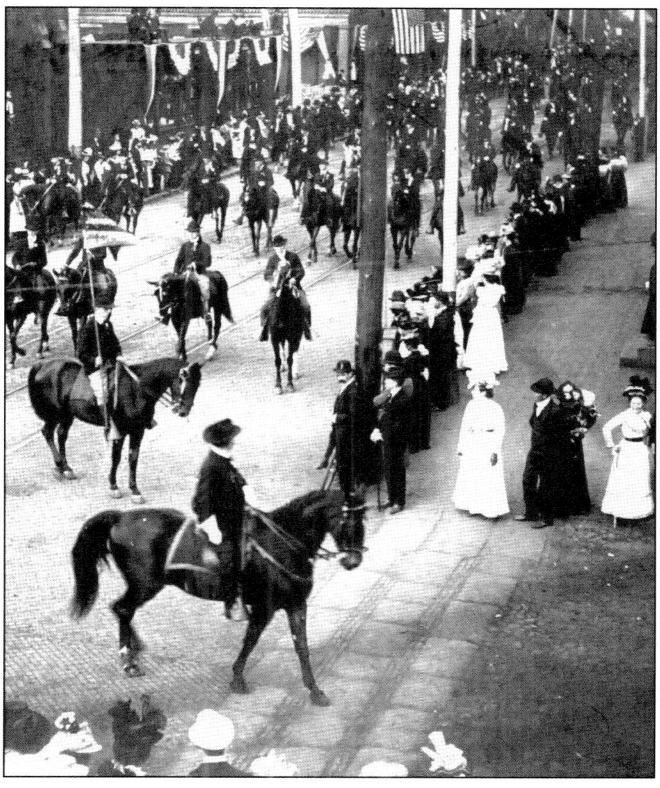

The 1893 Columbus Day parade turns the corner from Franklin to Vine Street, with grand marshal H. H. Kuhn leading the way on his grand horse. (Courtesy of the Johnstown Area Heritage Association archives.)

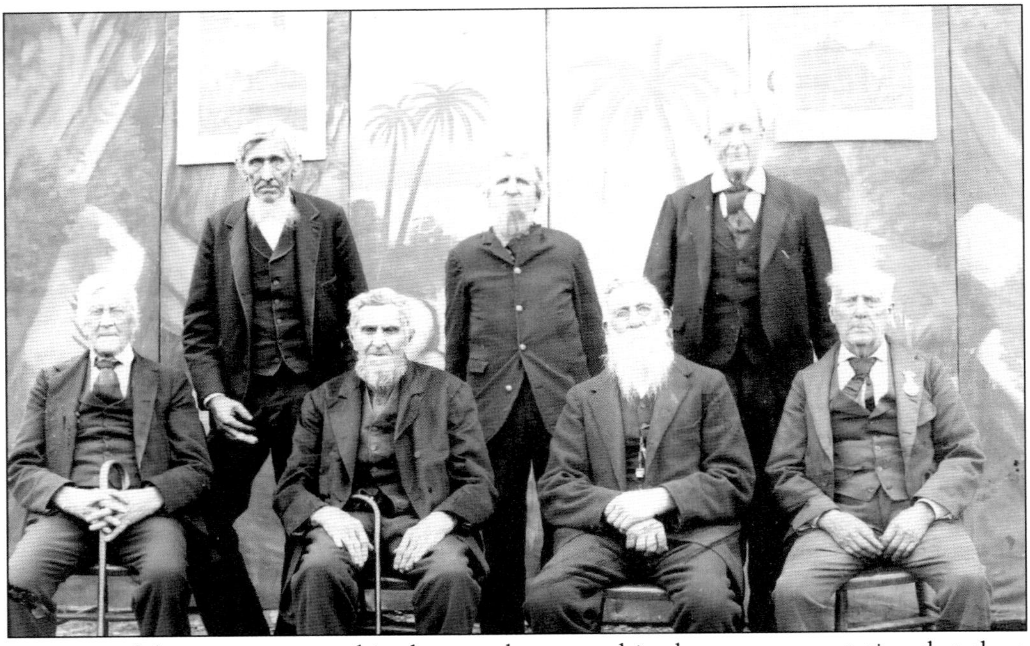

In a turn-of-the-century tease, this photograph appeared in the newspaper, stating that these 90-year-old voters sit with their favorite presidents. In fact, they sit in front of the portraits of Pres. Grover Cleveland, a Democrat, and Pres. William McKinley, a Republican. Although proud of their long voting record, these men were unwilling to say whom they had supported in past elections. (Courtesy of the Johnstown Area Heritage Association archives.)

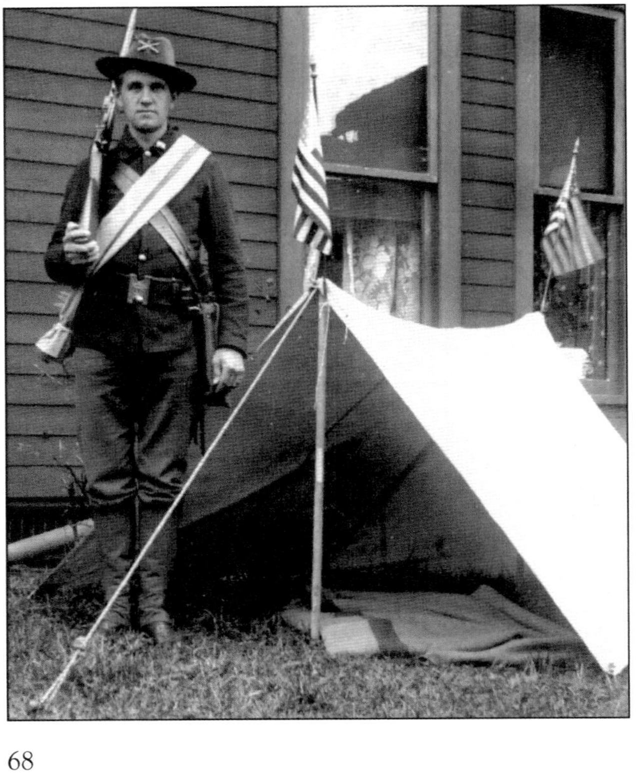

William West of Locust Street models a Spanish-American War uniform, complete with sashes, hat, and gun. It is not clear whether West was a veteran of the five-month war, which took place from April to August of 1898. (Courtesy of the Cambria County Historical Society, Emery West collection.)

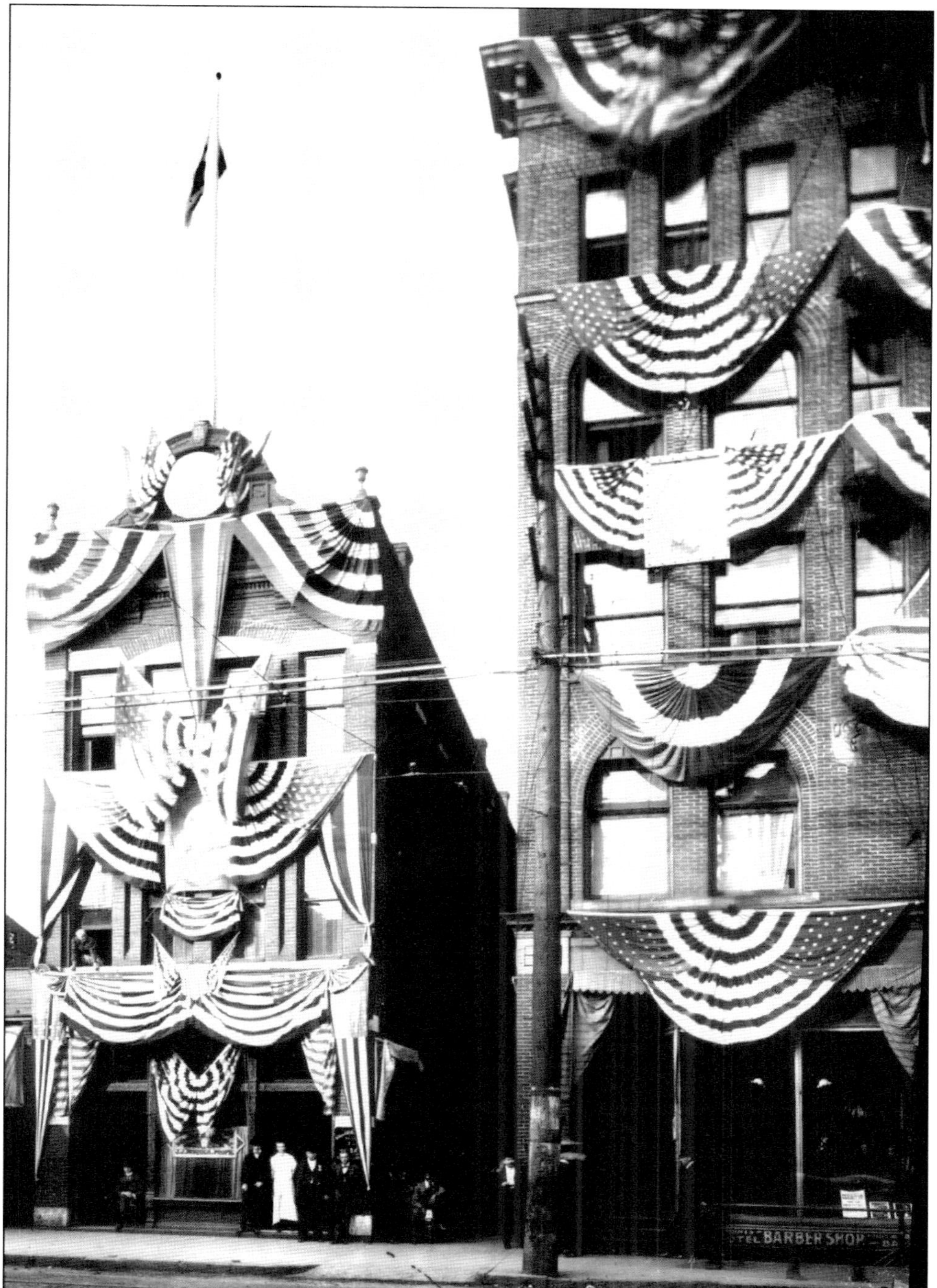

Considering that there were no super-sized cranes available to install these decorations in the 1900s, one wonders how John J. Hornick managed to hang all of the bunting and flags and a portrait of George Washington on the front of his Keystone Hotel, at 533 Main Street. The taller building next door, which houses a barbershop on the lower level, is also quite a patriotic sight. (Courtesy of the Johnstown Area Heritage Association archives.)

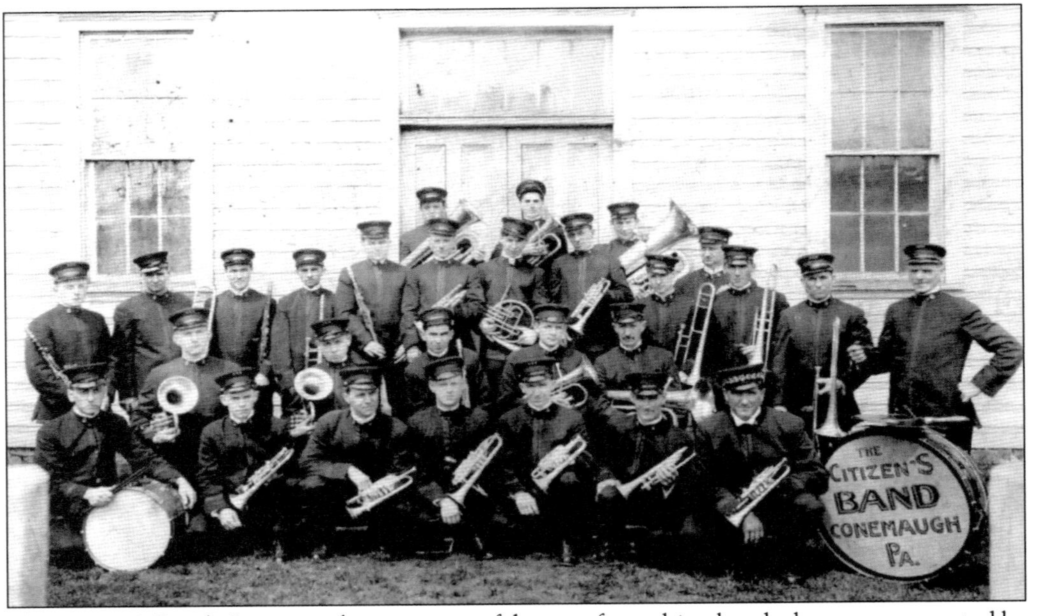

The Citizen's Band, Conemaugh, is just one of dozens of marching bands that were supported by community and ethnic groups, fire companies, or private individuals. These bands all marched in parades honoring veterans and celebrating city events. (Courtesy of the Johnstown Area Heritage Association archives.)

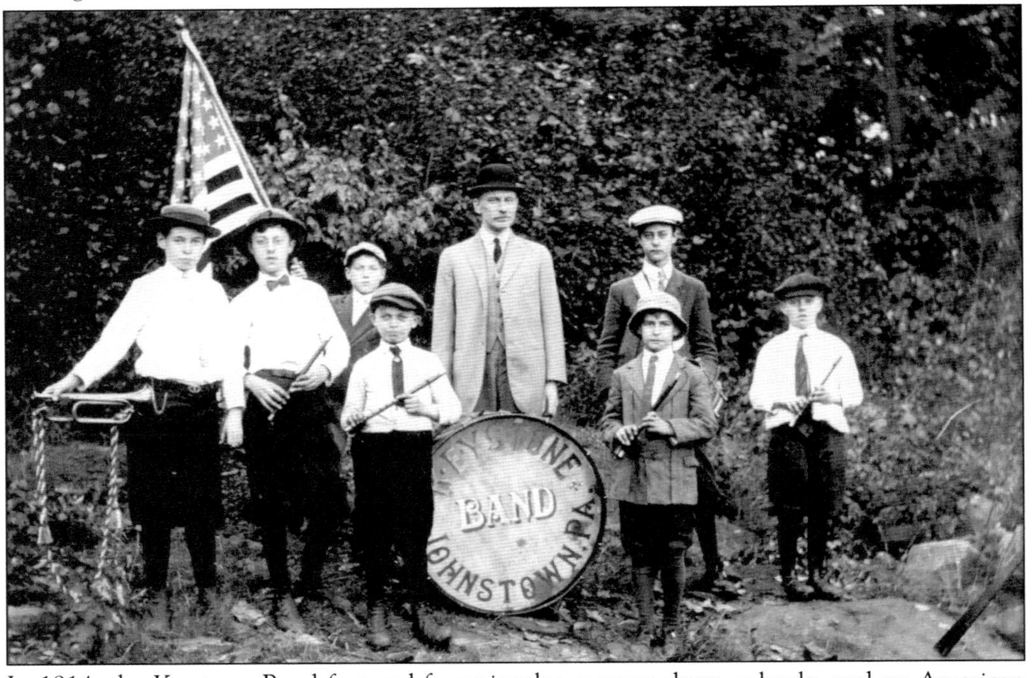

In 1914, the Keystone Band featured four piccolos, a snare drum, a bugle, and an American flag bearer. Specializing in Revolutionary War tunes, the band led by teacher and sponsor Harry Anderson marched in every parade possible. (Courtesy of the Johnstown Area Heritage Association archives.)

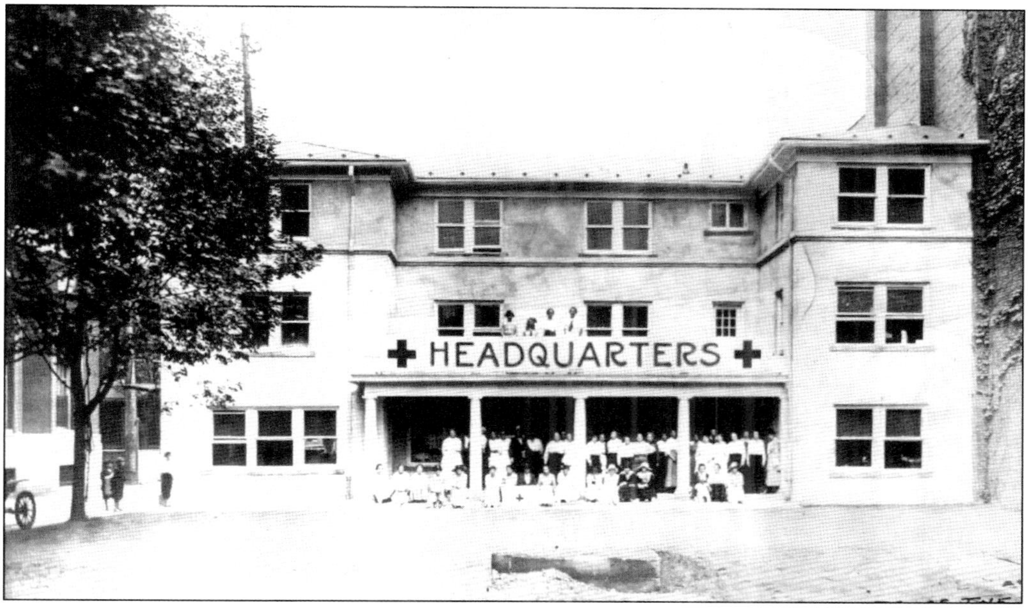

During World War I, the Cambria County chapter of the American Red Cross maintained its headquarters at the Lee Hospital Nurses Home in 1917–1918. (Courtesy of the Johnstown Area Heritage Association archives.)

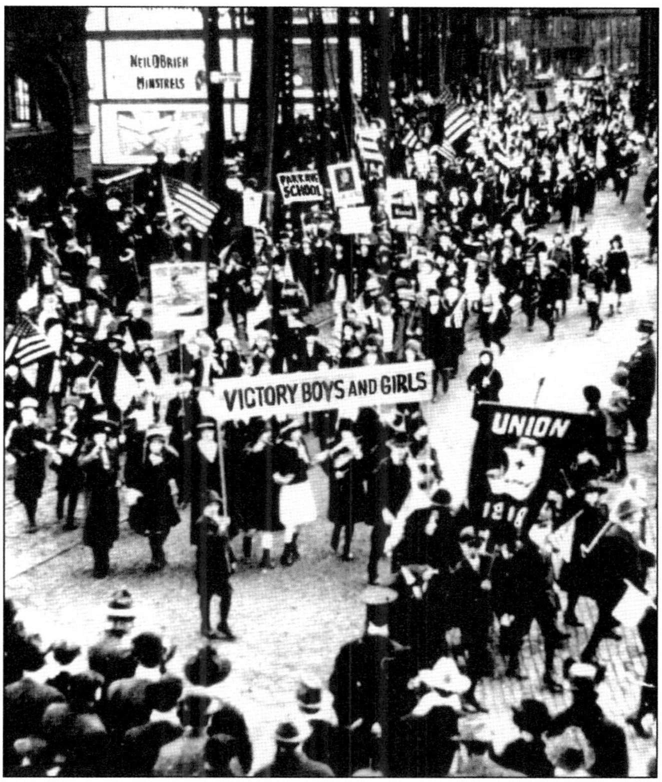

Schoolchildren wave flags and banners as they join in jubilation during the Armistice Day celebration in 1918. (Courtesy of the Johnstown Area Heritage Association archives.)

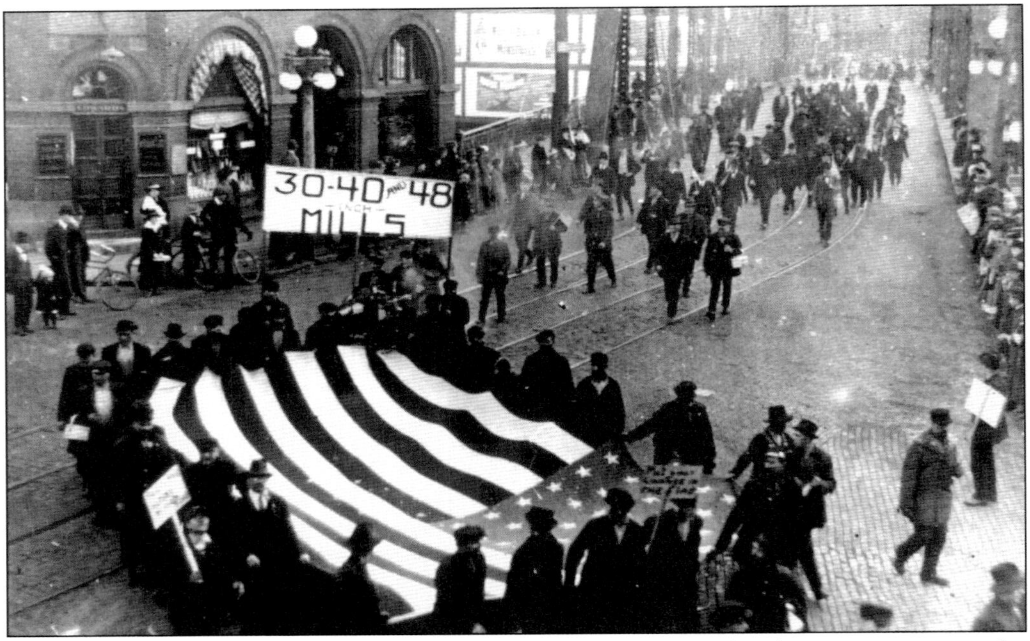

Celebrating the end of World War I in 1918, Johnstown's steelworkers stream across the Franklin Street Bridge and into downtown streets. Many carry signs proudly identifying the mill in which they work. Notice that the 30-inch, 40-inch, and 48-inch mills are represented. One sign next to the large flag says, "Put your courage in the Flag." (Courtesy of the Johnstown Area Heritage Association archives.)

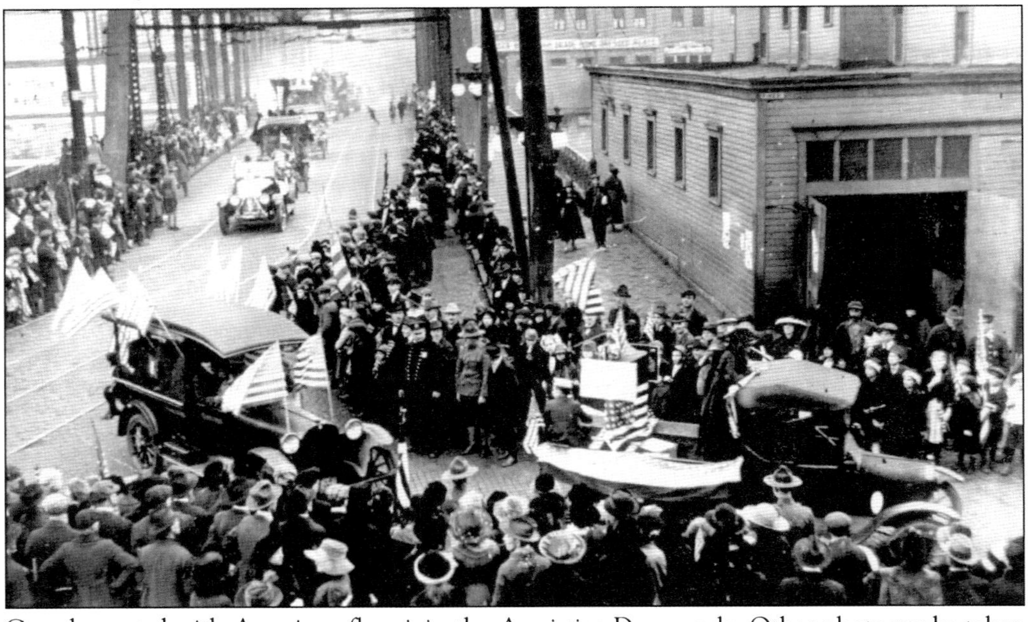

Cars decorated with American flags join the Armistice Day parade. Other photographs taken this day show steelworkers carrying signs announcing that they are "the men who rolled the bullets that licked the Kaiser." Other signs stated, "we rolled 1,000,000 tons." (Courtesy of the Johnstown Area Heritage Association archives.)

The doughboys come home to grateful crowds who lined the sidewalks so deep that the doorways of every store were blocked. (Courtesy of the Johnstown Area Heritage Association archives.)

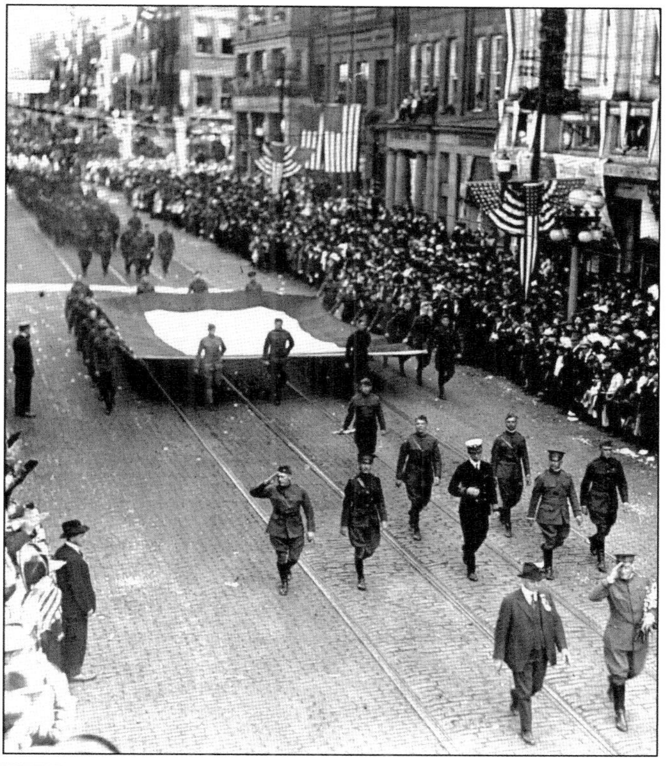

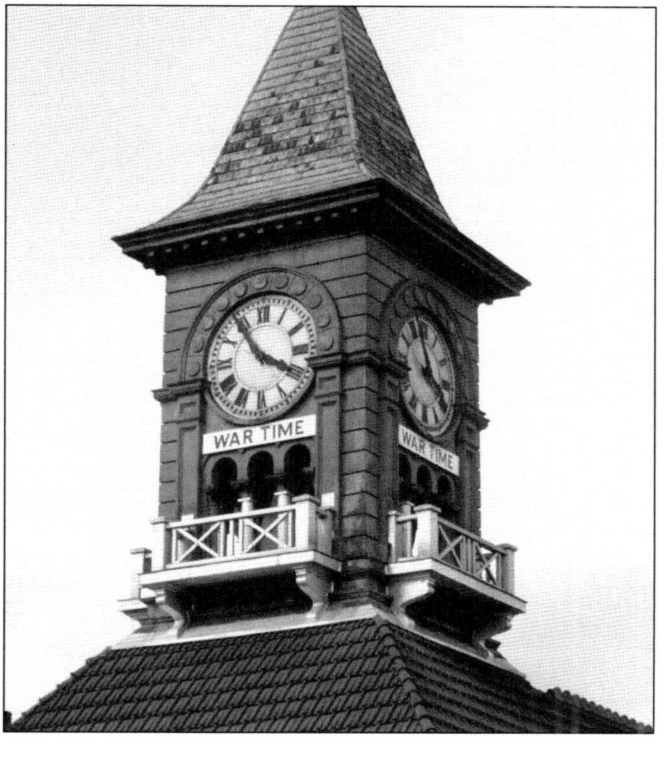

To outsiders, there would be no question that Johnstown supported the war effort, as the clock tower at city hall boldly makes a clear statement. (Courtesy of the Johnstown Area Heritage Association archives.)

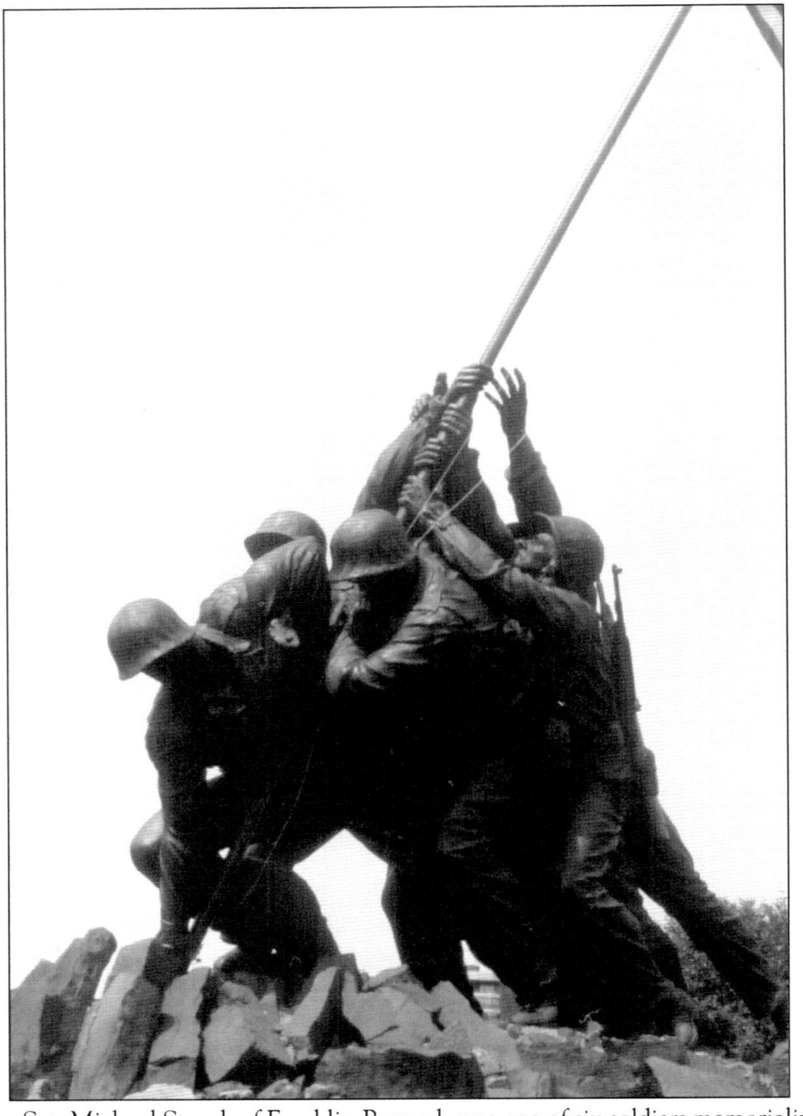

U.S. Marine Sgt. Michael Strank of Franklin Borough was one of six soldiers memorialized in this statue depicting the famous photograph of the raising of Old Glory on the peak of Mount Suribachi on Iwo Jima. Probably the most memorable image of World War II, the Pulitzer Prize–winning photograph shows just Strank's hands: one on the flagpole and the other supporting the wrist of a fellow soldier. In contrast, the above photograph of the back of the bronze and granite statue shows the figure representing Strank on the far right. Strank was killed in what was apparently a friendly fire incident on March 1, 1945, just days after the photograph by Joe Rosenthal of the Associated Press first appeared in the *New York Times* (February 25, 1945). Known as the U.S. Marine Corps Memorial, the $850,000 statue by sculptor Felix de Weldon was dedicated at Arlington National Cemetery on November 10, 1954—the anniversary of the Marine Corps's inception and the birthday of Michael Strank. Among those attending the dedication were Strank's parents, Martha and Vasil Strank, and his siblings Pete, John, and Mary. The inscription on the statue reads, "Uncommon Valor was a Common Virtue," a quotation by Adm. Chester Nimitz. (Photograph by Ellyn Henderson, 2003.)

A portrait of Sgt. Michael Strank shows the youthfulness of a dedicated soldier. Although he was an immigrant, born in Jarabenia, Czechoslovakia, in 1919, he made the supreme sacrifice at Iwo Jima as an American soldier. He was 26 years old. (Photograph by Ellyn Henderson, 2003.)

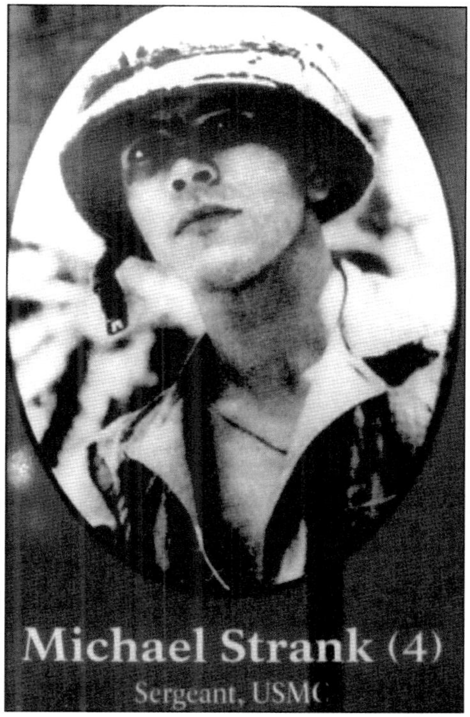

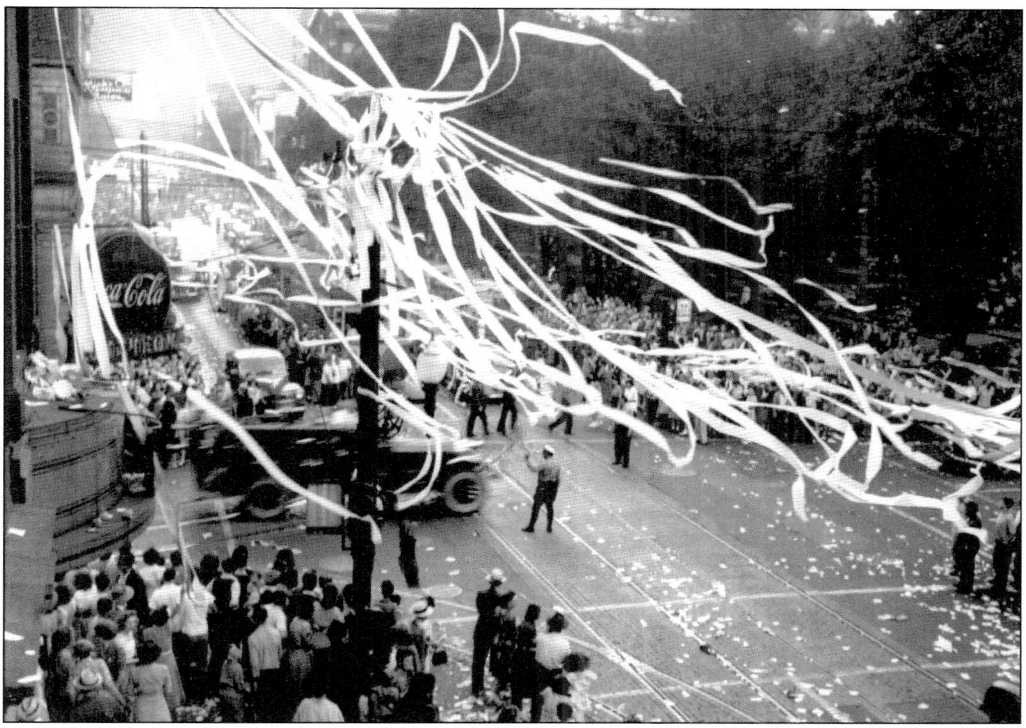

As residents gather to celebrate V-J Day in 1945, police try to contain the crowds, as confetti and streamers spill into the streets at Main and Franklin. (Courtesy Park Cove:, Cover Studio.)

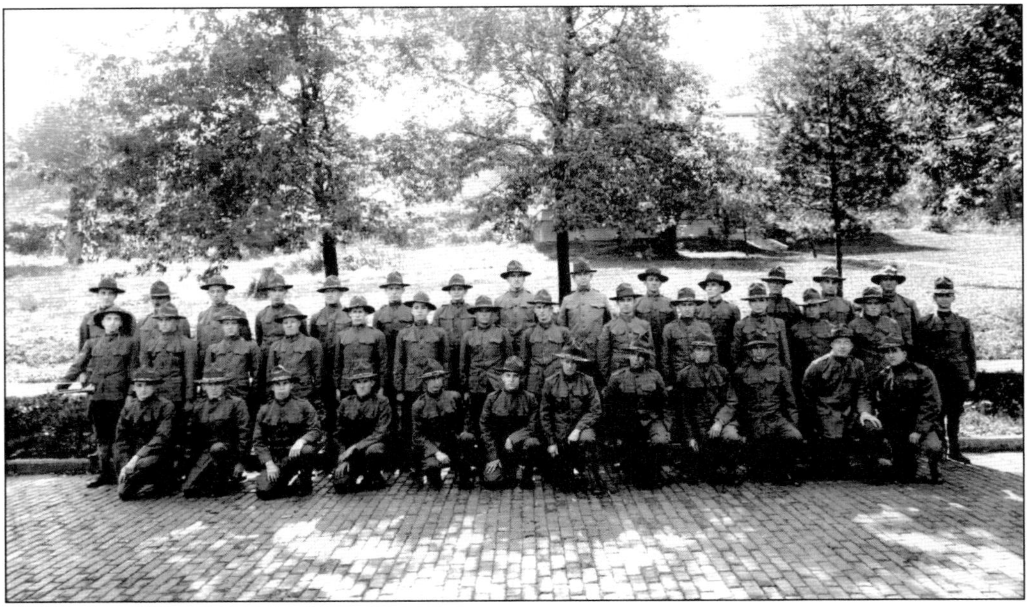

A division of the home guard was formed in Johnstown after World War I. The organization is considered the precursor of today's National Guard. Many residents from Ferndale appear in this photograph, which was taken apparently in the 600 block of Vickroy Avenue. (Courtesy of Jeanne D. Buck.)

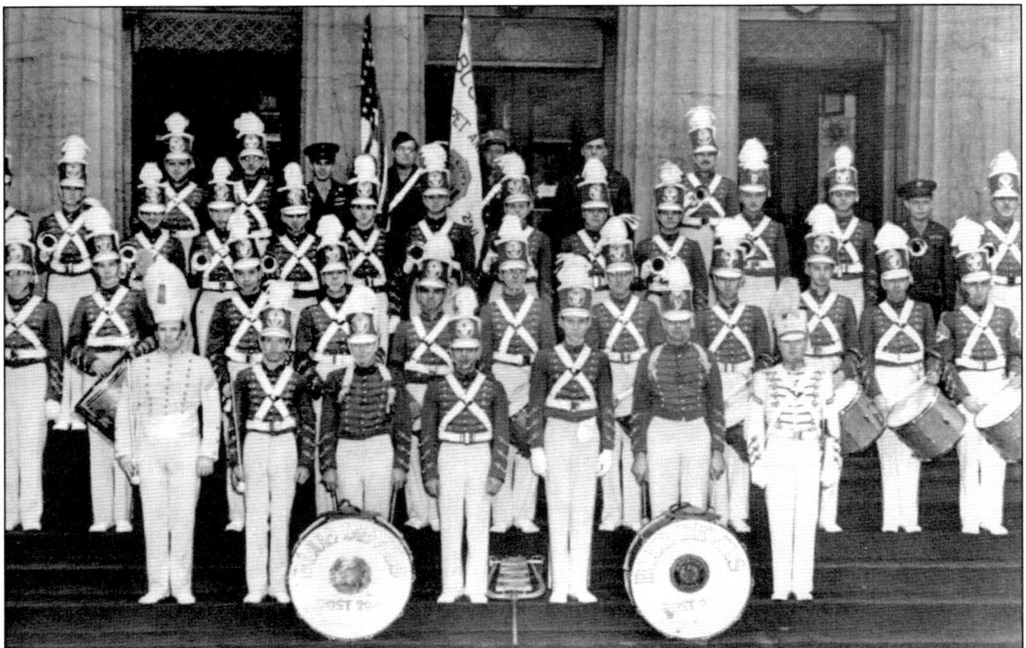

The Blue Devils Trumpet and Drum Corps formed before 1920 and was sponsored by American Legion Post No. 294. The trumpets had just one valve, which made them more difficult to play, much like a bugle. This photograph was taken in 1935. (Courtesy of Merle Showalter.)

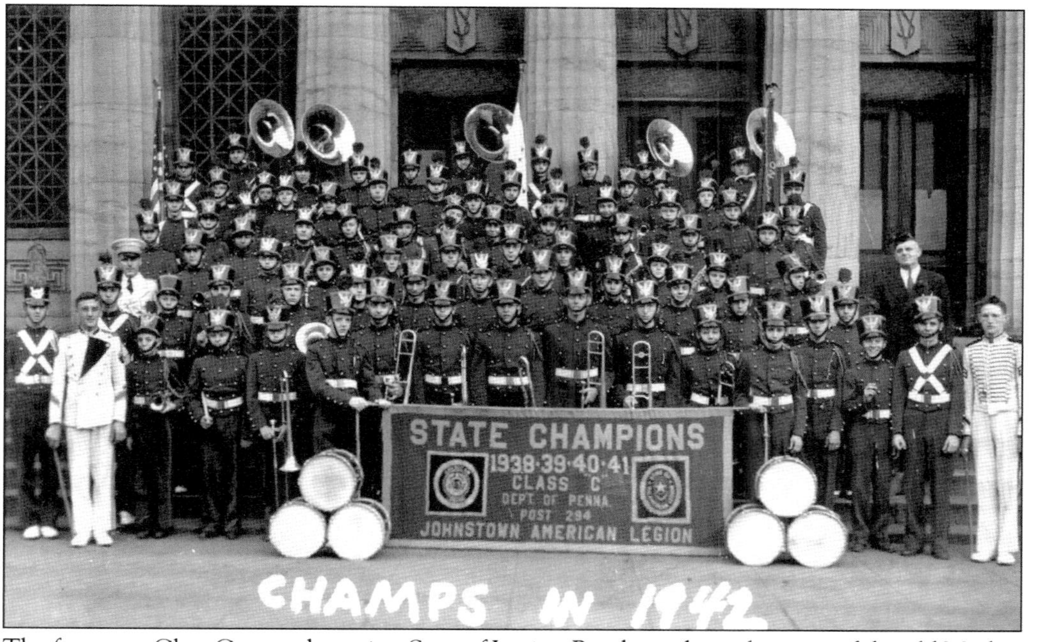

The four-year Class C state champion Sons of Legion Band stands on the steps of the old Market Street post office in 1941. The Johnstown American Legion Post No. 294 also supported this group and the American Legion Youth Chorus beginning in 1937. The American Legion believed that participation in such groups encouraged civic duty and patriotism. (Courtesy of the Johnstown Area Heritage Association archives.)

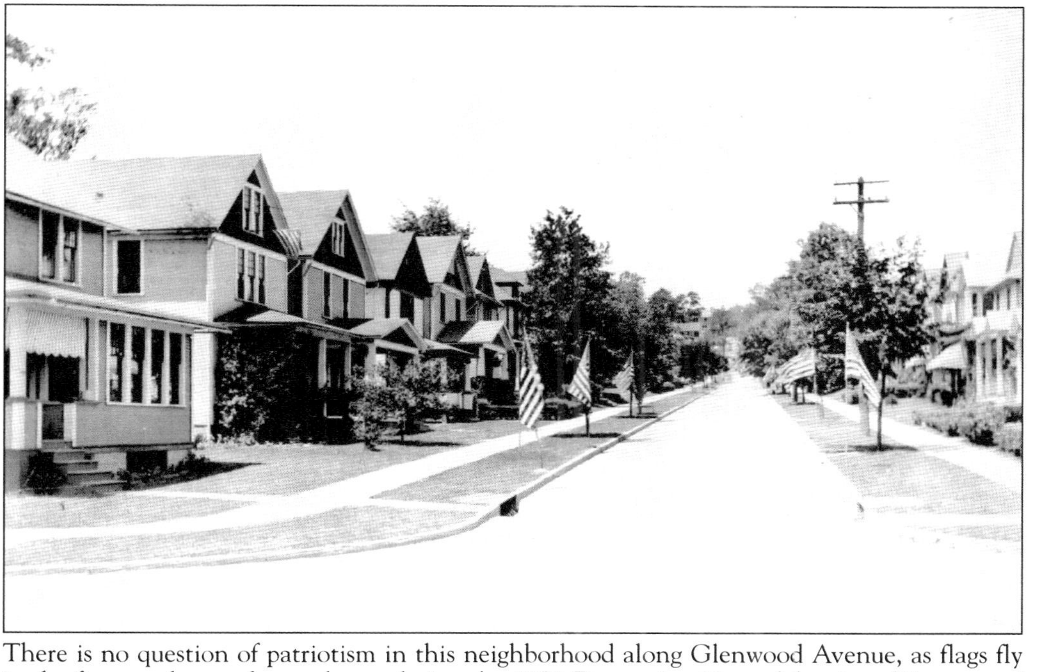

There is no question of patriotism in this neighborhood along Glenwood Avenue, as flags fly in the front parkway of every home during the 1939 Decoration Day celebration. (Courtesy of Jeanne D. Buck.)

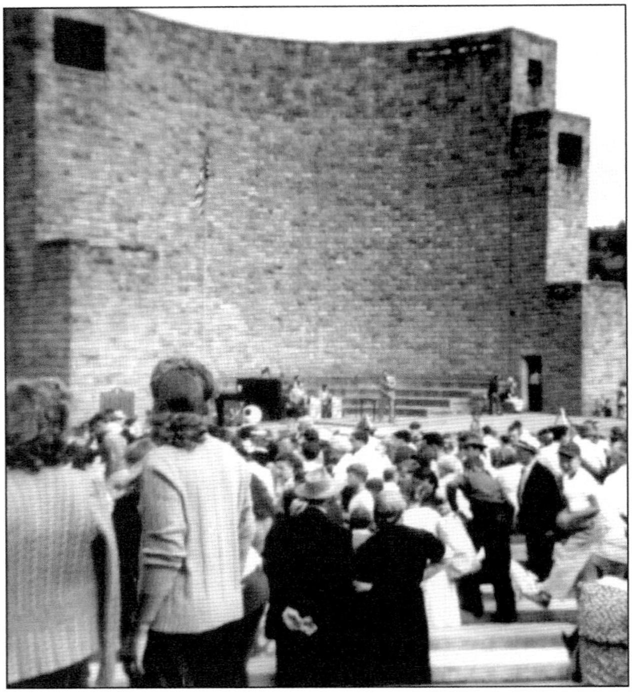

Crowds gather at the Roxbury band shell, ready to celebrate Labor Day 1948 with a picnic lunch and holiday concert. Formally named the Municipal Music Pavilion, the structure was dedicated in June 1940 with seven days of festivities, including concerts, dancing, and dignitary speeches. (Courtesy of the Johnstown Area Heritage Association archives.)

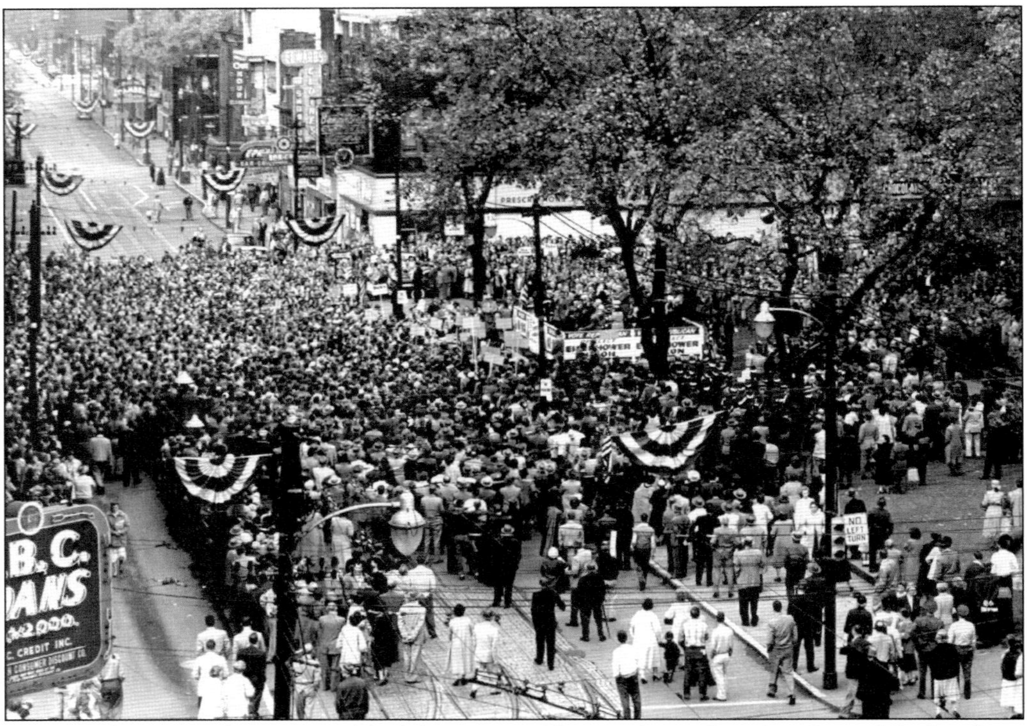

Apparently, some Johnstowners liked Ike, as a sizable crowd is gathered at Central Park to hear presidential candidate Dwight D. Eisenhower stump for votes in 1952. Eisenhower won the state of Pennsylvania in his presidential bid. (Courtesy of Park Cover, Cover Studio.)

Six

Main Street

Clattering ice wagons, teams of unruly horses, and mud-covered boots were a way of life in 1800s Johnstown. Sidewalks were often boards balanced from street to doorway. The variety of available foods was somewhat limited, but foods were fresh. Neighborhood grocers knew people by name and were happy to put purchases on account.

As the population grew, the demand for goods and services expanded. The first store was reportedly a trading post that carried minimal supplies. All changed quickly when the canal was built, bringing traffic and travelers to town. Hotels and restaurants began springing up to accommodate visitors. Demand for better selections and good-quality products inspired a wide variety of businesses. Shoppers in early Johnstown could purchase a fine cut of meat or handsome handmade boots. There were everyday necessities available, like cooking utensils and pottery, made on-site at places like Swank's Johnstown Pottery. Hardware stores carried everything from lumber to nails, as would be expected in today's stores. Johnstown had print shops, clothiers, and confectioners. Everything needed for convenient living could be found downtown.

Grand stores like Penn Traffic Company offered upscale customers fine silver, linens, and clothing. A tearoom was on the premises, and helpful professional sales clerks offered personal service. Glosser Brothers became known for great bargains and ample inventory. As locals said, "If Glosser's didn't have it, you just didn't need it."

Today, landmarks like the inclined plane have become tourist attractions, but even residents visit the upper platform to enjoy the view of the city below. There is great power in the quietness of the city. Although the downtown has changed over the years, no matter from calamity or economic downturn, the buildings below remind us that "this town won't die."

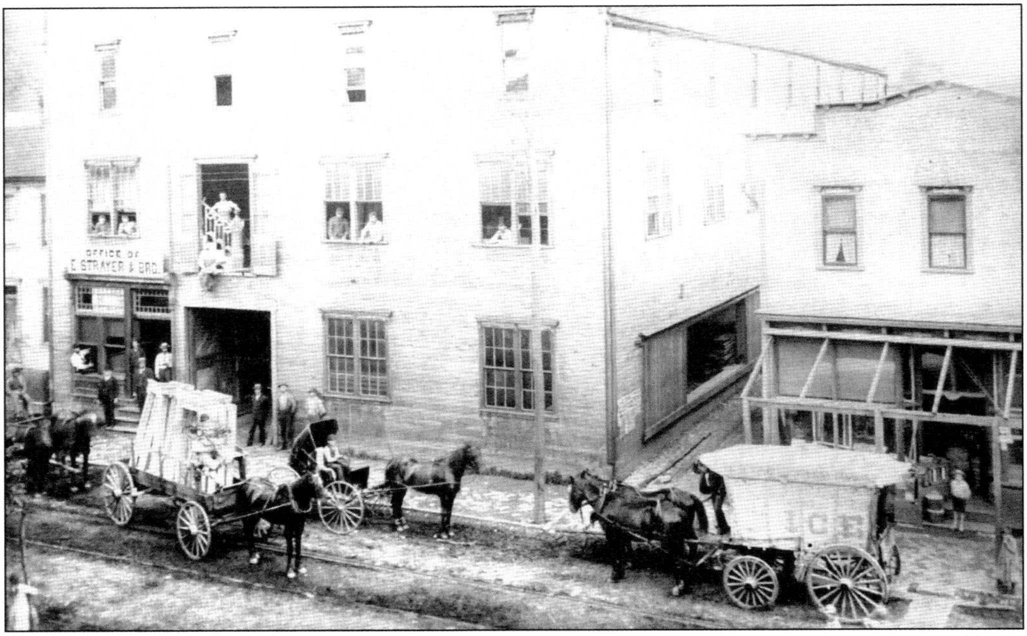

As neighbors pause to watch the street activity, this could be the start of any day in 1880s Johnstown. An ice-delivery wagon stops at one store while another wagon, transporting windows, navigates past the watchful eyes. (Courtesy of the Johnstown Area Heritage Association archives.)

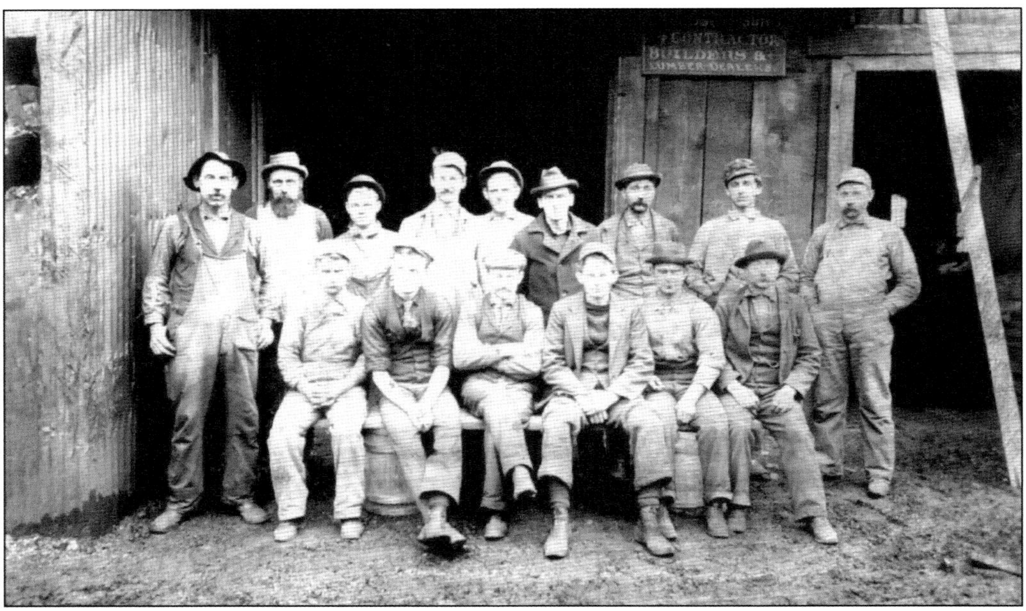

Workers from W. J. Rose and Sons (contractors, builders, and lumber dealers) pose at the main lumberyard and mill on Baumer Street. The firm maintained an office and a second, smaller lumberyard on Lincoln Street between Market and Walnut Streets. The 1869 Johnstown directory indicates that W. J. Rose, who was a talented carpenter, also owned a hardware store with John E. Frey at 200 Main Street. (Courtesy of the Johnstown Area Heritage Association archives.)

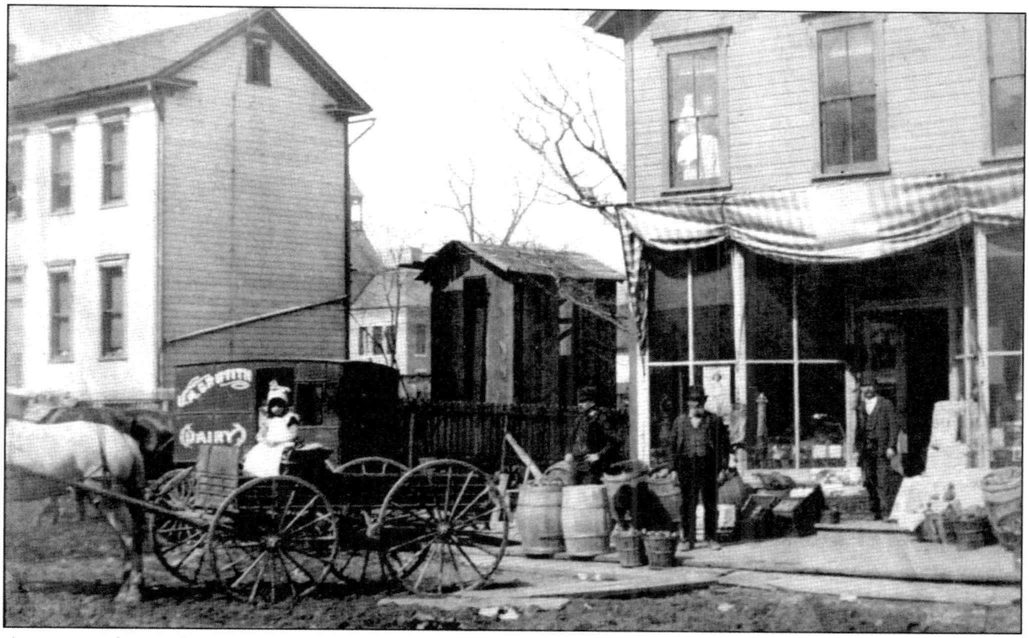

A wagon from the Griffith Dairy delivers products to George Glenn Groceries in 1891. Take note of the rut-filled street and the wooden sidewalk into the store. The neighbor's privy in the yard next door does not look as though it provided much privacy. Glenwood Avenue was named for George Glenn and was initially spelled Glennwood. (Courtesy of Jeanne D. Buck.)

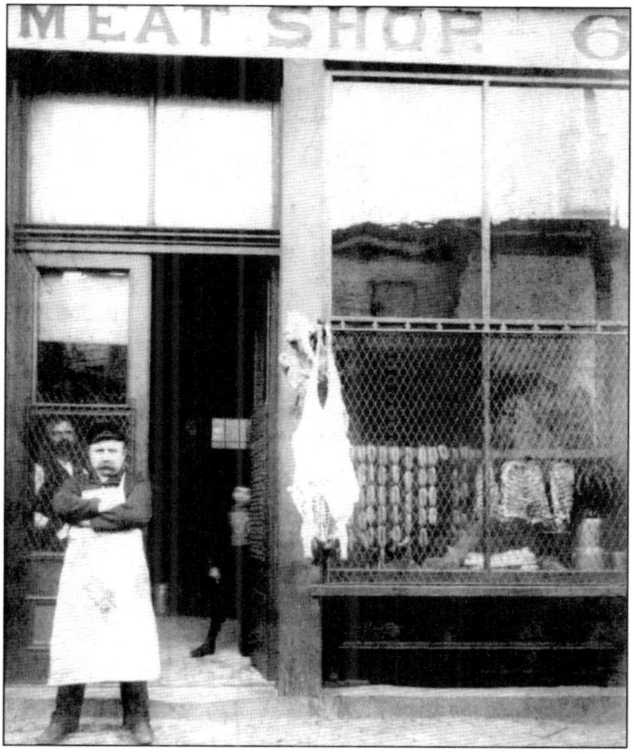

Is there any doubt that customers were on time with their payments to this butcher? (Courtesy of the Johnstown Area Heritage Association archives.)

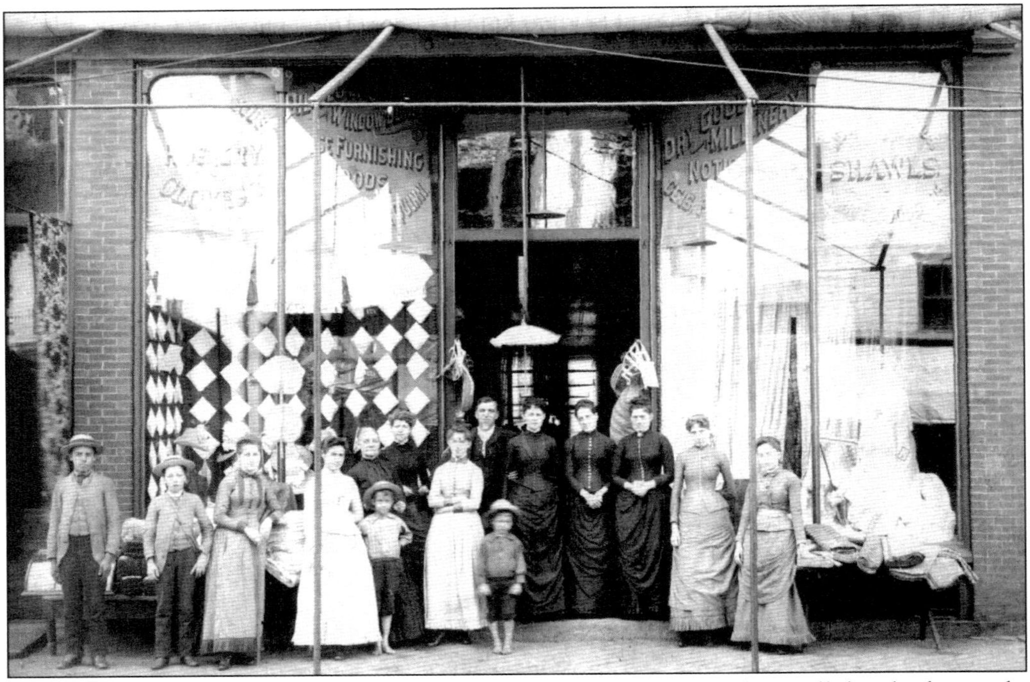

The friendly sales staff of Geis, Foster and Quinn, *c.* 1884, stands ready to sell shawls, dry goods, millinery, and house furnishings. Situated at Clinton and Bedford Streets, the No. 113 address sold wholesale and the No. 115 side sold retail. (Courtesy of the Johnstown Area Heritage Association archives.)

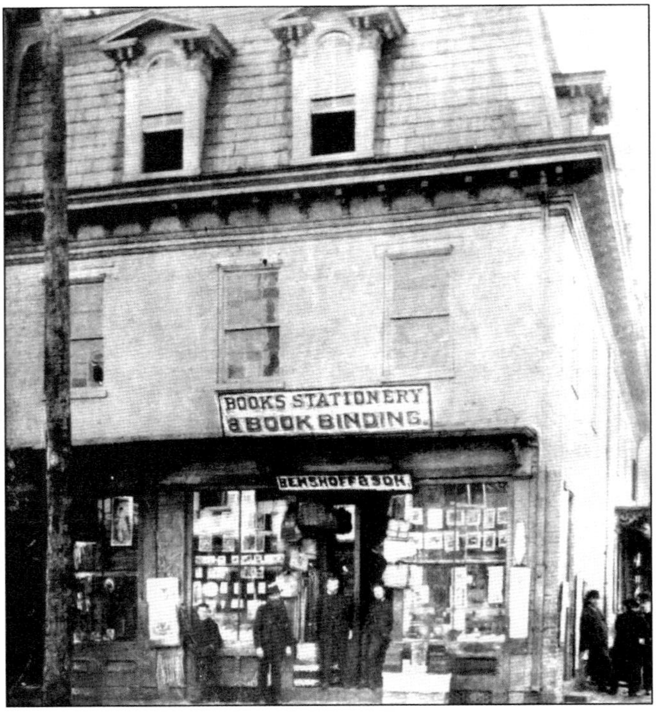

Benshoff and Son opened for business in 1867. By the time this photograph was taken in 1886, the store had expanded substantially. The company was expert in bookbinding and printing and sold ready-made stationery and cards. (Courtesy of the Johnstown Area Heritage Association archives.)

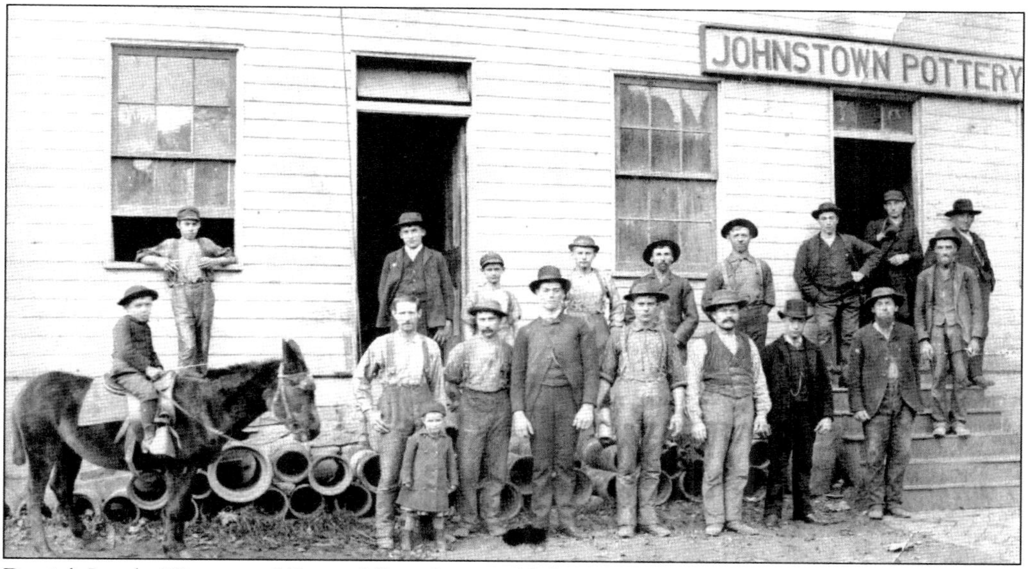

Daniel, Jacob, Hiram, and Samuel Swank owned Johnstown Pottery. The brothers opened their production plant on Morris Street (Franklin Street) *c.* 1860. Although most of their crocks were utilitarian, they did create some pieces considered unique in shape and color design. In the past, their pottery was used every day, but today a Swank crock is considered a collector's item. (Courtesy of the Johnstown Area Heritage Association archives.)

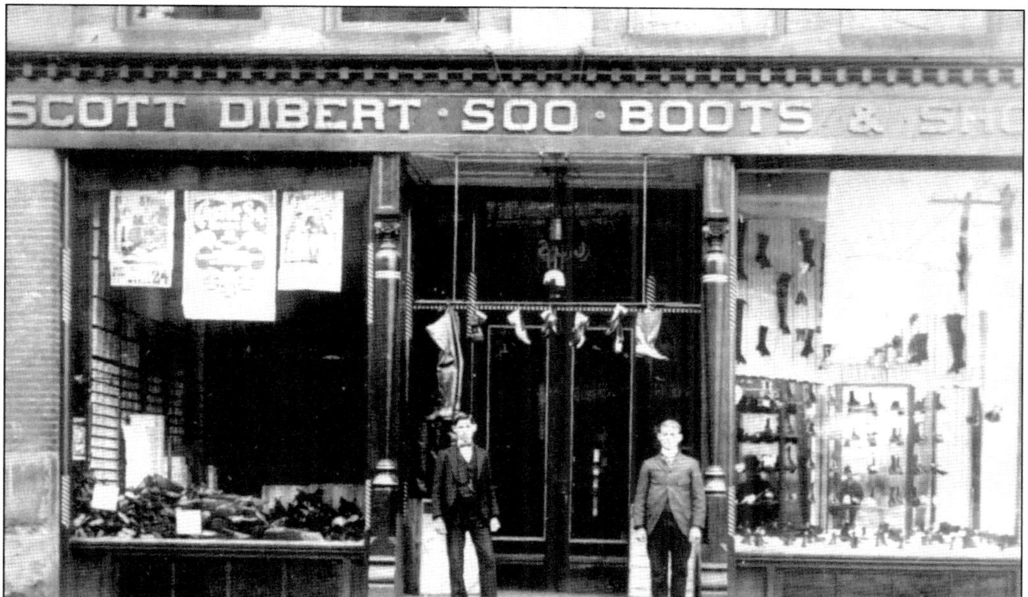

Johnstown native Scott Dibert was a business school graduate who confidently started several endeavors, including a livery and two brick companies. He helped organize the U.S. National Bank and served as the 17th Ward councilman and the director of Johnstown Light, Heat and Power. Scott Dibert Boots and Shoes at 215 Main Street was his first business venture. After 1889, he moved the shoe store to the corner of Franklin and Main Streets, where it remained into the early 1900s. (Courtesy of the Johnstown Area Heritage Association archives.)

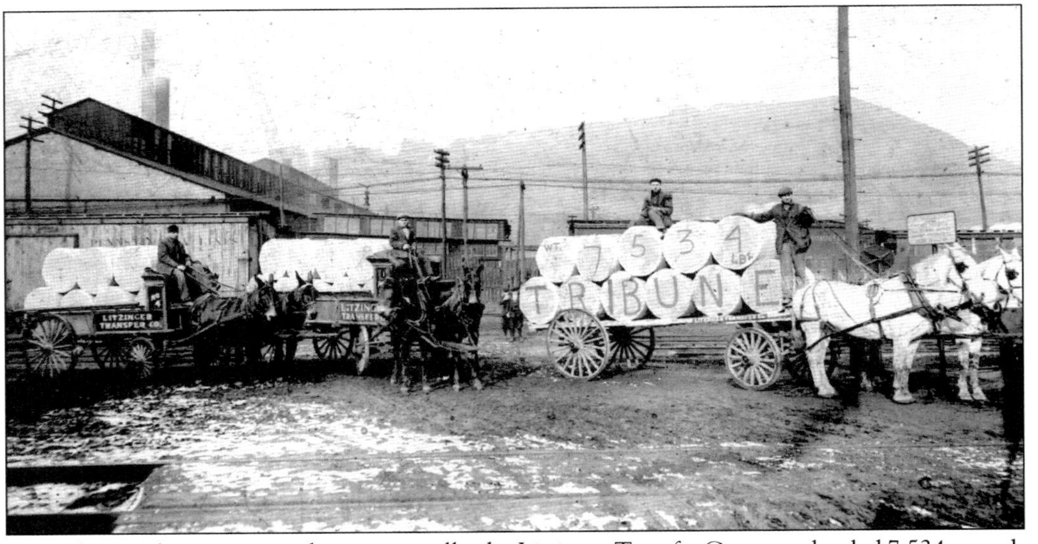

According to the writing on these paper rolls, the Litzinger Transfer Company hauled 7,534 pounds of paper from the Pennsylvania Railroad depot to the *Tribune* newspaper. Not to be outdone, the rival newspaper, the *Democrat*, also ran photographs of massive rolls of paper transported by carriage, boasting that eight such rolls were needed just for their Wednesday edition. (Courtesy of the Johnstown Area Heritage Association archives.)

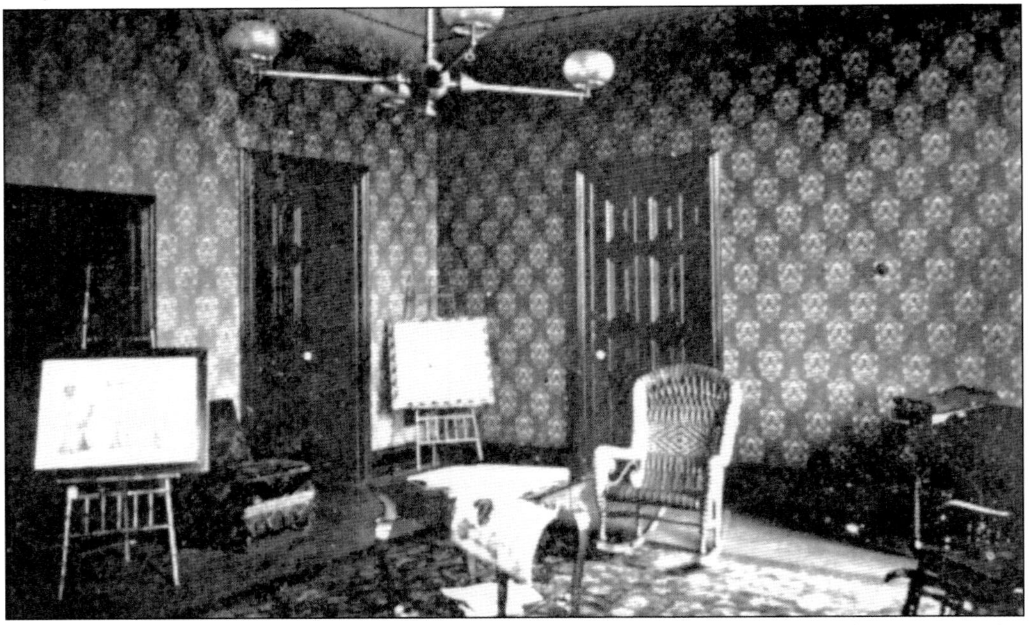

Cambria Iron's company store sold goods under the name Wood, Morrell and Company. On August 1, 1891, Daniel J. Morrell sold the business to Penn Traffic Company. Very quickly, the store became a showcase known for carrying the finest goods and providing personal service. The store's reputation attracted upscale clientele from Pittsburgh, Harrisburg, and surrounding communities. This photograph shows the tasteful Victorian décor of the ladies waiting room. Here, long-distance customers could relax and admire their purchases while waiting for their train home. (Courtesy of the Cambria Library System, Johnstown.)

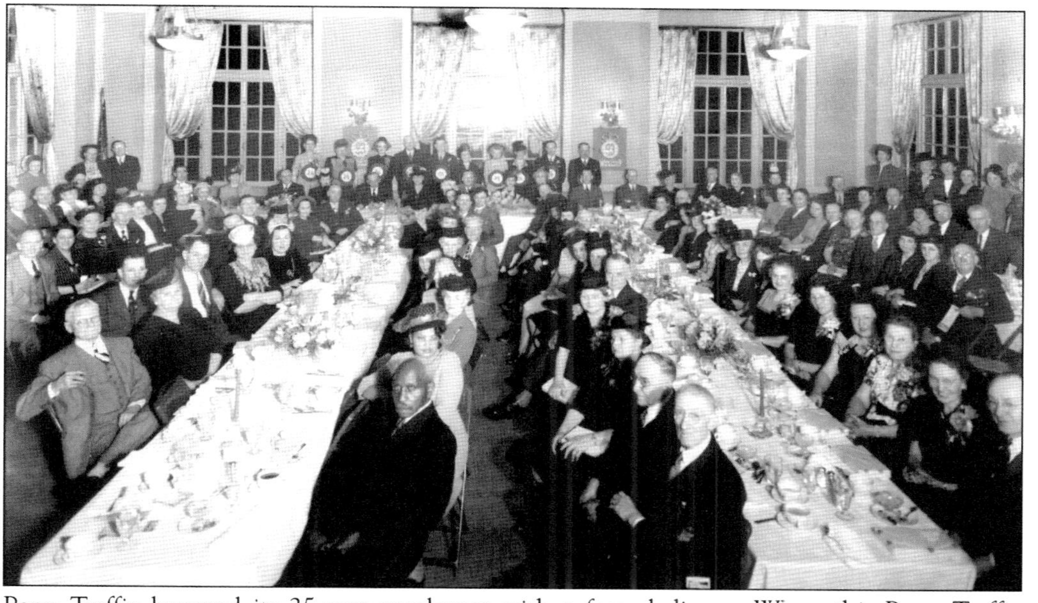

Penn Traffic honored its 25-year employees with a formal dinner. When this Penn Traffic Quarter Century Club banquet was held in February 1947, the store had already been in business for 93 years. The store closed after the 1977 flood. (Courtesy of the Johnstown Area Heritage Association archives.)

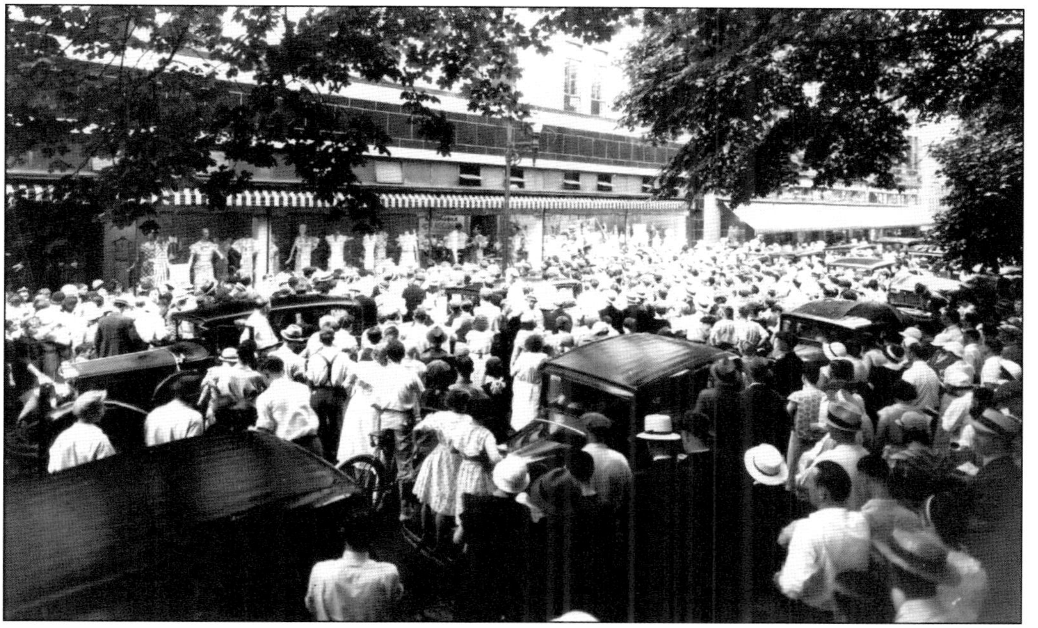

The 1910 Glosser Brothers tailoring business expanded into a store renowned for its scramble-table bargains, wooden floors that squeaked beneath high-heeled shoppers, and smell of freshly roasted red-skinned peanuts. In 1933, large crowds attended the grand opening of this addition, which doubled the store's size. The city felt a great loss when Glosser's closed in 1989, and the pigeons that lived across the street in Central Park probably wondered what happened to their peanut lunches. (Courtesy of the Johnstown Area Heritage Association archives.)

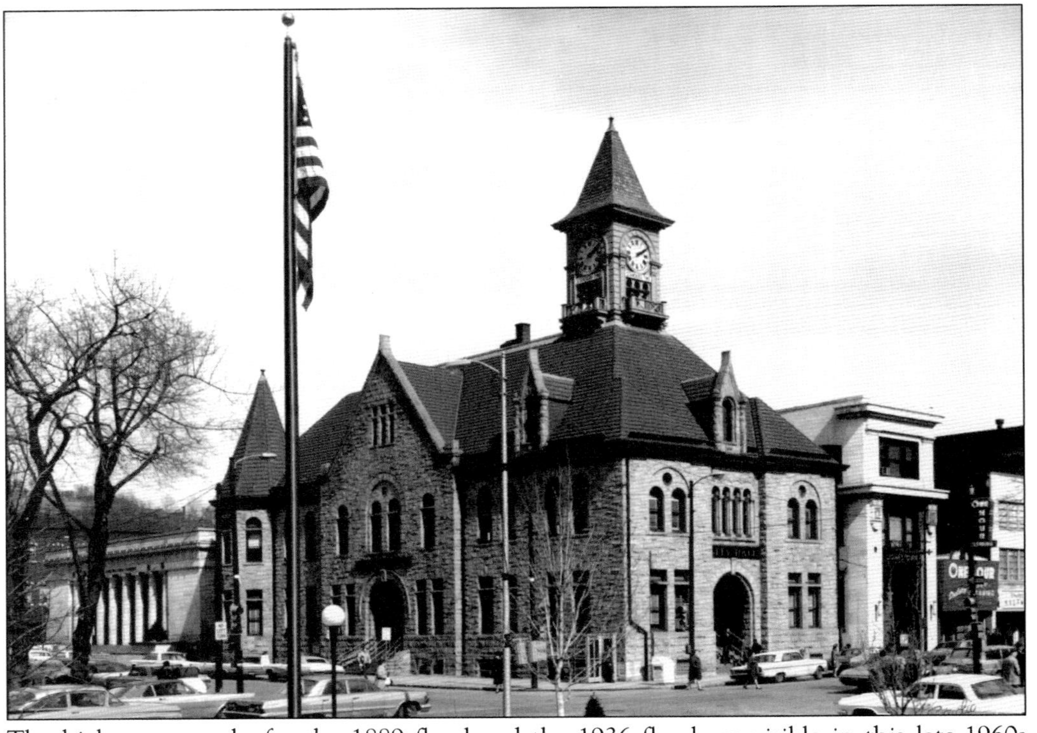

The high-water marks for the 1889 flood and the 1936 flood are visible in this late-1960s picture of city hall. The building was constructed at its Market and Main Street location after the 1889 flood, but the watermark was painted to help passersby visualize the water height of the great flood. Today, there are three labels, with the last one commemorating the 1977 flood. (Courtesy of Jim Cover Jr.)

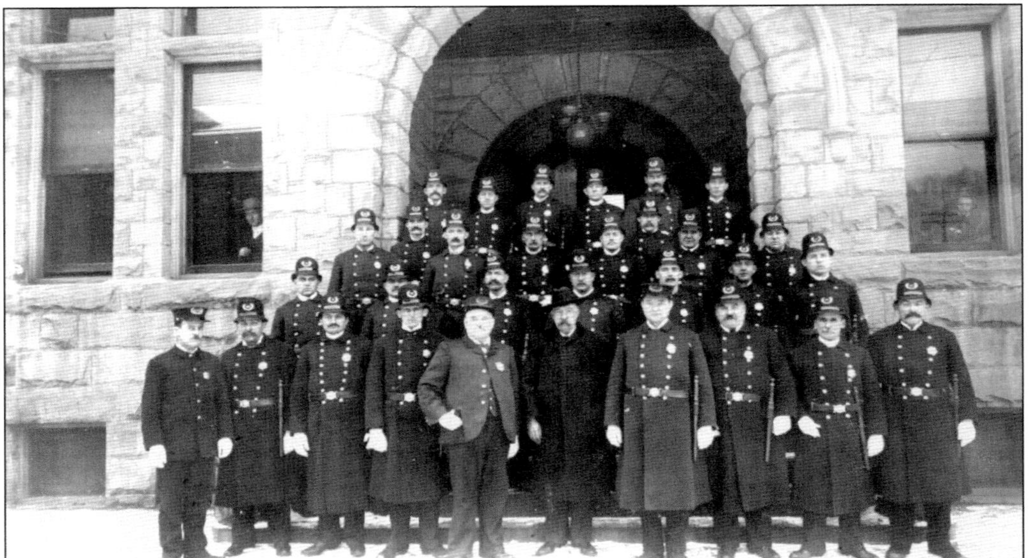

In this view, 31 members of the robust-looking Johnstown police force stand ready to fight crime and keep the peace in 1903. (Courtesy of Park Cover, Cover Studio.)

This picture debunks the dreamy legend that the zinc statue known as Morley's Dog was something other than a lawn ornament. The manager of the Cambria Iron mines, James Morley, purchased the figure in 1870 and displayed it, as seen here, in front of his Main Street home. Washed away in 1889, it was rescued from rubble and returned to his property. Morley's daughter donated it to the city in 1944, and it guarded a small park across from city hall until 2004. (Courtesy of the Johnstown Area Heritage Association archives.)

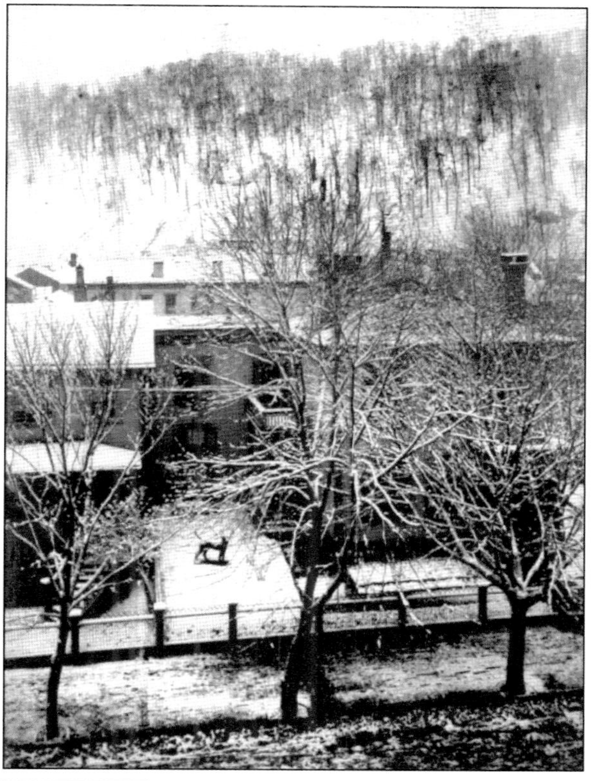

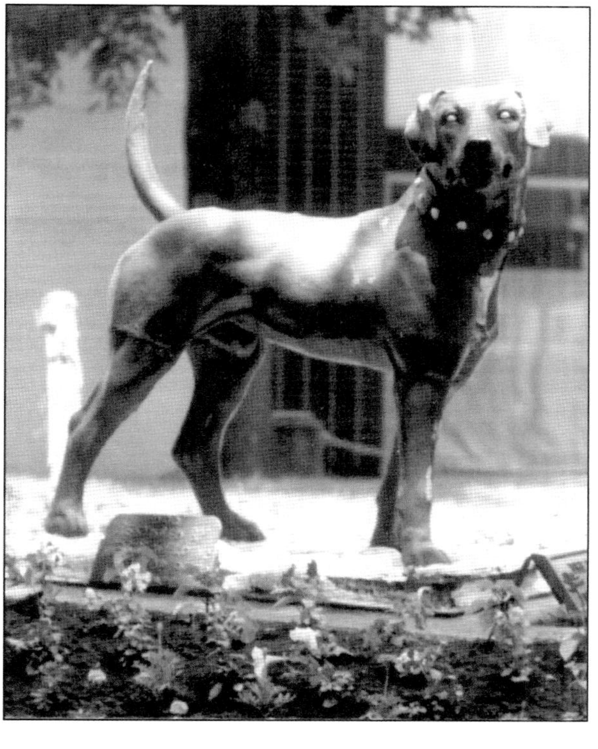

Tales of dogs saving their masters during the flood grew into an urban legend that stuck with Morley's Dog. It was a rumor perpetuated by the 1977 movie *Slap Shot*, which was filmed in Johnstown. In the movie, Paul Newman's character mentions that the statue was dedicated to dogs saving lives during "some big flood." (Courtesy of Jim Cover Jr.)

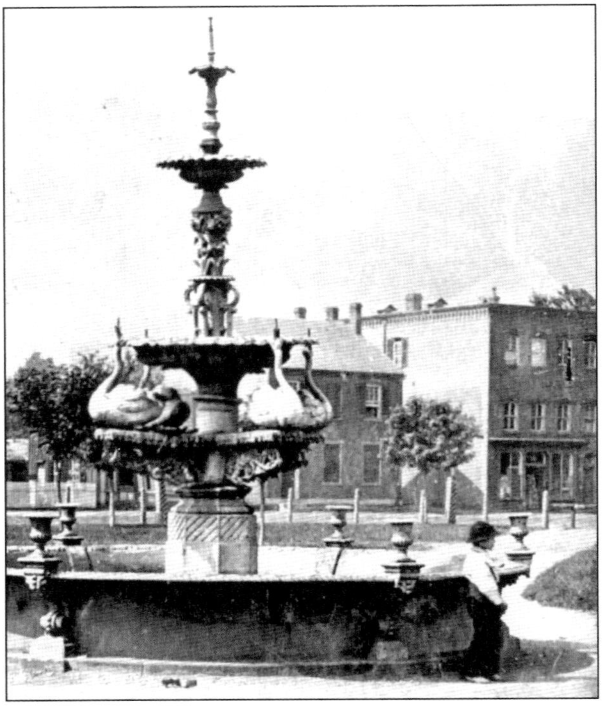

Founder Joseph Johns expected Johnstown to become the county seat, so he designated a public square for the construction of a courthouse. When that dream failed, several buildings, including a garage for the hand-pump fire engine, meat markets, and even a small lockup were built there instead. By 1880, many of those buildings had been removed and the park had become a place for residents to congregate. This fountain, with its glorious swans, attracted visitors in 1880. (Courtesy of the Johnstown Area Heritage Association archives.)

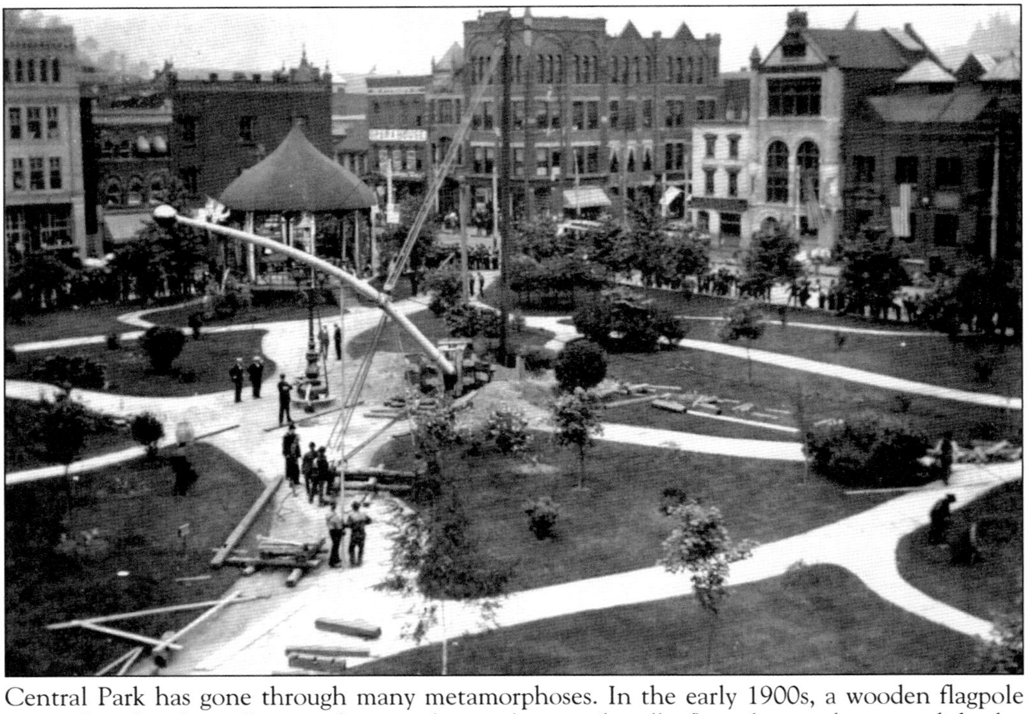

Central Park has gone through many metamorphoses. In the early 1900s, a wooden flagpole was replaced with a taller metal one and meandering sidewalks flowed around trees and shrubs, a decorative pavilion, a new fountain, and several statues. (Courtesy of the Johnstown Area Heritage Association archives.)

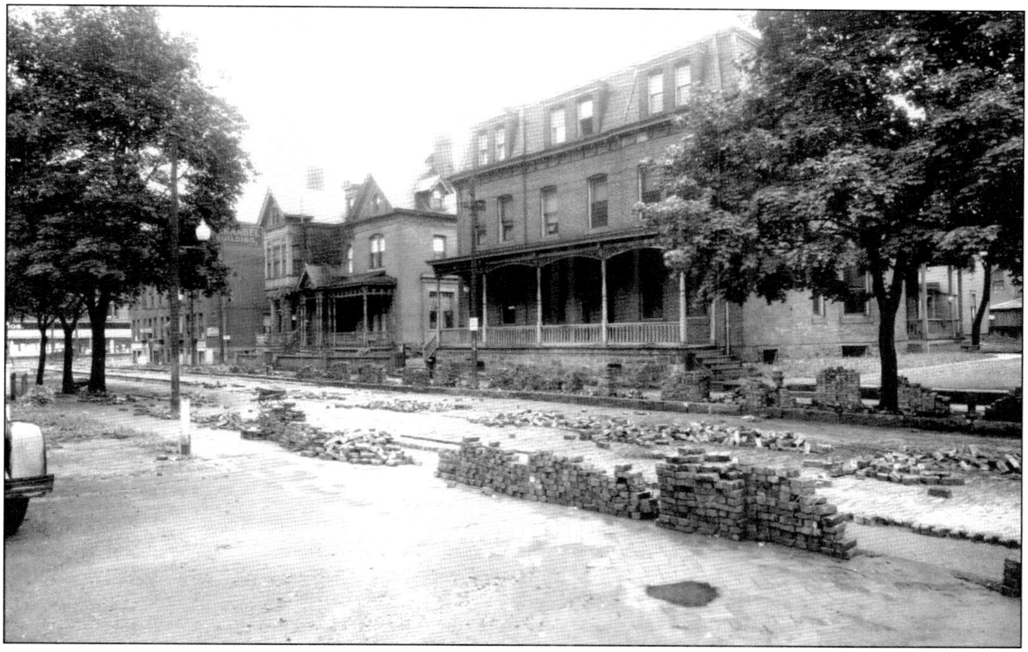

Brick pavers were tough to maintain in light of frequent floods and heavy traffic. Installation of rail tracks, beginning in 1882, required that bricks be removed and reset for horse-drawn trolley cars. Later, the lines were electrified, and motorcars powered from a station at Baumer Street used the rail system beginning in 1891. (Courtesy of the Johnstown Area Heritage Association archives.)

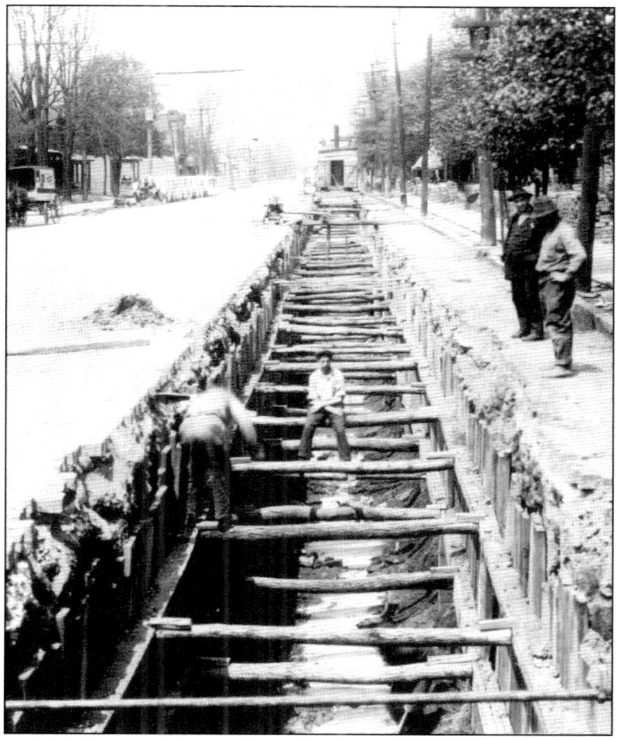

Like most cities, Johnstown constantly worked to upgrade and maintain roads. In May 1918, workers take a breather from the open trench created on Cooper Avenue for installation of a 63-inch sewer main. (Courtesy of the Johnstown Area Heritage Association archives.)

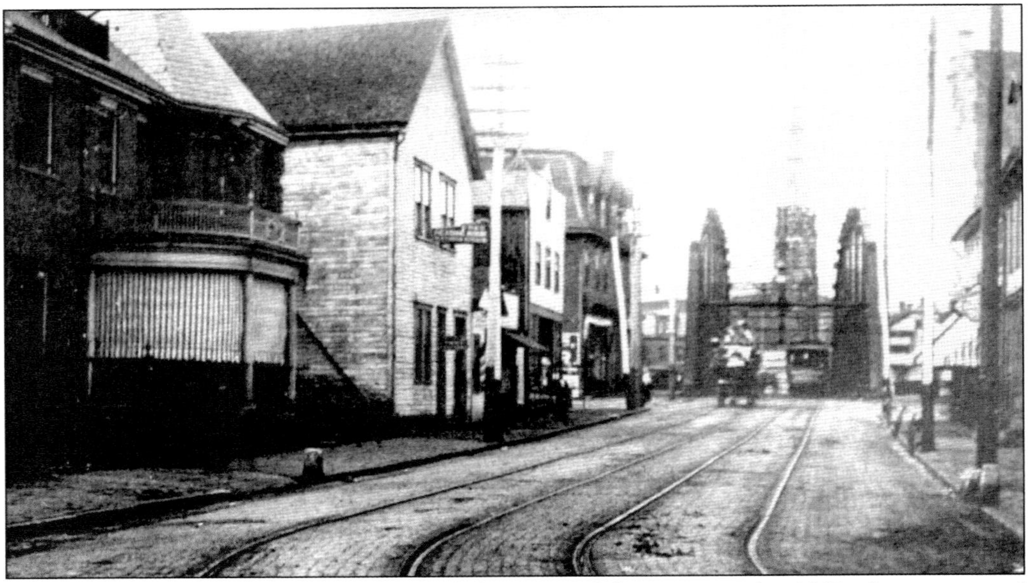

In the distance, a trolley proceeds toward downtown Johnstown in the 1880s, having wound past homes and businesses located on the south side of the Franklin Street bridge. (Courtesy of the Johnstown Area Heritage Association archives.)

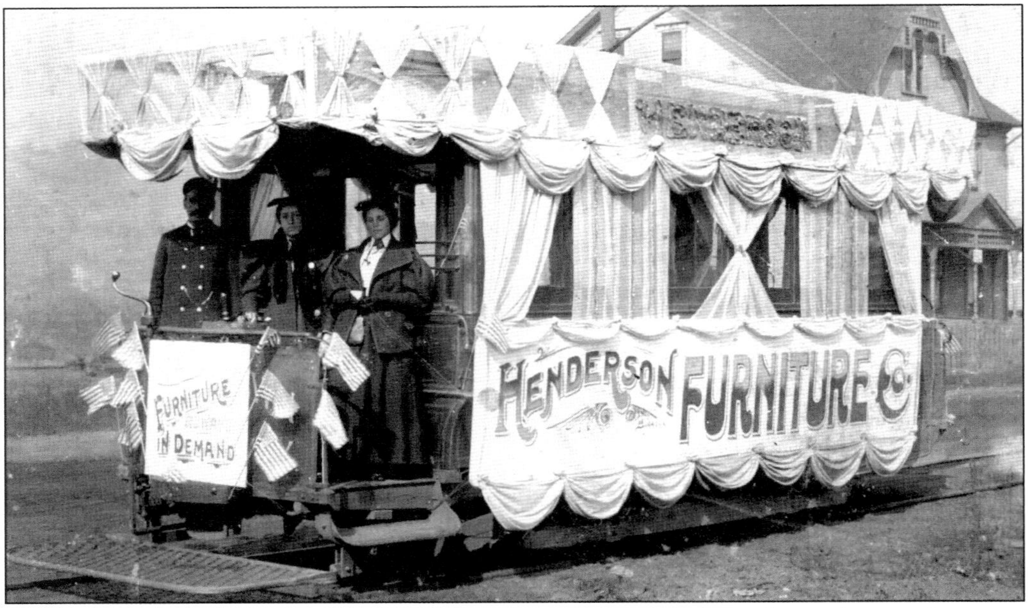

A moving advertisement, this Mineral Point streetcar is dressed in the proclamation "Henderson's Furniture always in demand." In 1889, Henderson and Alexander Furniture opened at 328–330 Main Street. Robert Henderson renamed the business Henderson Furniture Company and served as sole proprietor for 29 years. Customers were probably confused about the store's location, as Henderson moved it frequently. In 1900, the store address was 527 Somerset Street; in 1901, the Main and Clinton corner; in 1903, 502 Somerset; from 1905 to 1908, 309 Fisher Building; from 1911 to 1912, 417 Lincoln; and in 1918, back in the Fisher Building. (Courtesy of the Cambria County Historical Society.)

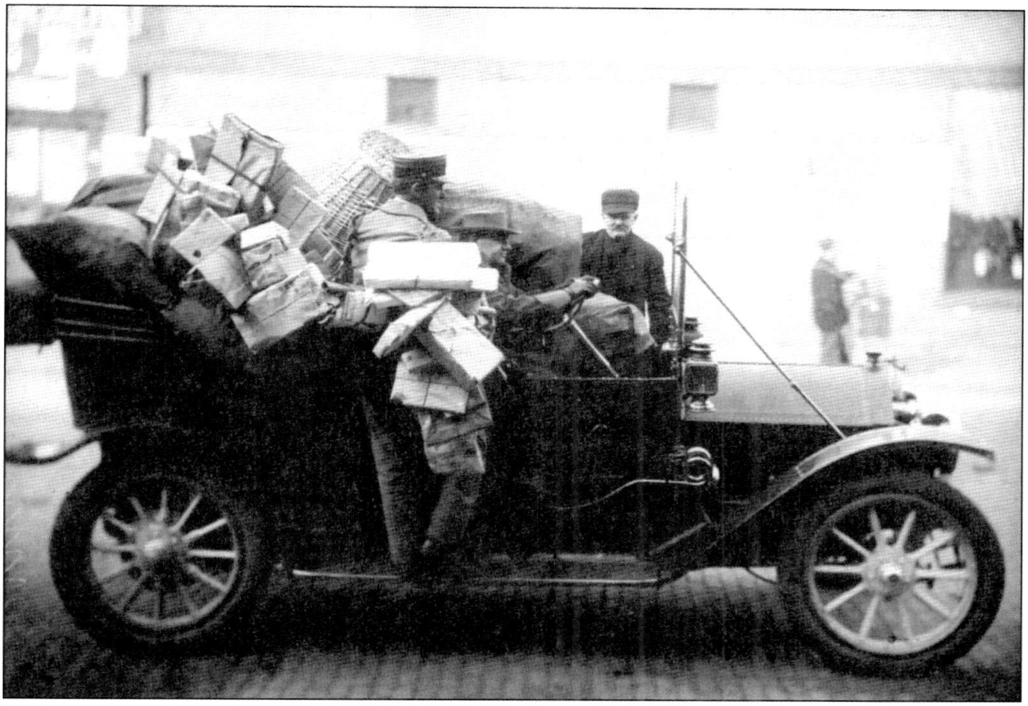

Packed beyond belief, it is a wonder that the men operating this parcel post delivery car could safely navigate around town, let alone find the correct package for delivery among this stack. Perhaps all of the packages were headed to Nathan's Clothing Store, which appears in the background. (Courtesy of the Johnstown Area Heritage Association archives.)

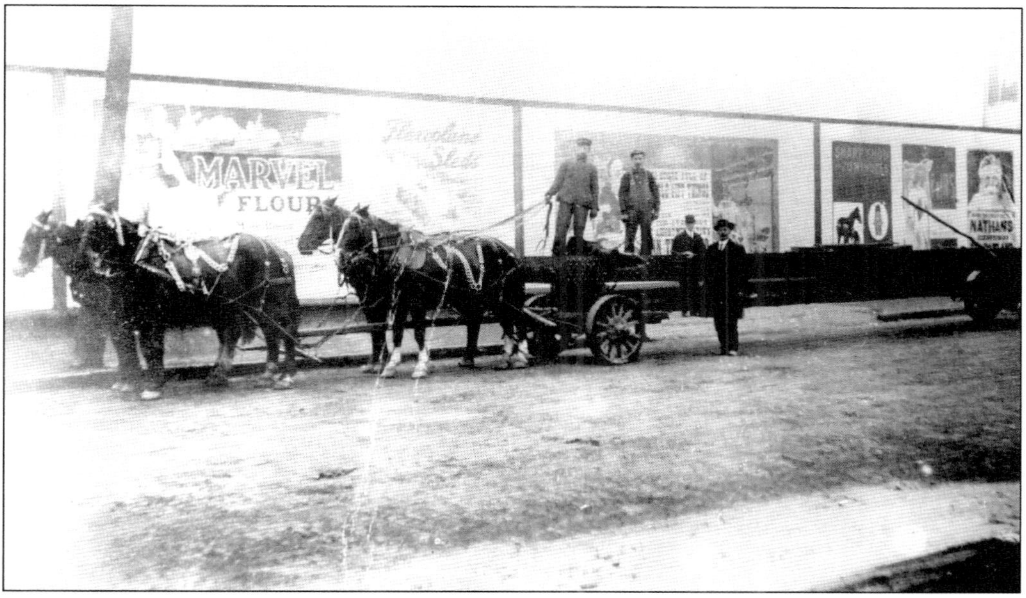

Never surprised at what might be coming down the street in such a busy steel town, residents undoubtedly ignored horse-drawn wagons loaded with rails or beams. (Courtesy of the Johnstown Area Heritage Association archives.)

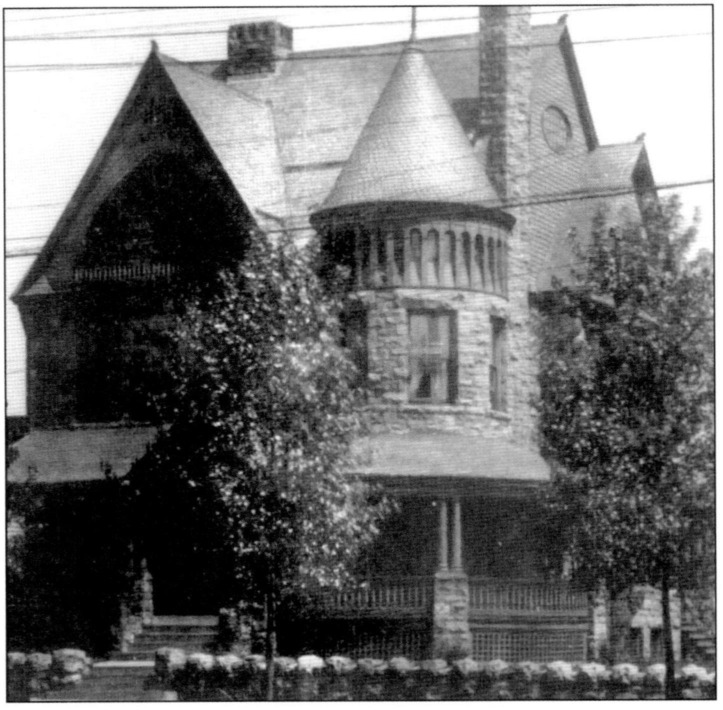

The former residence of the Honorable William Horace Rose, Johnstown's first mayor (1890–1893), is located at 229 Main Street and is currently home to the Knights of Columbus. William Rose suffered injuries during the Civil War and nearly succumbed during the 1889 flood. He rebuilt this home after it was destroyed in the flood to signal his confidence that another flood of that magnitude would never again threaten the city. (Courtesy of the Johnstown Area Heritage Association archives.)

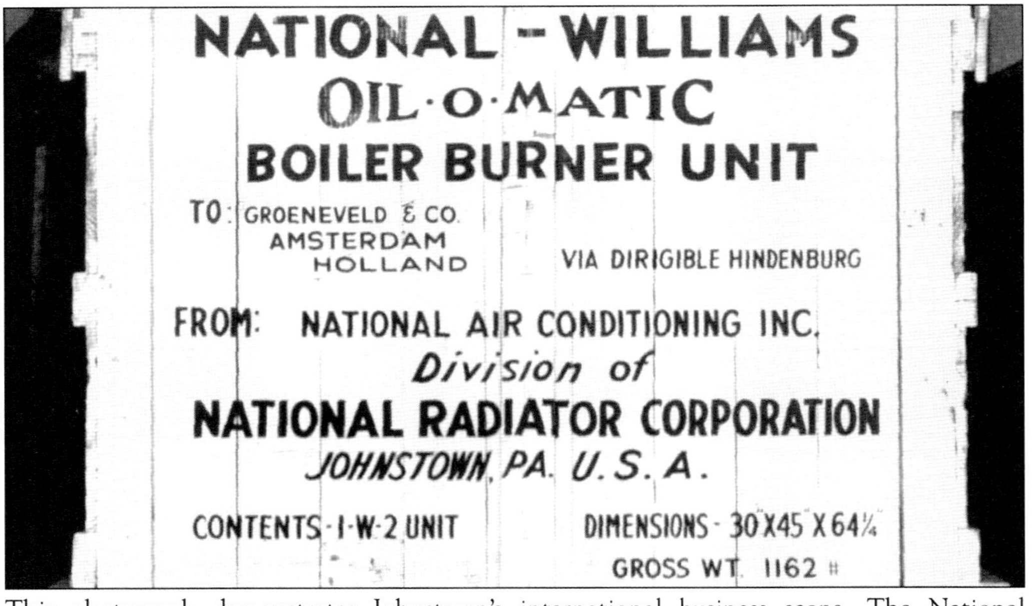

This photograph demonstrates Johnstown's international business scope. The National Radiator Corporation operated in Johnstown's Moxham section during the mid-1930s. This particular crate, containing an Oil-O-Matic boiler burner unit, was headed for Amsterdam, Holland. Note that the burner weighed 1,162 pounds and was destined for transport by the dirigible *Hindenburg*. It is doubtful that this package made it to its destination on the airship, as the *Hindenburg* exploded upon landing in an eastern airfield on May 6, 1937. (Courtesy of the Johnstown Area Heritage Association archives.)

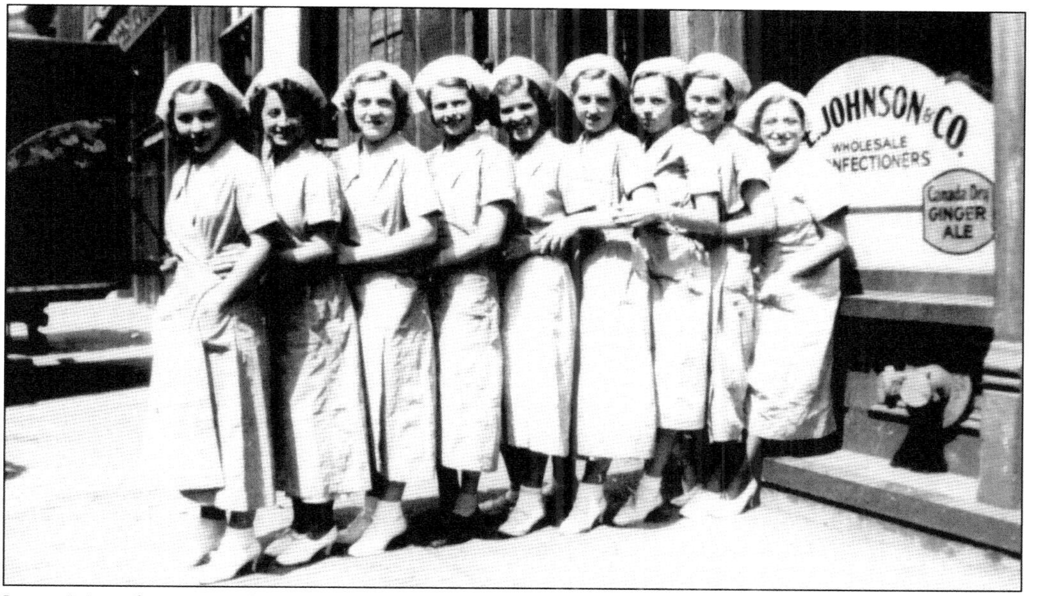

Love Manufacturing Company served as a wholesale confectionery from 1903 to 1942 at 621 Railroad Street. The employees in this July 1934 photograph, dressed in their white pressed dresses and hats, look more like nurses than confectionery experts. (Courtesy of the Johnstown Area Heritage Association archives.)

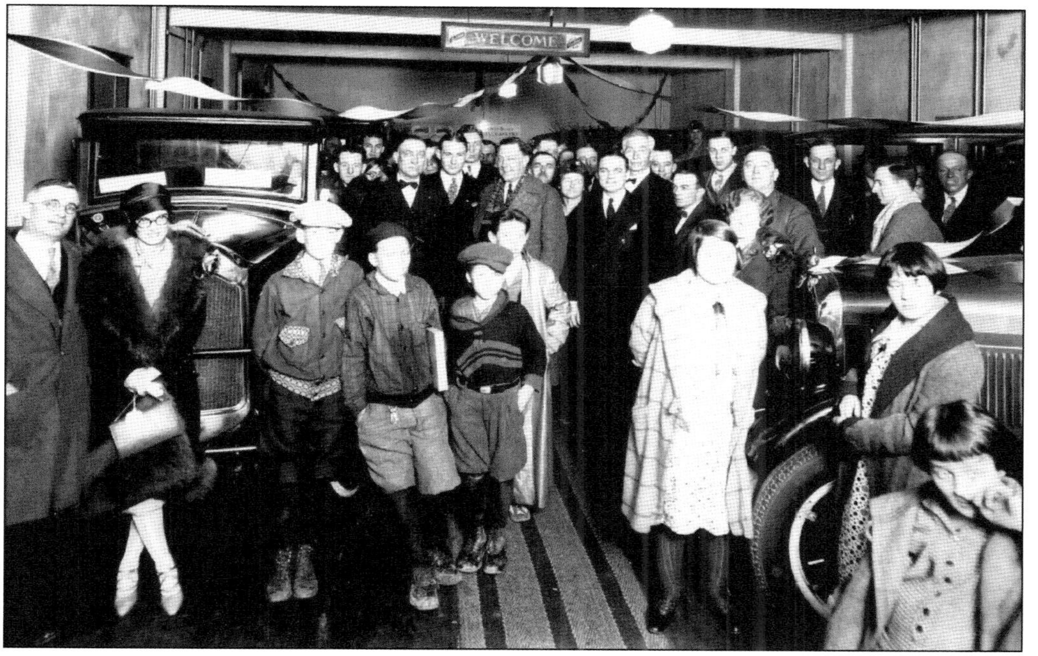

The 1922 city directory lists Johnstown Motor Company at 12 Iron Street as the area's "sole distributors of Unit-Built Studebakers." Probably celebrating the dealership's grand opening, these flapperish guests pose beneath crepe paper decorations and a welcome sign. The carpeted showroom contains new model cars waiting for a test drive. (Courtesy of the Johnstown Area Heritage Association archives.)

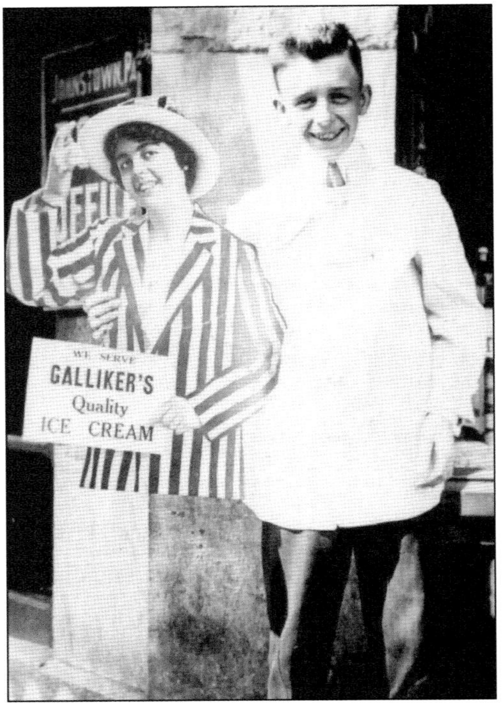

Johnstown loves its ice cream. Louis Galliker purchased the Shreve Ice Cream Company in 1914 and immediately started the Galliker Ice Cream Company. Galliker's ice-cream plant was located in the 450 block of Franklin Street. He sold products to restaurants and lunch counters, where soda jerks dipped cones and created sundaes for customers. Advertisements like this one in the mid-1920s encouraged patrons to indulge themselves. (Courtesy of Robert Snavely.)

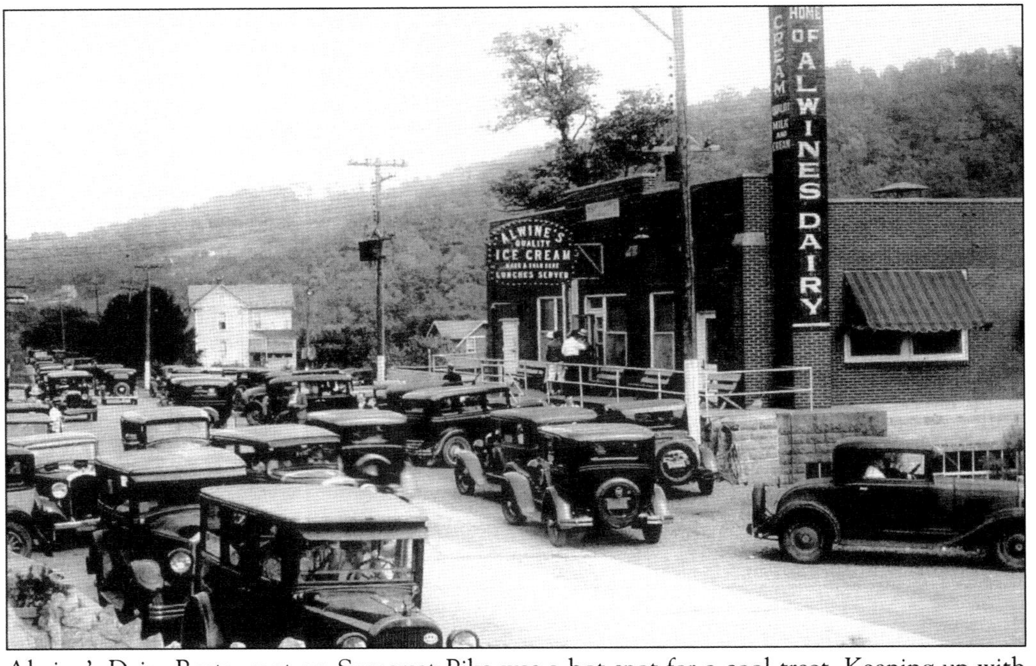

Alwine's Dairy Restaurant on Somerset Pike was a hot spot for a cool treat. Keeping up with customer demand was daunting, as lines formed for the giant 10¢ cones. Harry E. Alwine's dairy business boomed from 1914 to 1964. When he opened a restaurant across from the dairy, customers drove miles to eat Alwine's home cooking and sample the area's freshest milk and ice cream. Alwine's restaurant was razed in 1986. (Courtesy of Terry Alwine.)

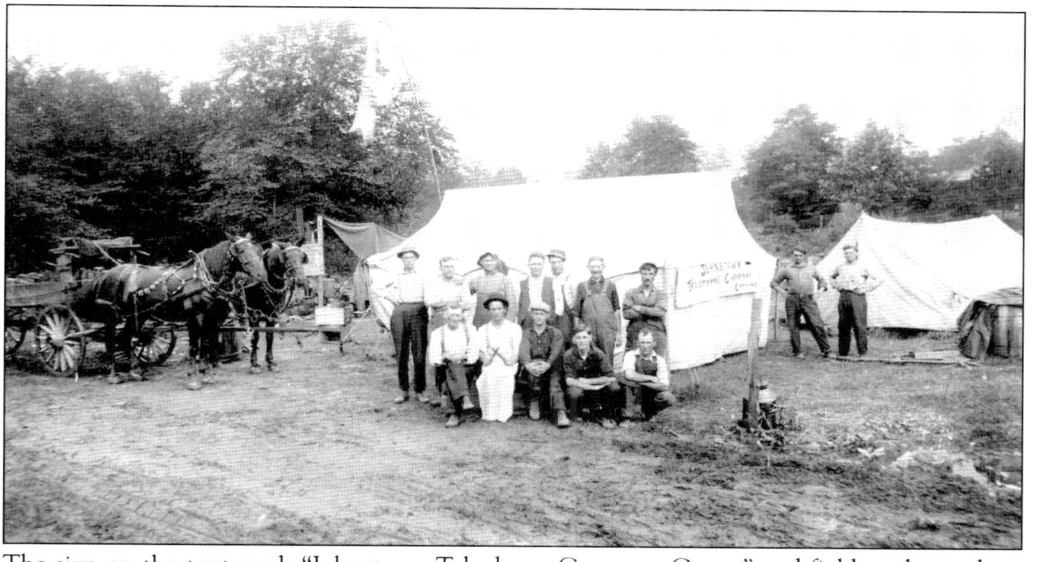

The sign on the tent reads "Johnstown Telephone Company Camp," and field workers take a break from installing poles and lines for telephone service to the greater Johnstown area. In 1915, there were more than 9,000 telephones ringing in Johnstown's homes and businesses. (Courtesy of the Johnstown Area Heritage Association archives.)

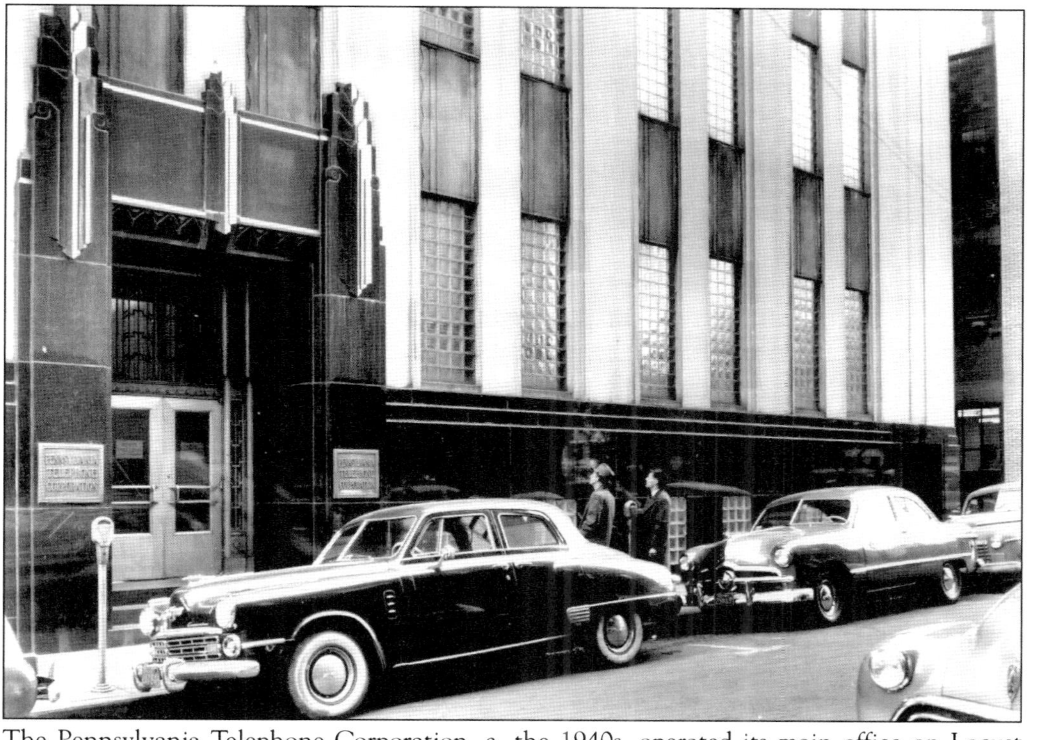

The Pennsylvania Telephone Corporation, *c.* the 1940s, operated its main office on Locust Street within this Art Deco structure, reminiscent of 1920s architecture. The building subsequently became home to General Telephone. (Courtesy of the Johnstown Area Heritage Association archives.)

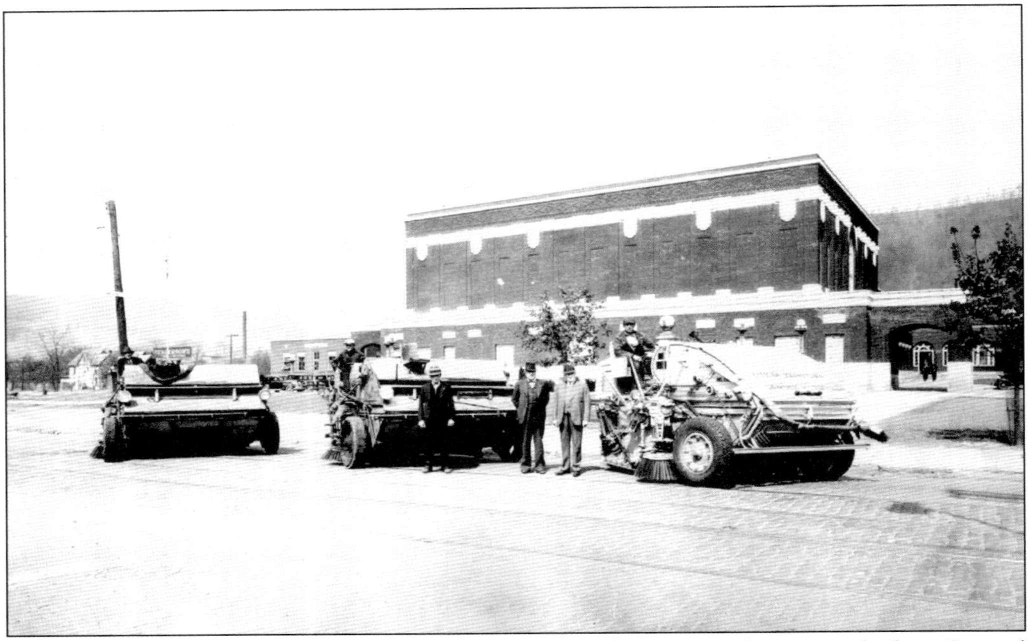

No excuses for dirty streets with this impressive street-cleaning machinery, parked on Central Avenue in front of then Cochran Junior High School *c.* the 1940s. (Courtesy of the Johnstown Area Heritage Association archives.)

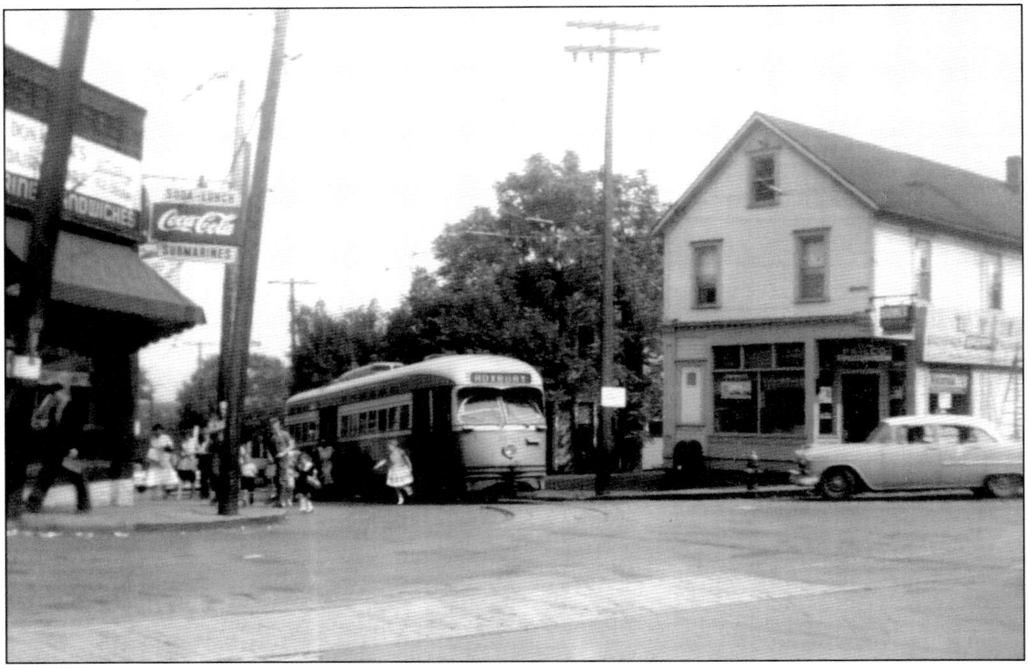

Beginning with livery service and then moving to trolley cars and finally to buses, dependable public transportation supported Johnstown's workers, schoolchildren, and shoppers in their quest to be mobile. Here, passengers bound down the steps of the last trolley to run the Roxbury circuit, as it stops at the corner of Strayer Street and Chandler Avenue. (Courtesy of Robert Snavely.)

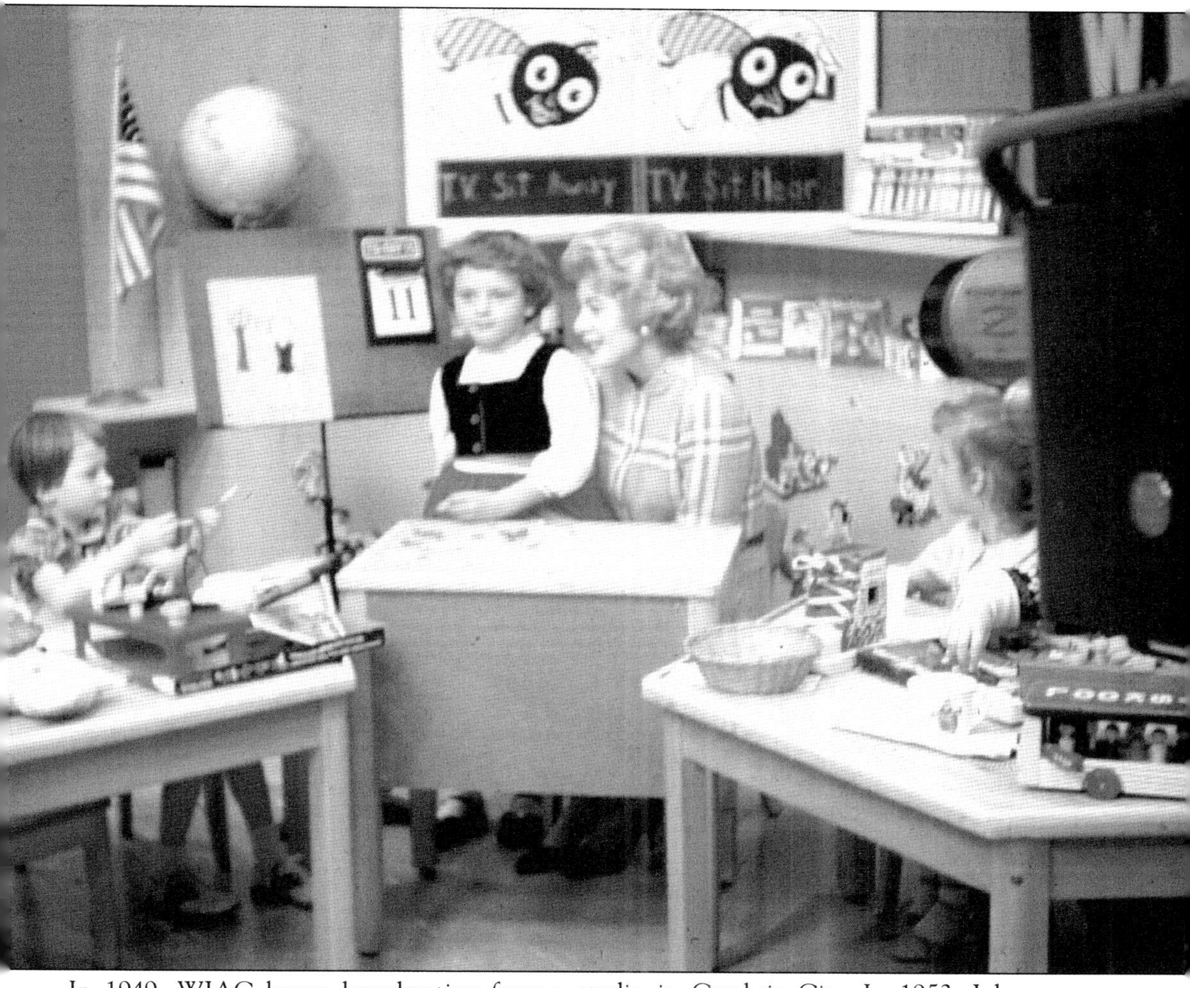

In 1949, WJAC began broadcasting from a studio in Cambria City. In 1953, Johnstown became the nation's first television marketplace to receive a permanent license from the Federal Communications Commission authorizing the station's use of expanded broadcasting. The station moved to its current location 10 years later. The then state-of-the-art facility, perched on a hill at the end of Old Hickory Lane in Upper Yoder, featured a dome that changed colors to indicate anticipated weather conditions. Before Mr. Rogers and public television, Johnstown's kids enjoyed the syndicated show *Romper Room*, c. 1954. The program incorporated canned cartoons, backdrops, and stage props but featured local children and on-air talent such as Miss Patty (Hewitt), seen here. During the magic mirror segment at the end of each show, the teacher looked through a hand mirror frame and greeted children at home by name. Johnstown's broadcast of *Romper Room* ended in 1975 and Sr. Mary Parks was the last teacher to look into the magic mirror and say goodbye. (Author's collection.)

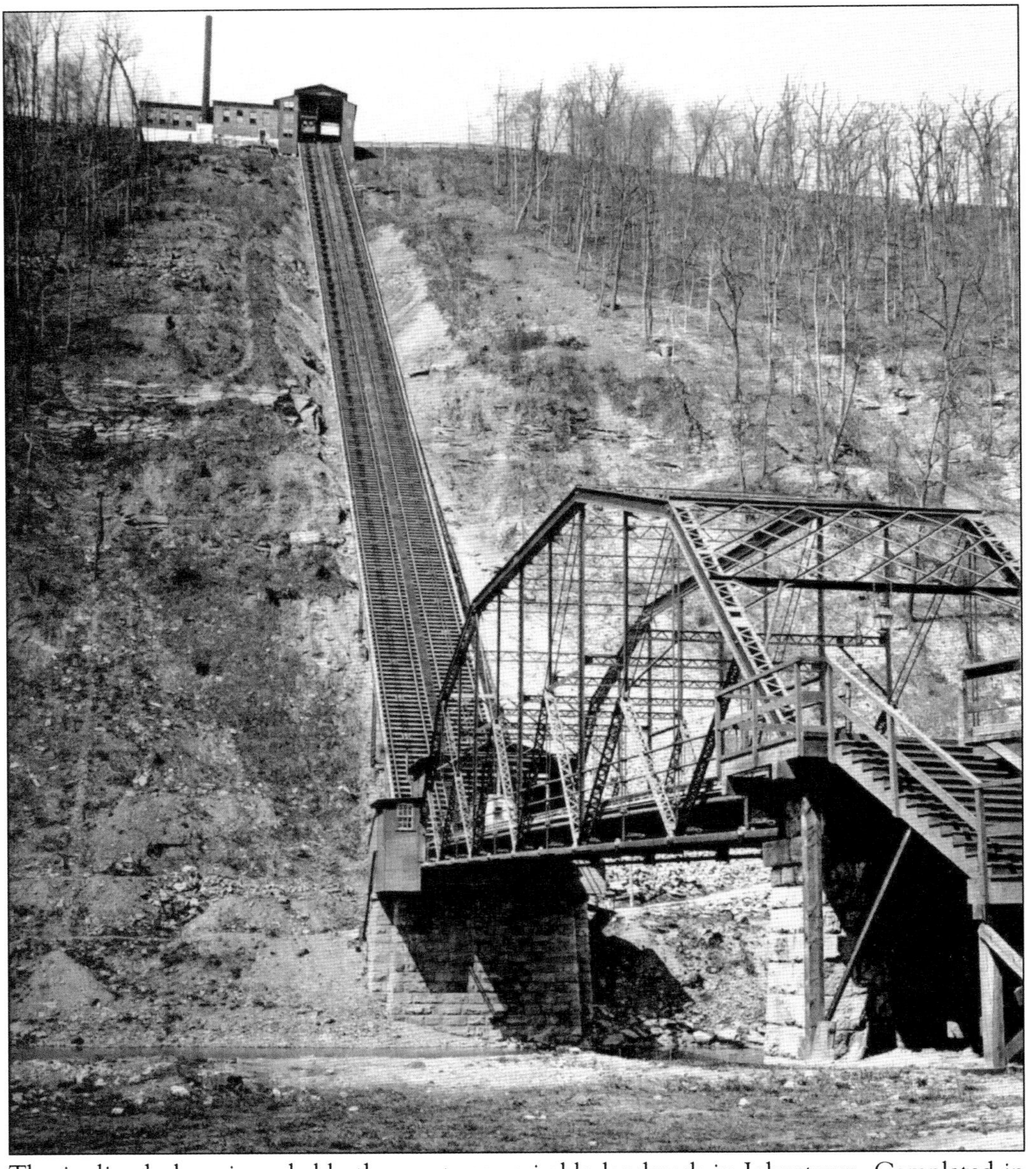

The inclined plane is probably the most recognizable landmark in Johnstown. Completed in 1891, Cambria Iron Company began its construction just months after the 1889 flood, although plans were on the drawing board years prior. The company was selling home sites in Westmont, but potential buyers complained about the lack of good roads downtown. Cambria Iron hoped the incline would overcome the transportation issue. Another benefit surfaced during both the 1936 and 1977 floods, when the inclined plane became an escape from rising floodwaters. Initially powered by steam, a stack is visible in this *c.* 1894 photograph. It was converted to electricity in the early 1900s, and the stack was eventually removed. *The Guinness Book of World Records* lists the Johnstown inclined plane as "the world's steepest vehicular inclined plane." The views of the city from the hillside platform are stunning, especially on a bright sunny day or when lights below are twinkling in the night. (Courtesy of the Cambria County Historical Society.)

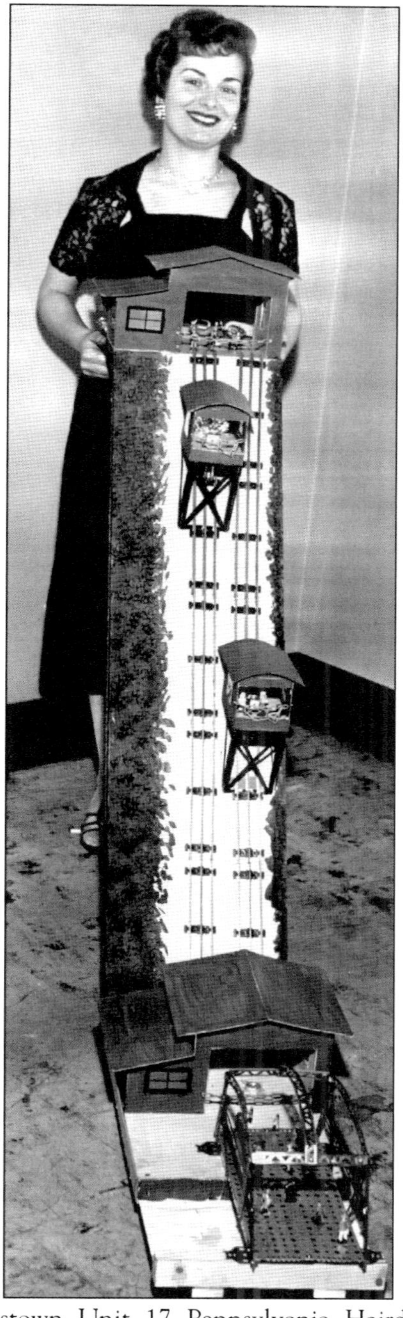

As a member of the Johnstown Unit 17 Pennsylvania Hairdressers and Cosmetologists Association, Marilyn Rehn McDermott was selected to represent Johnstown for the organization's state convention, which was held in Pittsburgh on April 5, 1959. Amazingly, the honor required that she wear this sizable model of Johnstown's inclined plane on her back while walking down a long stage runway. McDermott's brother-in-law Chuck McDermott built this version of Johnstown's most recognized landmark out of wood and an Erector set. (Courtesy of the *Tribune-Democrat*, the Marilyn McDermott collection.)

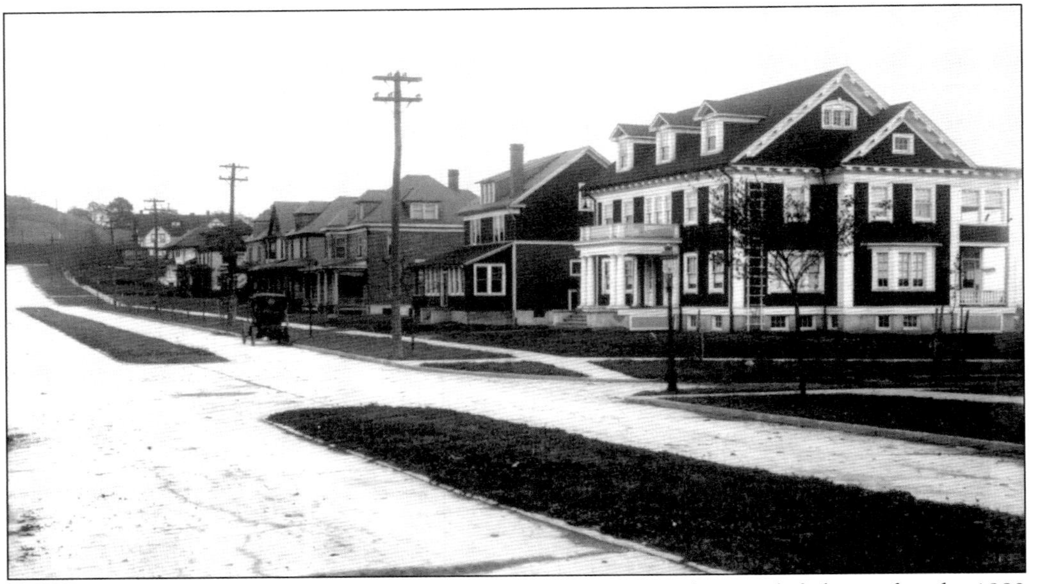

The Westmont area converted from potato fields to homes in rather quick fashion after the 1889 flood, as families escaped the downtown area with its temperamental rivers. The new hilltop homes ranged from modest to massive, traditional to classical, multifamily to single-family. The home prominently seen in this photograph still guards the corner of Luzerne and Dartmouth Streets. In this *c.* 1915 view, the American elms planted in the easements are young saplings. (Courtesy of the Johnstown Area Heritage Association archives.)

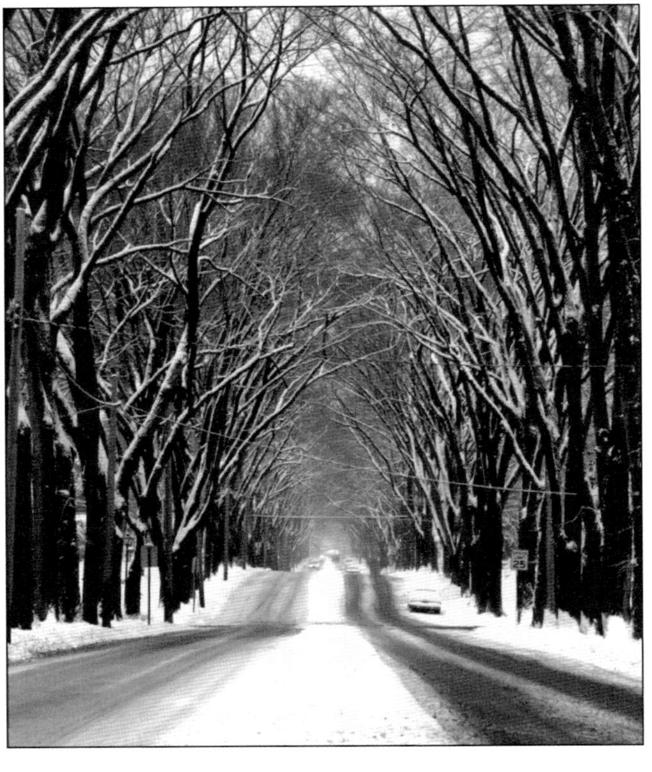

Luzerne Street continues to be one of the most picturesque locations around town. The trees, photographed here in the 1970s, are believed to be the longest stand of American elms found in the nation. The scene is often described as a cathedral of trees. (Courtesy of Park Cover, Cover Studio.)

Johnstown's first municipal airport was built on Bethlehem Steel land that was formerly the Stutzman's Westmont farm. The hilltop location, deemed safe from flooding, provided ample space for easy access by a variety of aircraft. The airport is seen in the upper right side of this 1929 aerial view. (Courtesy of Ray Clites.)

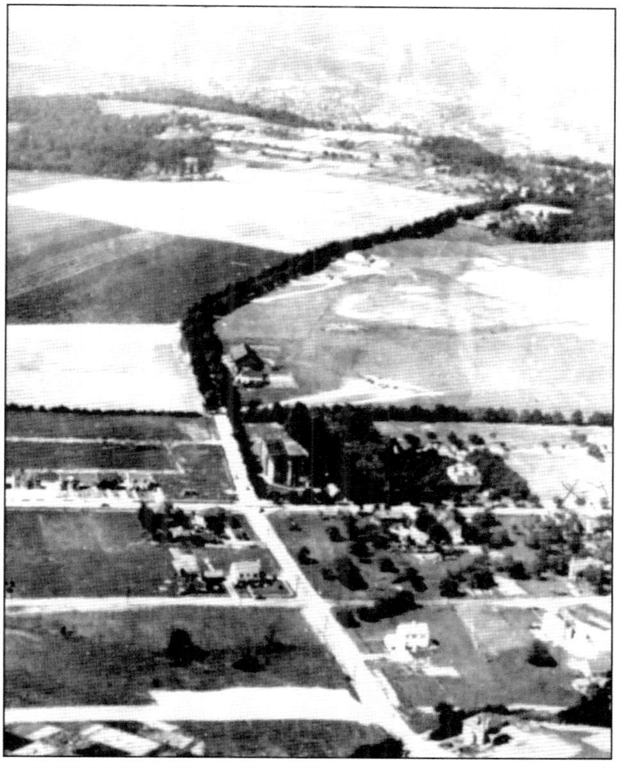

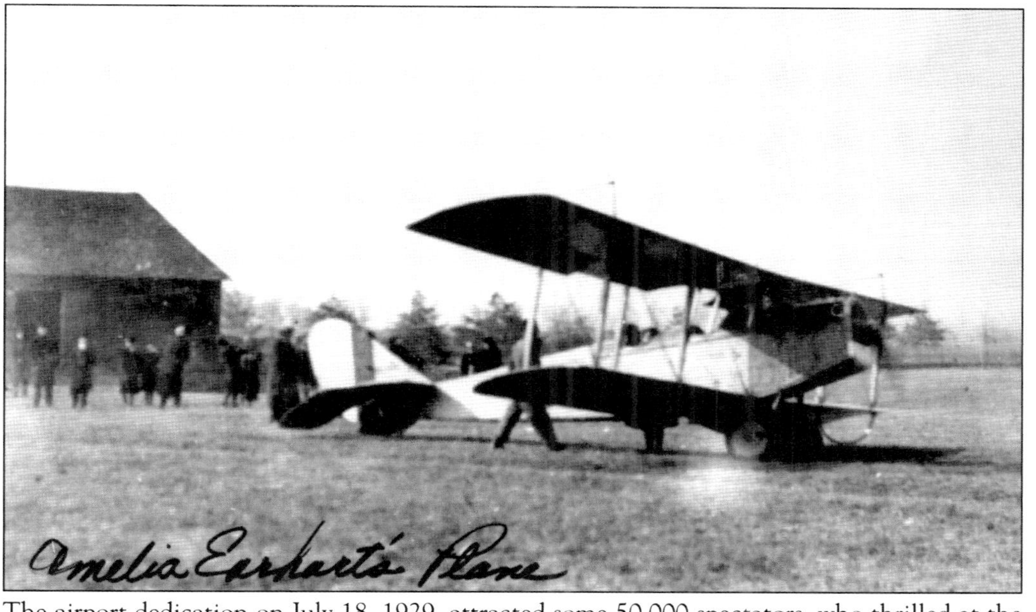

The airport dedication on July 18, 1929, attracted some 50,000 spectators, who thrilled at the arrival of 36 airplanes, including the one pictured here, the Lockheed Vega of the nation's premier aviatrix, Amelia Earhart. For die-hard shoppers, downtown retailer Glosser Brothers ran advertisements in the *Daily Tribune* that offered with every $2 purchase a free airplane "that really and truly flies." (Courtesy of Ray Clites.)

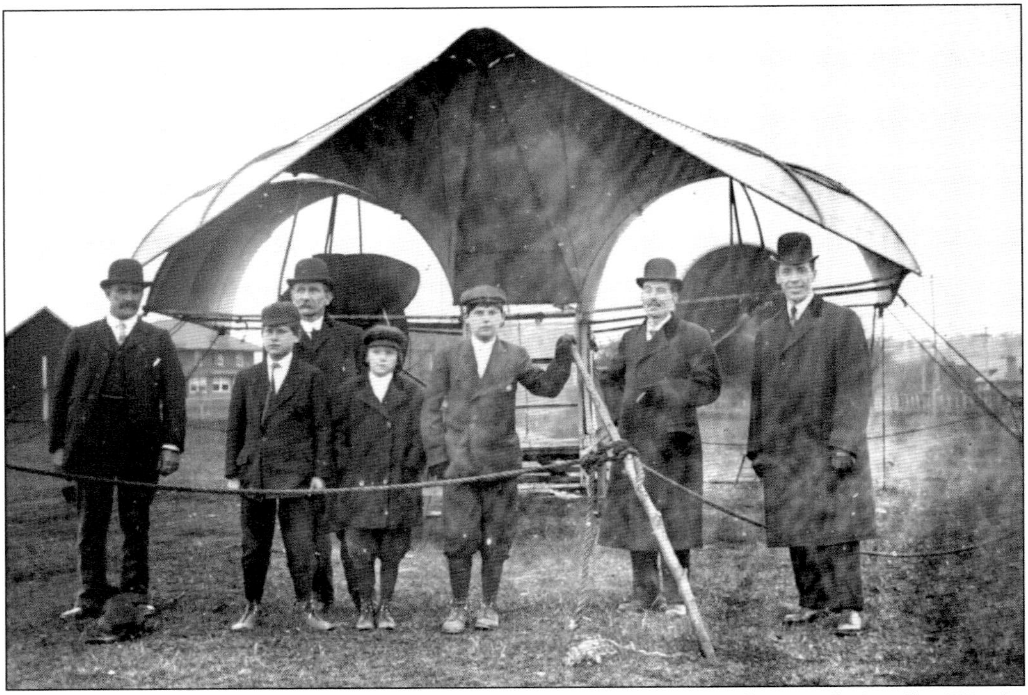

December 17, 1903, a pivotal date in air travel, is when Wilbur and Orville Wright demonstrated the first controlled flight of an engine-powered airplane. By 1910, the brothers acquired financing and formed the Wright Brothers Areoplane Company. It is a puzzle, then, why Johnstown businessman Daniel R. Schnabel backed Fritz Russ in building this machine, described in the local media as "part airplane, part parachute." "Uncle Dan's folly" was plagued by a lack of foresight. Built in Schnabel's Seventh Ward carriage shop, the oversized bird's first flight occurred with the aid of pulleys, as it required lifting through a hole cut in the roof since the width exceeded the door exits. A tow to Westmont via automobile snapped the ship's axle, and a wagon ride to the launch site forced additional repairs. In August 1910, the thrill of victory turned into the agony of defeat, as the behemoth lifted off the ground a mere 2 feet, traveled 15 feet, and thumped back to earth. Apparently, Schnabel got the message, as the plane was abandoned after its dismal maiden voyage. (Courtesy of the Johnstown Area Heritage Association archives, Irving London collection.)

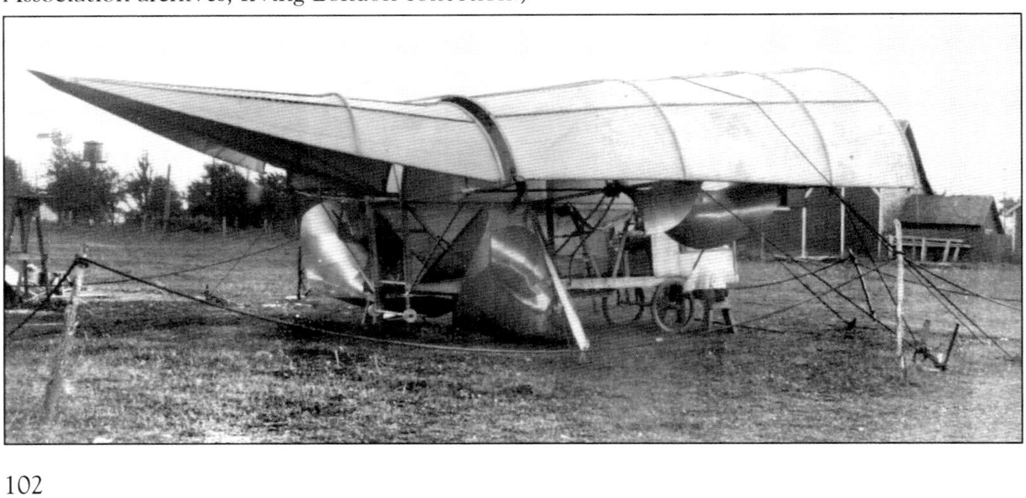

Seven

Everyday Life

Growing up in early Johnstown meant learning family values, religious training, and hard work. Youngsters were free to play and explore. Holidays were events to cherish. Sunday was truly the day of rest, and school primers and sports were put aside as family time took precedence over play.

Organizations like the YMCA and YWCA provided a place to go for assistance, exercise, or education. Other groups, including fraternal and religious organizations, reinforced ethnic, religious, and philanthropic ideals, supporting the community when times were tough, providing time and money when needs arose, and celebrating when a victory was won.

Sports played a large part in city life, as rivals met on the baseball field and school teams defended hometown honor. After competitions, kids cooled off in neighborhood watering holes. A taste of professional sports was provided by the Johnstown Blue Birds hockey team and, later, by the Johnstown Jets and Chiefs. The Johnstown Johnnies and All American Amateur Baseball Association (AAABA) gave residents the opportunity to see budding stars and true legends of the game. If the children of immigrants were given the chance, music, dance, and ice-skating filled hours that would have otherwise been spent idly, something that work ethics in the mills and mines would never have tolerated.

Over the years, Johnstown has supported a number of amusement and swimming parks and festivals. Walking along the river and touring the town via bicycle or car continues to be a form of entertainment for today's residents. The natural beauty in Johnstown's surrounding hillsides is splendid no matter what time of year.

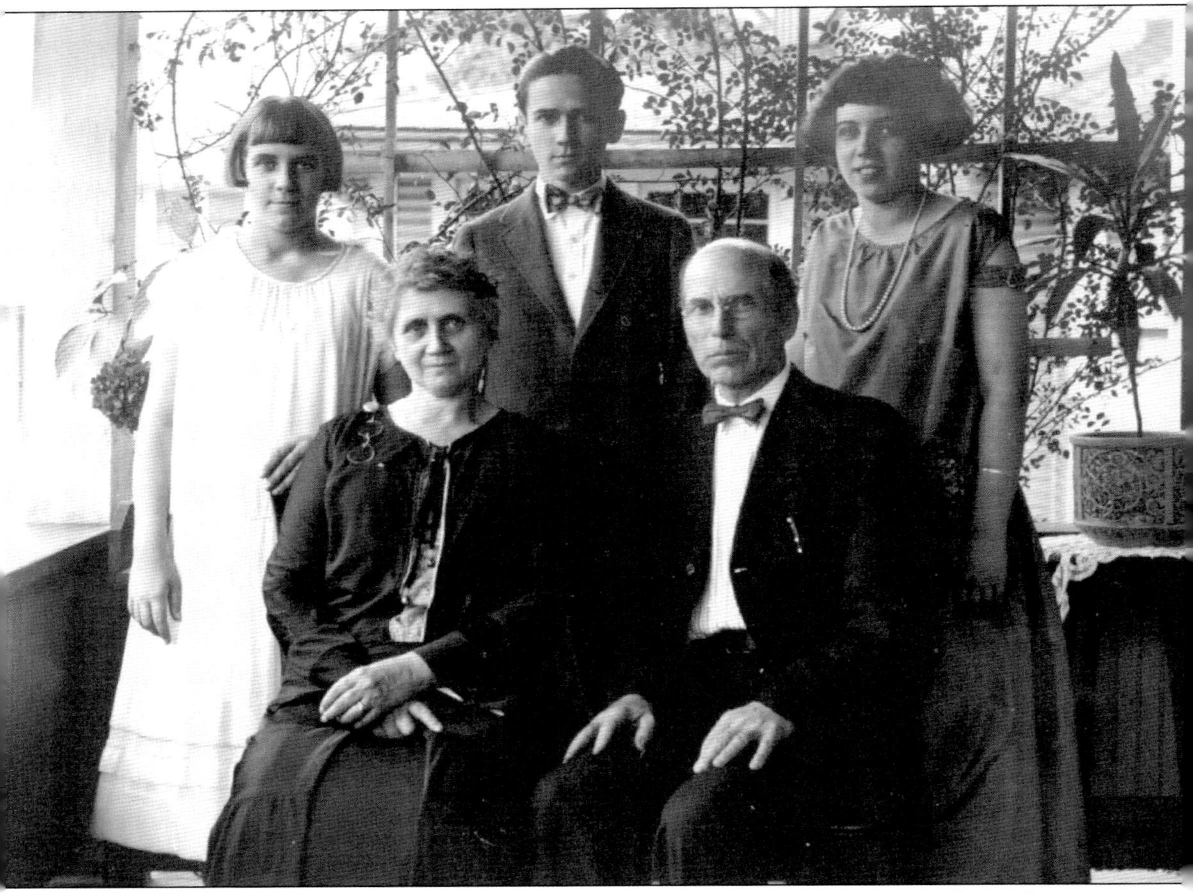

Members of the Kemery family pose for a formal portrait on the front porch of their home, at 726 Glenwood Avenue, c. 1925. From left to right are the following: (front) Nora and V. Max Kemery; (back) Vera, Fred, and Katharine. Kemery often photographed his three children, and many of his images are featured on the following pages. Although he possessed a photographer's eye, Kemery's full-time employment was as a draftsman in the Lorain Steel Company's engineering department. The Kemery homestead was the first home built on the street. As a young man, Kemery originally hailed from Renova before relocating to the area. His first job in Johnstown was at the Moxham store of George Glenn in 1891. (Courtesy of Jeanne D. Buck.)

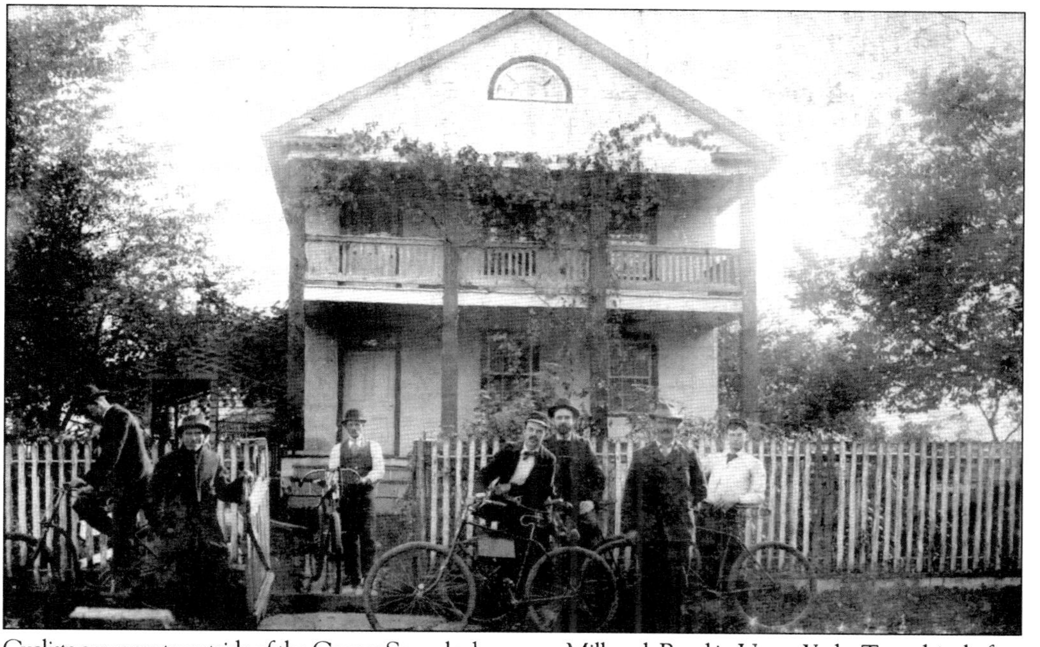

Cyclists congregate outside of the George Spangler home, on Millcreek Road in Upper Yoder Township, before heading off on a jaunt into town. Note that neither George Spangler, second from the left, nor any of his friends are wearing helmets, although their stiff bowlers probably afforded plenty of head protection. (Courtesy of the Johnstown Area Heritage Association archives.)

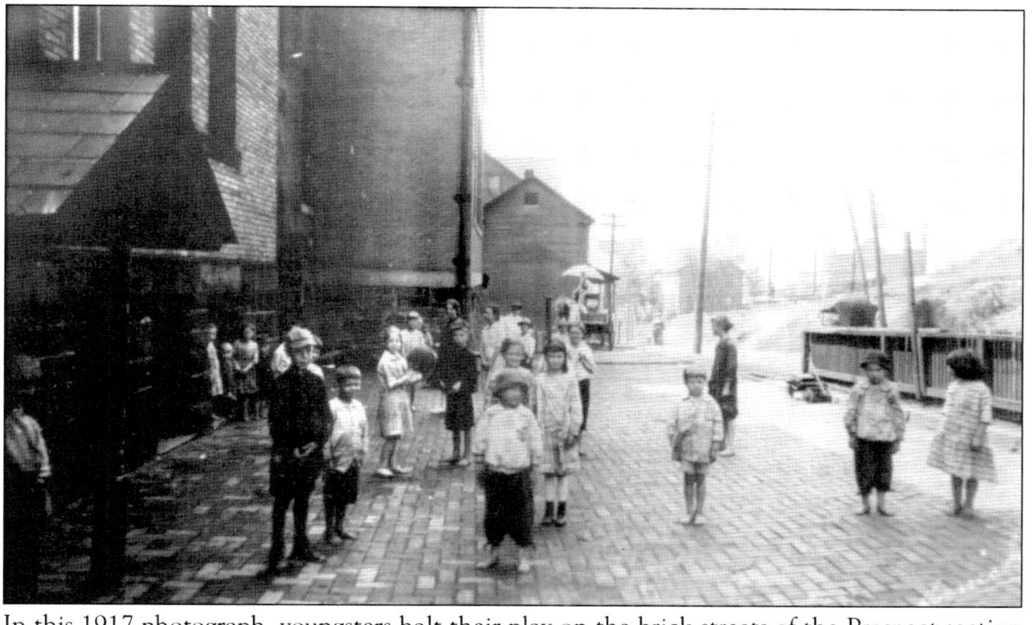

In this 1917 photograph, youngsters halt their play on the brick streets of the Prospect section of town and obediently wait for the cameraman's cue to continue. Note that although many of the children sport bare feet, they are neatly dressed with hats and well-kept clothing. For many, shoes were a prized accessory spared from play for use in school and church. (Courtesy of the Johnstown Area Heritage Association archives, Hornick Studio.)

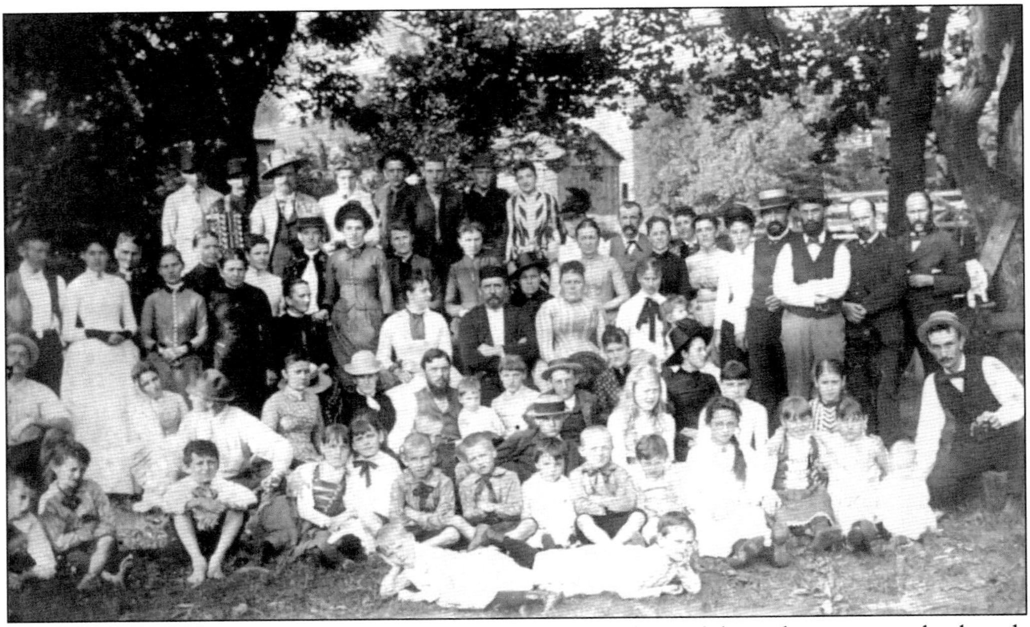

Picnics were a popular diversion from work, and families often celebrated reunions in backyards or local parks. Here is a 1905 photographic record of the gathering of the Fronheiser and Zimmerman families. (Courtesy of the Johnstown Area Heritage Association archives.)

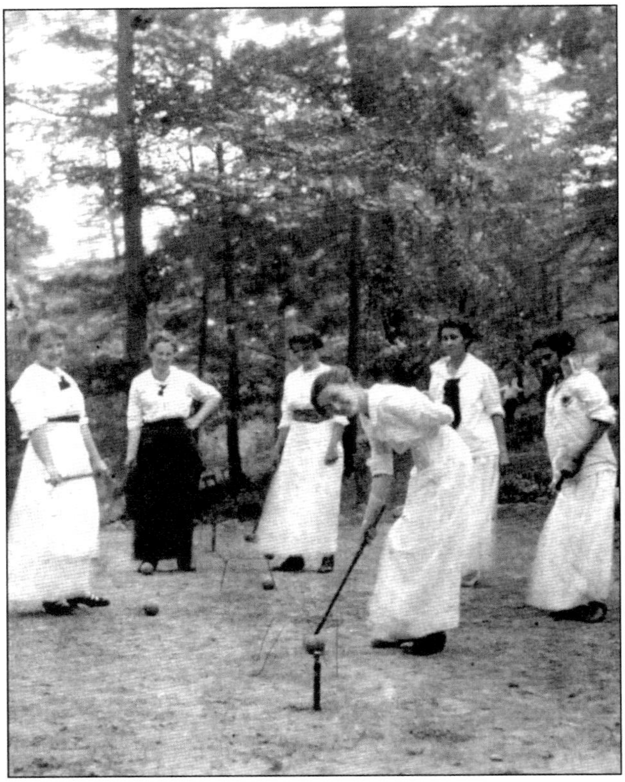

Fresh-air games such as croquet were enjoyed at the cottages and tennis court of the North Fork Country Club, off old Route 219, now Route 985. (Courtesy of the Johnstown Area Heritage Association archives.)

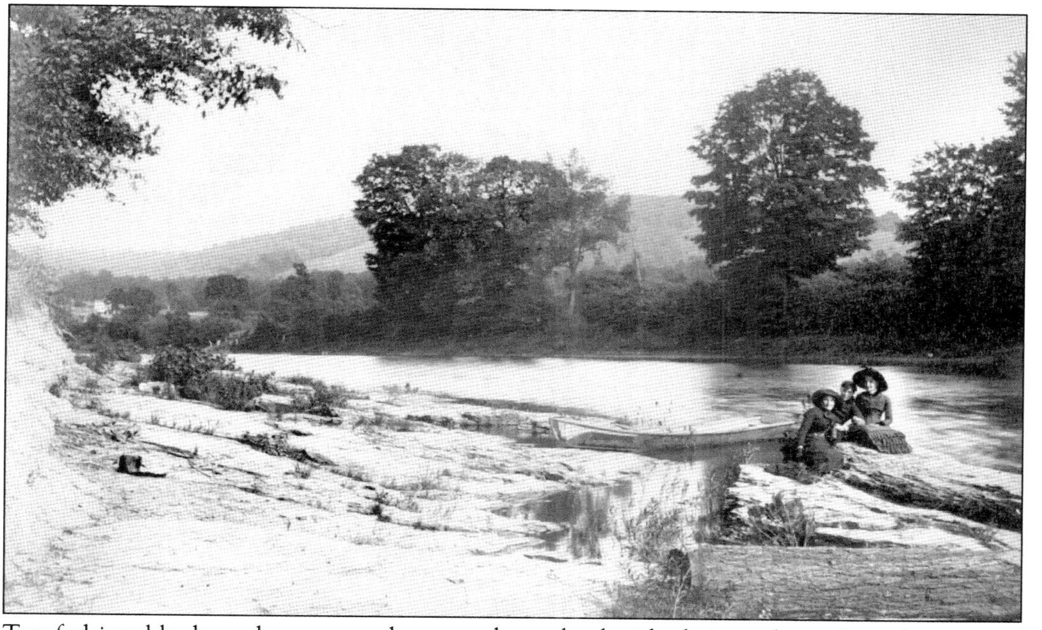

Two fashionably dressed women and a young boy relax beside their rowboat along the rocks of the Stonycreek near Johnstown in July 1886. The Stonycreek was often tame in the summer heat, affording leisure boating and swimming as entertainment. (Courtesy of the Johnstown Area Heritage Association archives.)

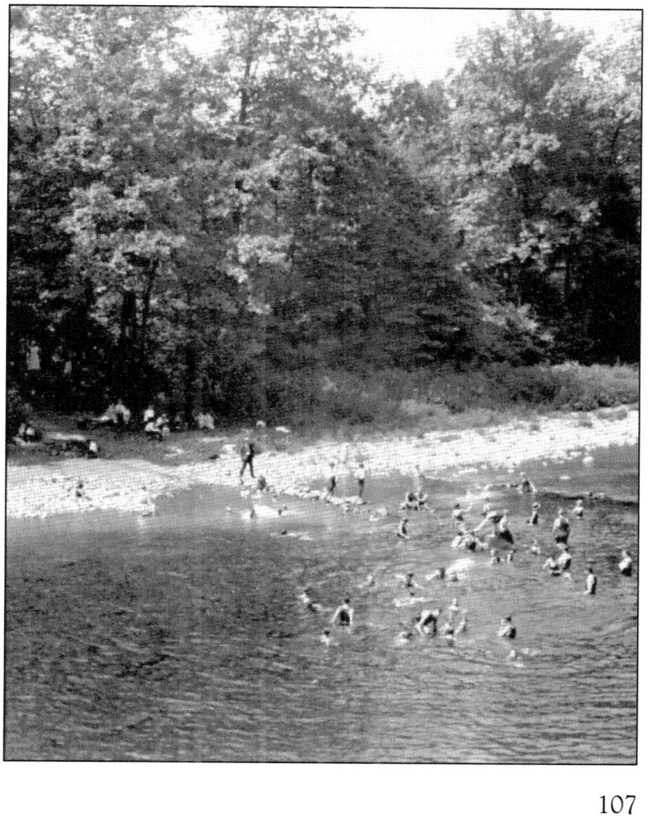

Parents stand guard *c.* 1905, as children splash in the Stonycreek at Ferndale Beach. The swimming spot was also called Red Rock because there was a reddish colored rock in the middle of the river. Unfortunately, due to mining in the area, the river became full of sulfur, sewage, and slag, which ended swimming activity. This photograph makes it clear why the river was known as Stonycreek, as stones clog the banks, diverting the water around them. (Courtesy of Jeanne D. Buck.)

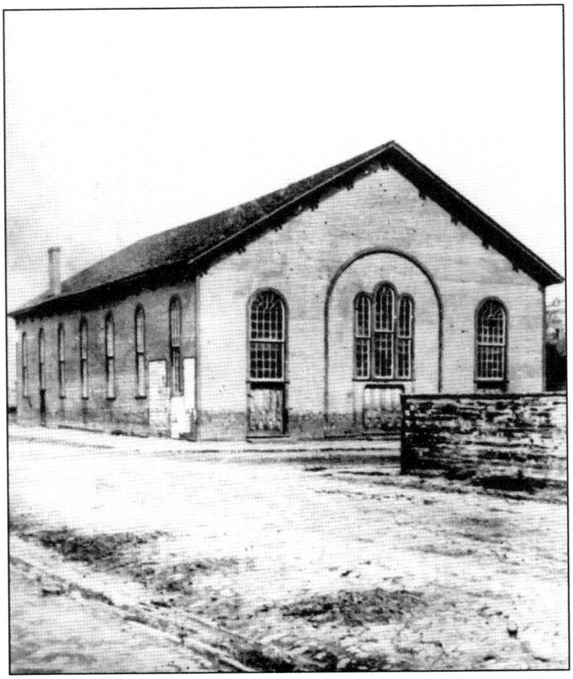

Johnstown residents supported a wide variety of theaters. Union Hall, despite its austere and modest exterior *c.* 1880, had a large interior that provided seating for over 2,000 people—1,500 on the main floor and 500 in the balcony. (Courtesy of the Johnstown Area Heritage Association archives.)

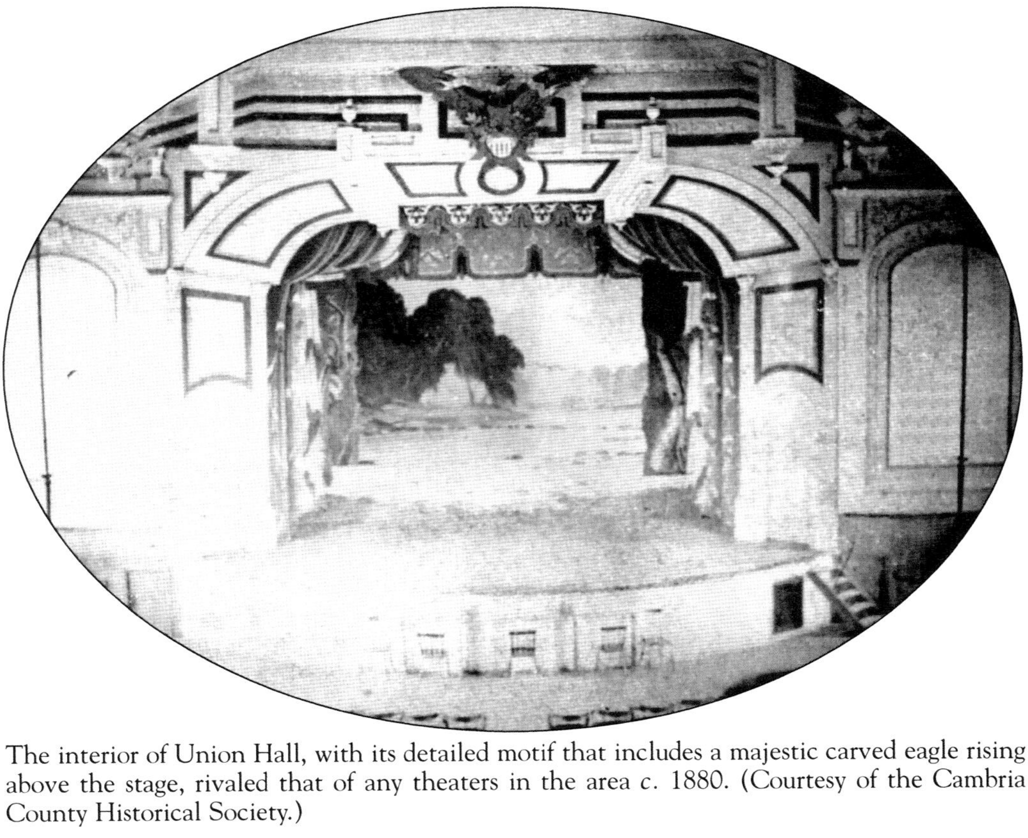

The interior of Union Hall, with its detailed motif that includes a majestic carved eagle rising above the stage, rivaled that of any theaters in the area *c.* 1880. (Courtesy of the Cambria County Historical Society.)

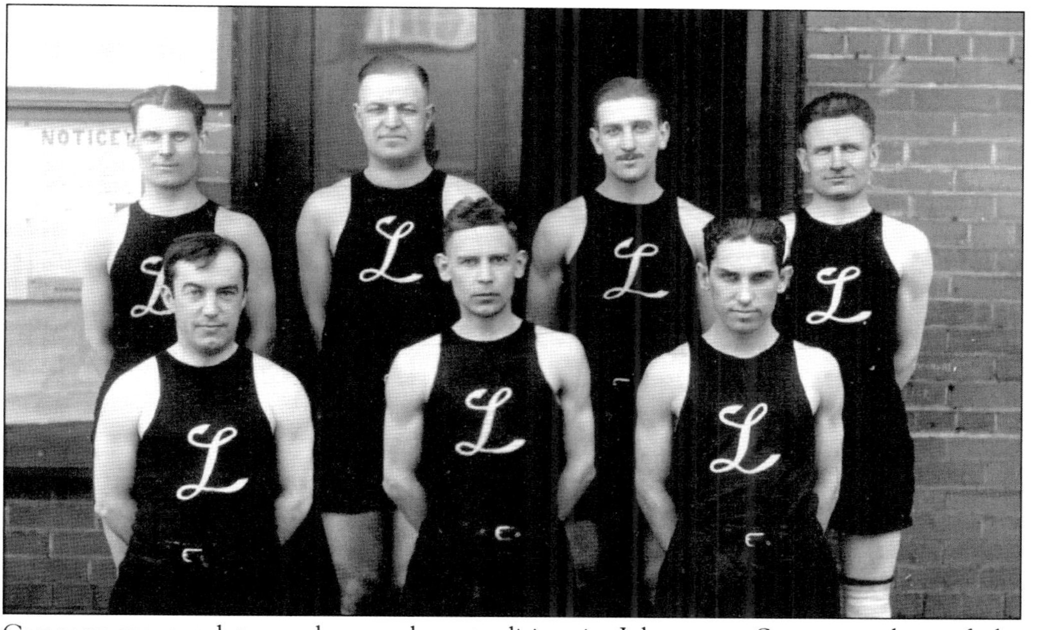

Company-sponsored teams have a long tradition in Johnstown. Seven members of the Lorain Steel Company basketball team stand in front of Lorain offices as proud winners of the title Industrial Champions of 1922–1923. (Courtesy of the Johnstown Area Heritage Association archives.)

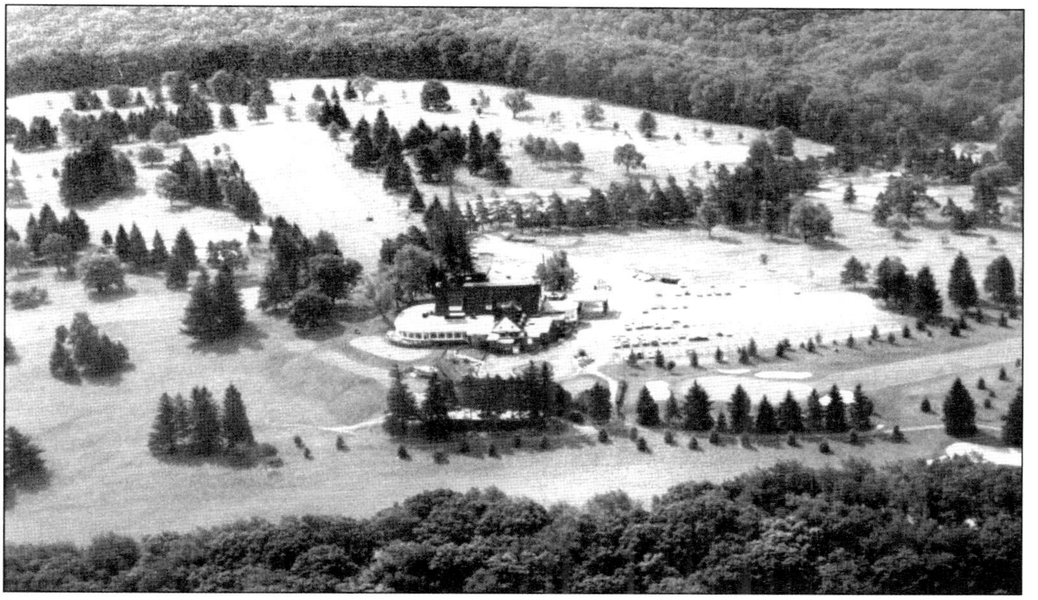

A 1960s aerial view of Sunnehanna Country Club shows the breathtaking beauty of the golf course, tucked away among trees and the rolling terrain of Westmont. A. W. Tillinghast designed the 18 holes, and architect Henry Rogers created the clubhouse, which sits prominently in the middle of the greens. Play at Sunnehanna began in August 1923, and in 1954, the Sunnehanna amateur 72-hole competition became the first such event in the United States. (Courtesy of Jim Cover Jr.)

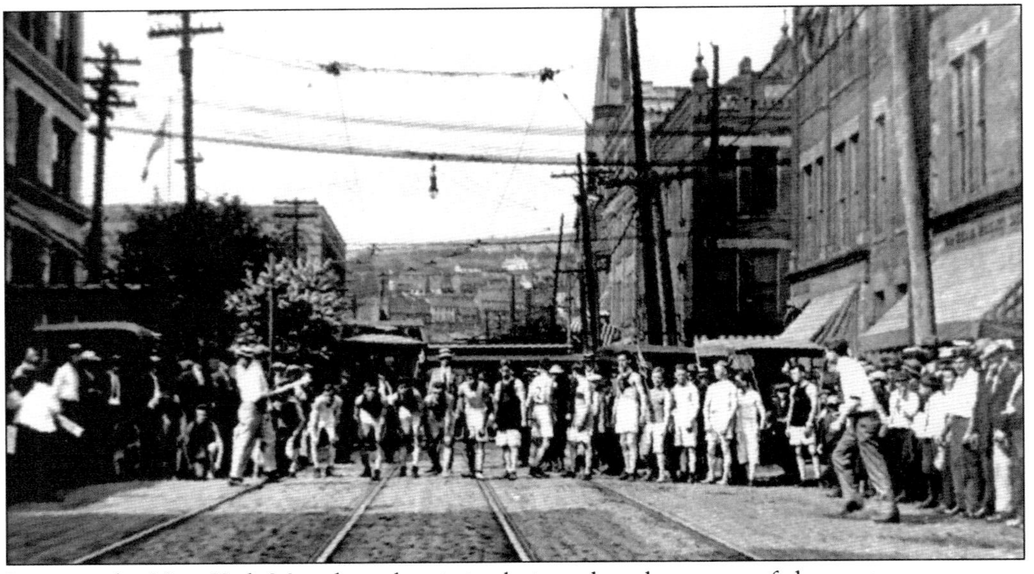

It is not the New York Marathon, but it is obvious that these turn-of-the-century racers are serious about their sport, as they bend in anticipation of the starter's gun. This footrace starting line is just south of Main Street on Franklin Street heading toward the Franklin Street bridge. (Courtesy of the Johnstown Area Heritage Association archives.)

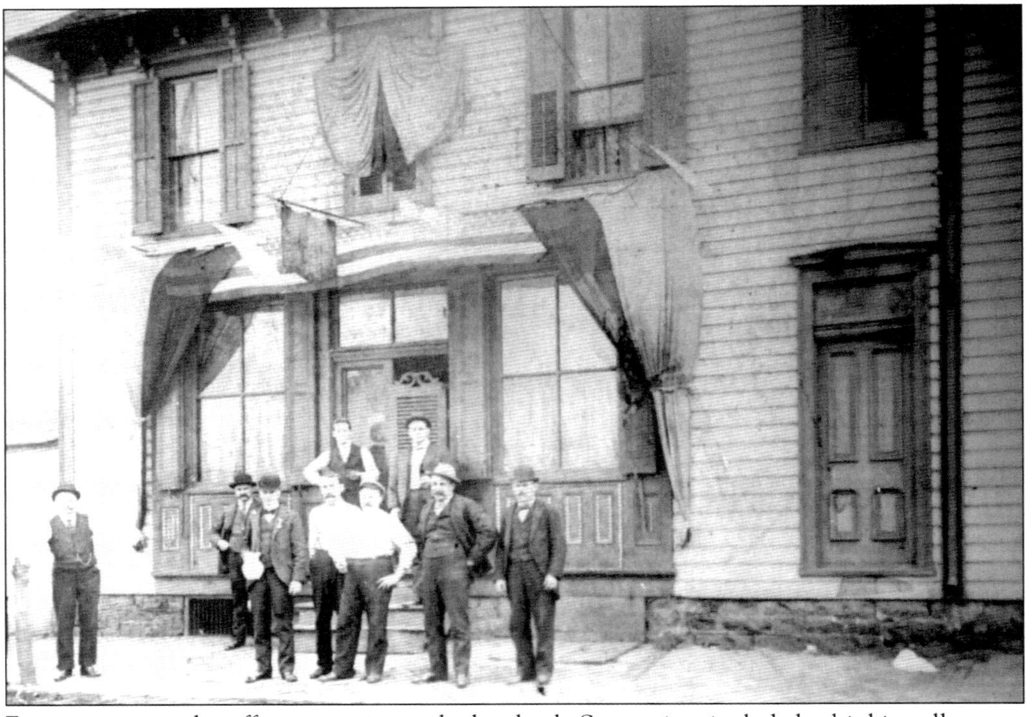

For many men, a day off meant a visit to the local pub. Some wives included a drinking allotment in the family budget. These gents stand in front of a commercial bar in 1880, some wearing their best three-piece suit and hat. One patron casually or defiantly shows off a full pitcher of liquid respite for the camera. (Courtesy of the Johnstown Area Heritage Association archives.)

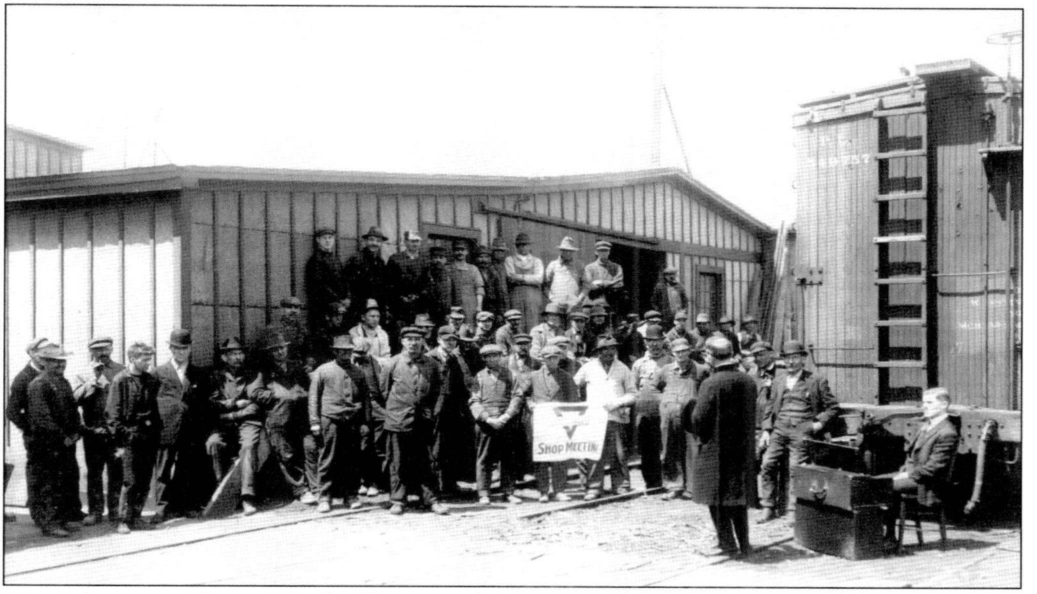

The Johnstown Young Men's Christian Association (YMCA) incorporated in December 1869, just four years after the end of the Civil War. Probably photographed c. 1900, workers from the Conemaugh yards hold a sign which says, "YMCA shop meeting." In May 1914, the organization settled in its first permanent location, on Market Street. Benefits of membership included social services, health counseling, and activities for all ages. Programs expanded when the YMCA opened a new building at 100 Haynes Street in 1979. (Courtesy of the Johnstown Area Heritage Association archives.)

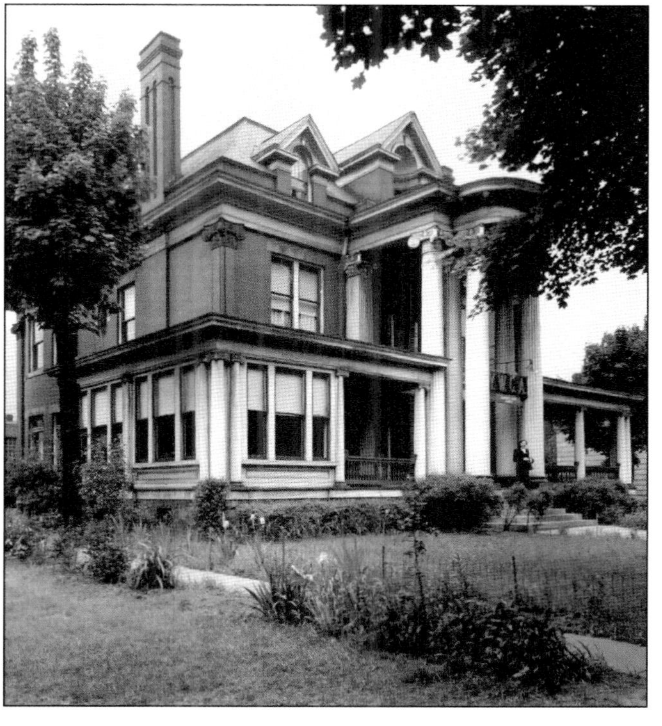

Originally a private residence for James P. Thomas, the vice president of the Imperial Coal Company, this building, at 526 Somerset Street in the Kernville section of Johnstown, became home to the Young Women's Christian Association in November 1918. Johnstown's YWCA began in 1914 and continues operations from this classically designed structure. (Courtesy of the Johnstown Area Heritage Association archives.)

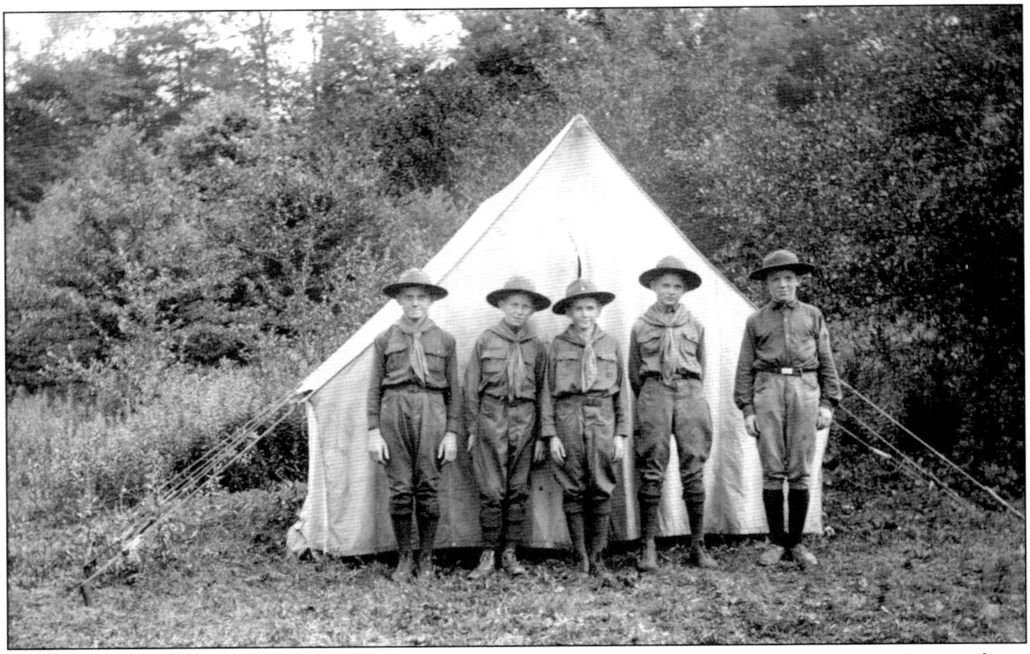

They pledged on their honor to do their best for God and their country. These Boy Scouts from Troop 9 stand at attention, in full uniform, in front of their campsite tent *c.* 1920. (Courtesy of Jeanne D. Buck.)

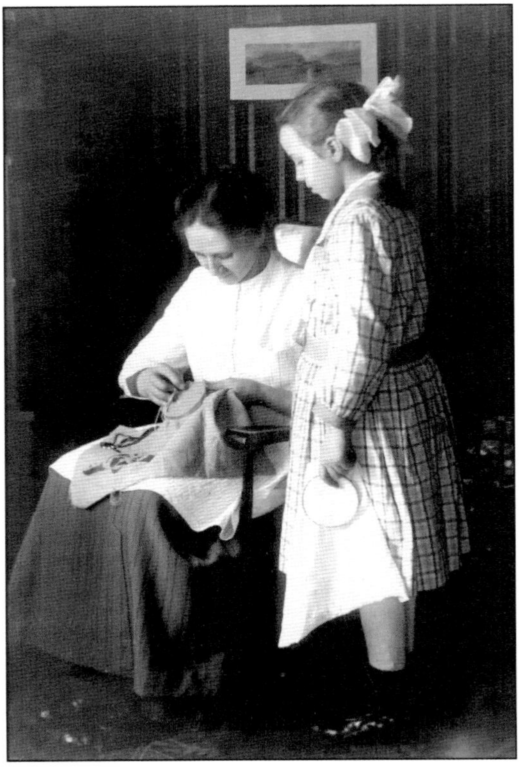

Learning needlework at the knee of a mother, grandmother, or aunt was a common activity for girls at the turn of the century and served as a matter of practicality, as well as a lesson in patience. Here, mother Nora Kemery teaches daughter Katharine the fine art of embroidery *c.* 1912. (Courtesy of Jeanne D. Buck.)

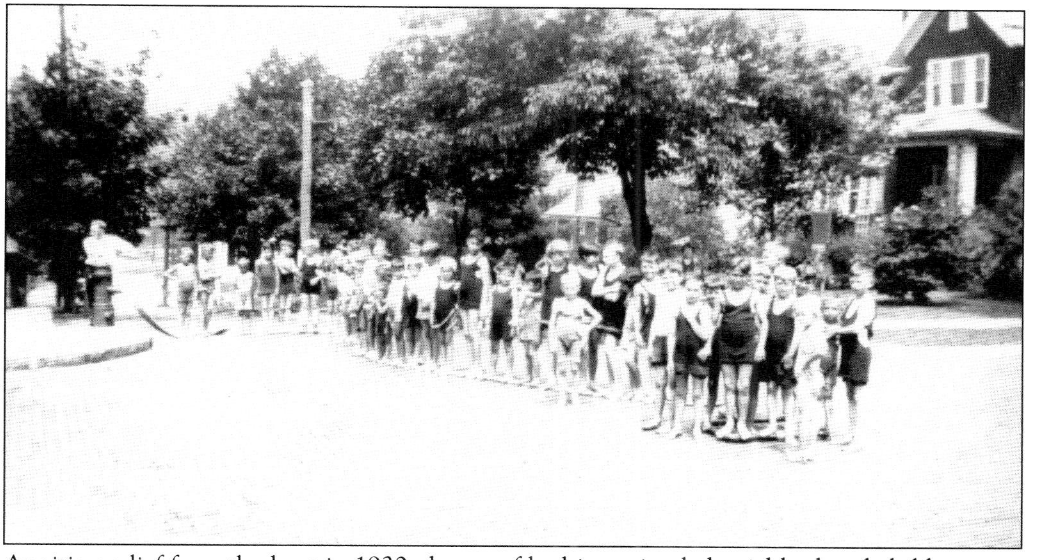

Awaiting relief from the heat in 1930, dozens of bathing suit–clad neighborhood children pose politely on the corner of Vickroy Avenue and Station Street in front of the home of David Weimer, the Cambria County district attorney. (Courtesy of the Ferndale Historical Society.)

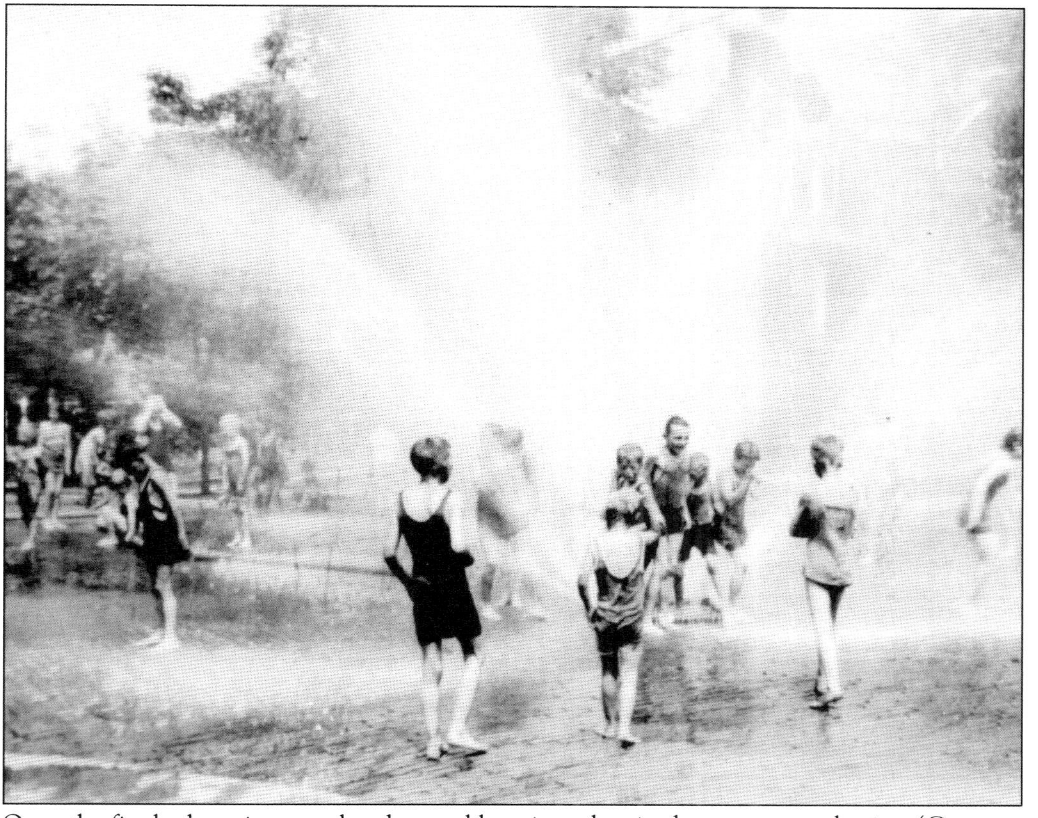

Once the fire hydrant is opened and water blasts into the air, the street party begins. (Courtesy of the Ferndale Historical Society.)

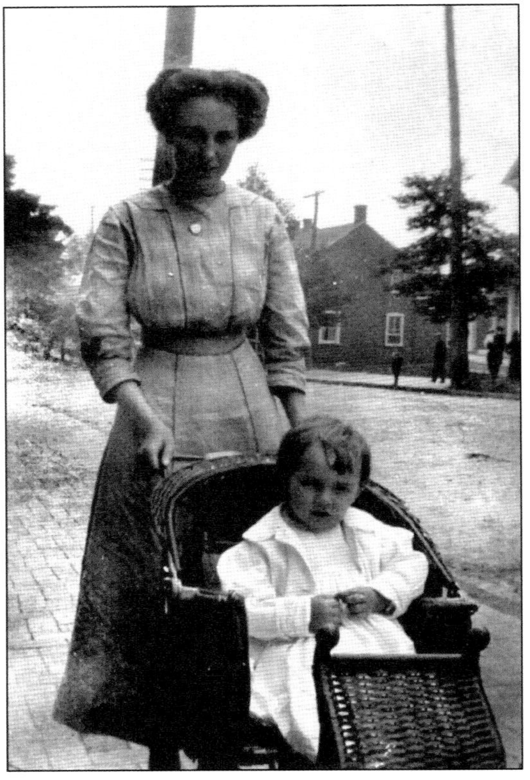

Strolling the street with her baby in the comfort of an elaborate wicker carriage, this Gibson girl mother navigates her charge over an undoubtedly bumpy brick sidewalk *c.* 1910. (Courtesy of the Cambria County Historical Society.)

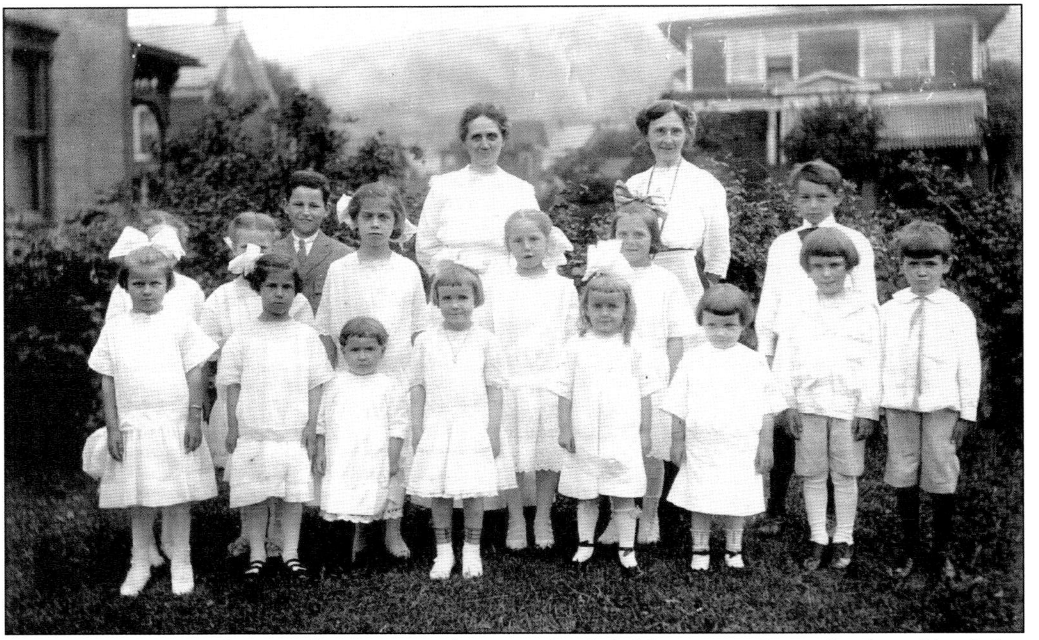

Not everyone is smiling in this *c.* 1910 photograph of children attending a backyard birthday party at a Grove Avenue home in the Moxham area of town. Perhaps the ice cream was melting. (Courtesy of Jeanne D. Buck.)

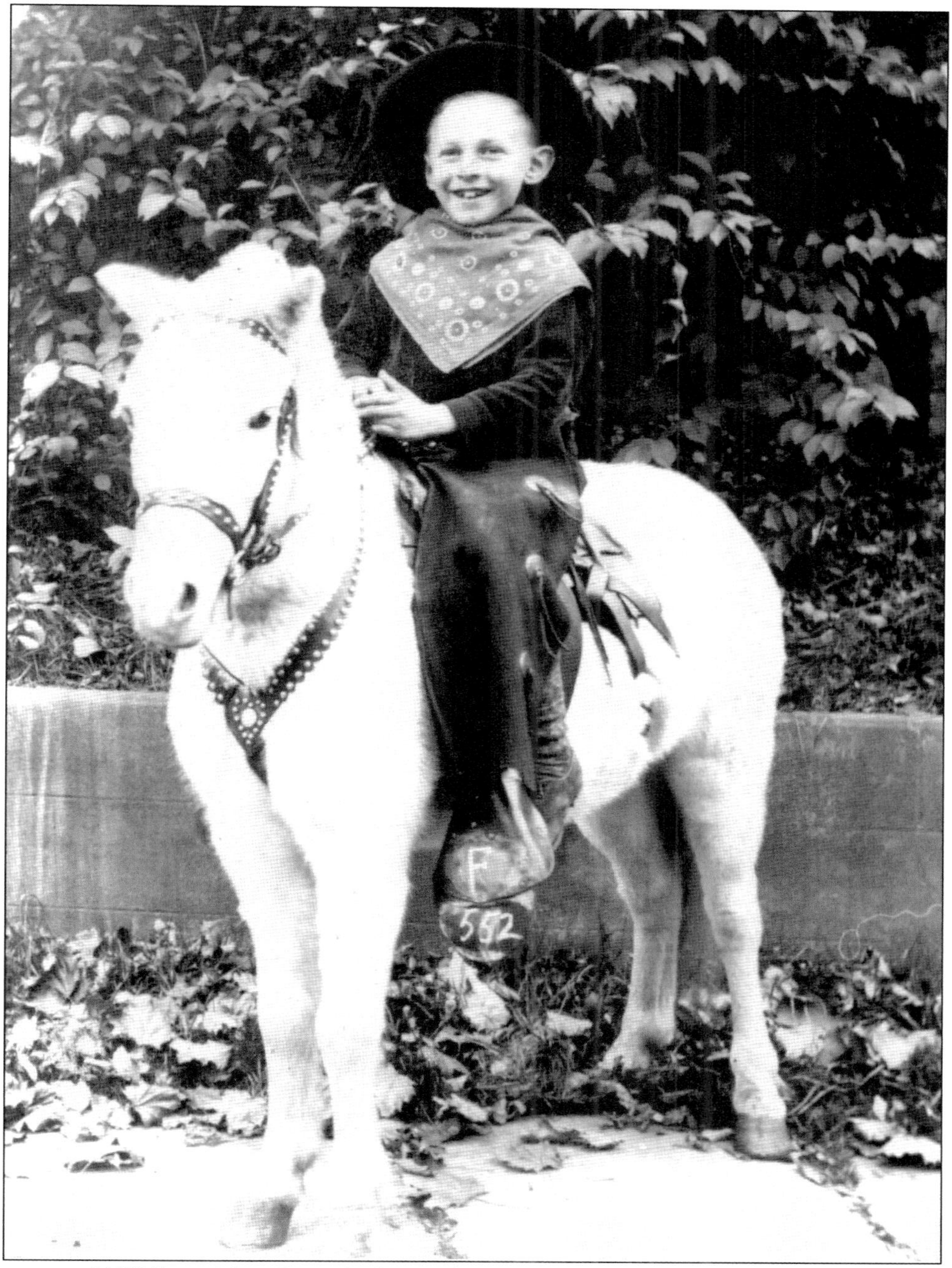

Five-year-old Wilbert Adam Boerstler beams from ear to ear as he sits upon the beautiful white pony of every young cowboy's dreams. Enterprising photographers from out of town often brought a pony into a neighborhood and outfitted children in official cowboy hats, chaps, and neckerchiefs for the photograph of a lifetime. Mothers lined up their children who patiently waited their turn in the saddle. A week after the photograph session, the developed print, which cost 10¢ in 1936, was delivered to the home of the lucky cowpoke. These photo opportunities continued in the Johnstown area through the 1940s. (Courtesy of Wilbert A. Boerstler.)

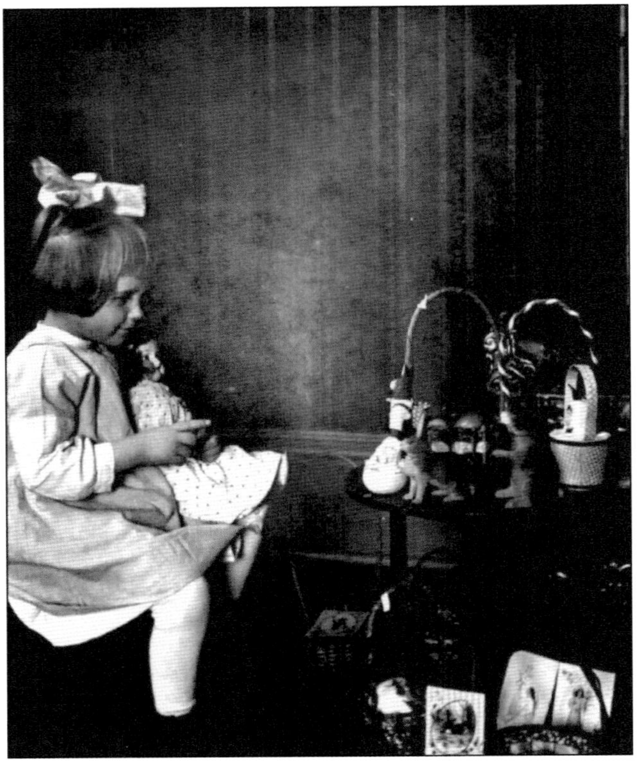

The Easter bunny treated Vera Kemery quite well, as verified by this 1912 photograph taken in the parlor of the family home. Traditions such as decorating eggs and symbols of rabbits were popular in Victorian times. (Courtesy of Jeanne D. Buck.)

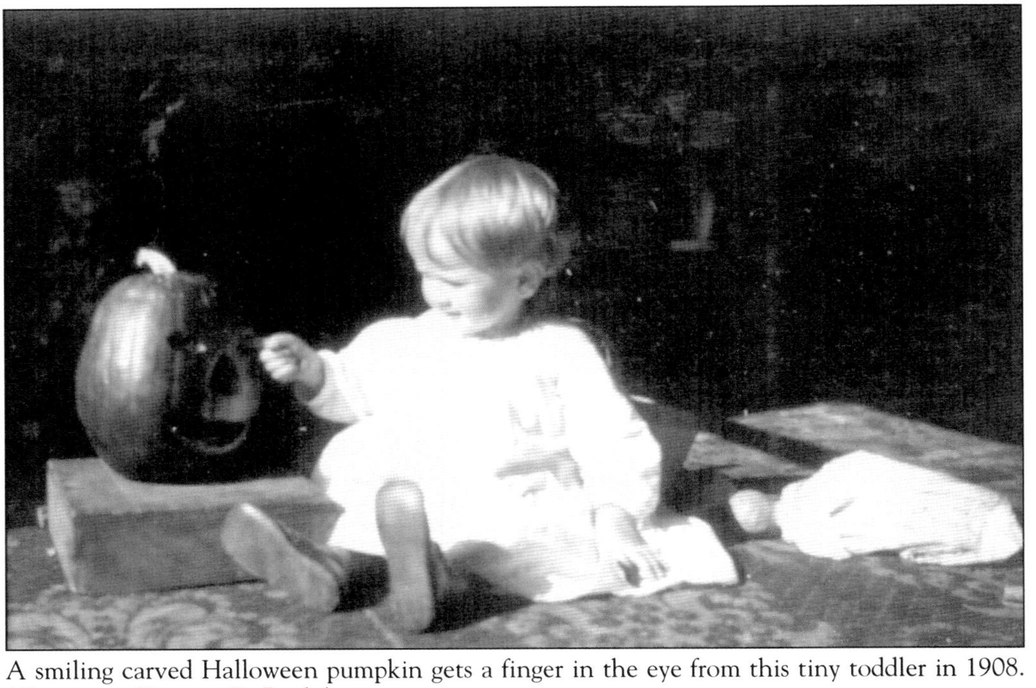

A smiling carved Halloween pumpkin gets a finger in the eye from this tiny toddler in 1908. (Courtesy of Jeanne D. Buck.)

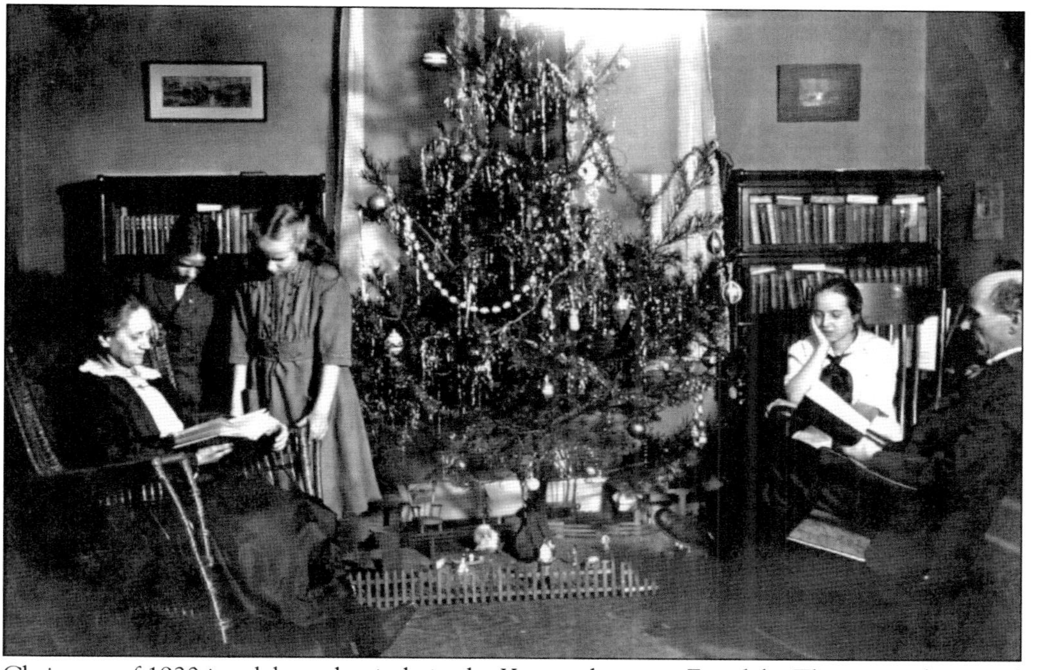

Christmas of 1920 is celebrated quietly in the Kemery home in Ferndale. The tree is decorated with garlands and tinsel, and a small fence encloses figurines. Without television or radio for entertainment, the children gather to hear stories read by their parents. Note the large book collection in the barrister cases against the walls. Lacking the commercialization so prevalent in today's Christmas celebrations, religious holidays tended to revolve around sacred messages. (Courtesy of Jeanne D. Buck.)

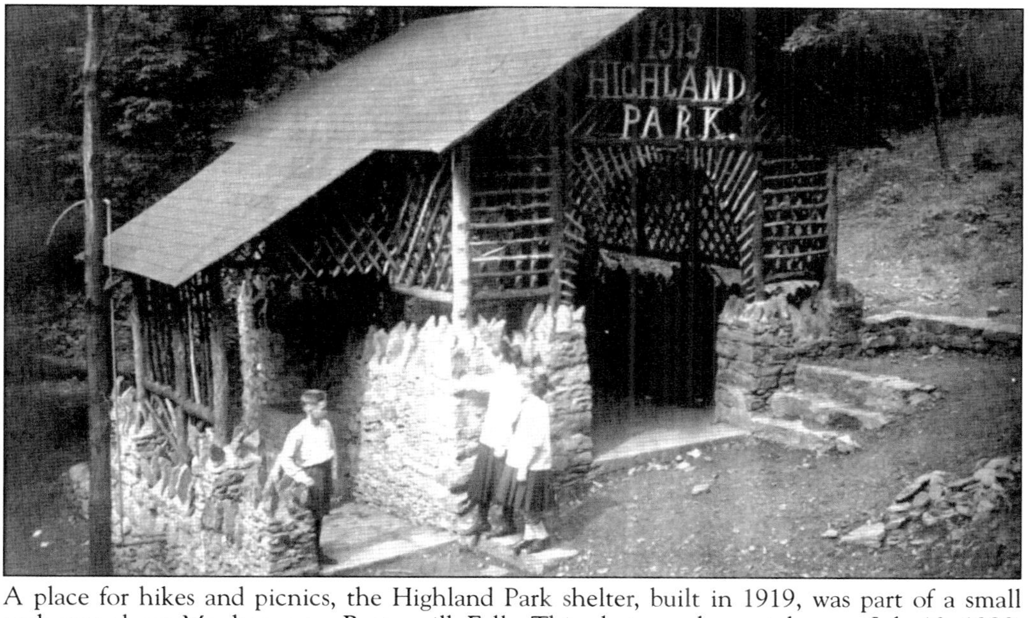

A place for hikes and picnics, the Highland Park shelter, built in 1919, was part of a small park area above Moxham near Buttermilk Falls. This photograph was taken on July 10, 1920. (Courtesy of Jeanne D. Buck.)

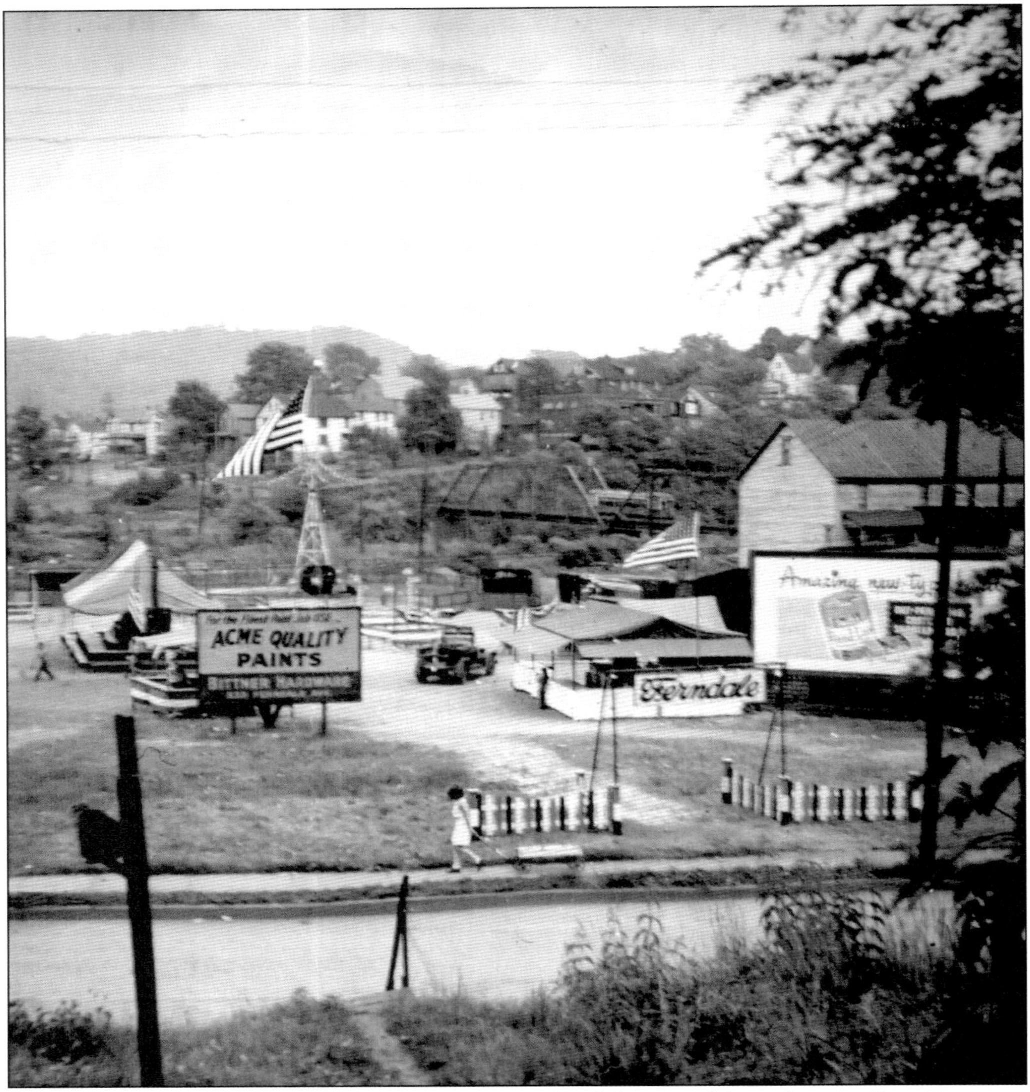

This *c.* 1942 view is the oldest known photograph of the Ferndale Volunteer Fire Company jubilee grounds. The jubilee premiered in 1930, making it the oldest city carnival in Johnstown. Originally held in the 300 block of Ferndale Avenue near Ogle Street, it was moved to the 800 and 900 blocks of Ferndale Avenue to accommodate the expansion of entertainment and food areas, as well as crowds. Note the Johnstown Traction Company bridge in the background. The bridge was built in 1901. Streetcar No. 352 crosses nearby, as men unload a truck, in the center of the scene. A young girl pulls her wagon past the concession tent and the chair plane ride. A row house sits near the American flagpole. The Johnstown area continues to celebrate with festivals year-round, the largest being FolkFest, held in the late summer in the Cambria City neighborhood. (Courtesy of the Ferndale Historical Society.)

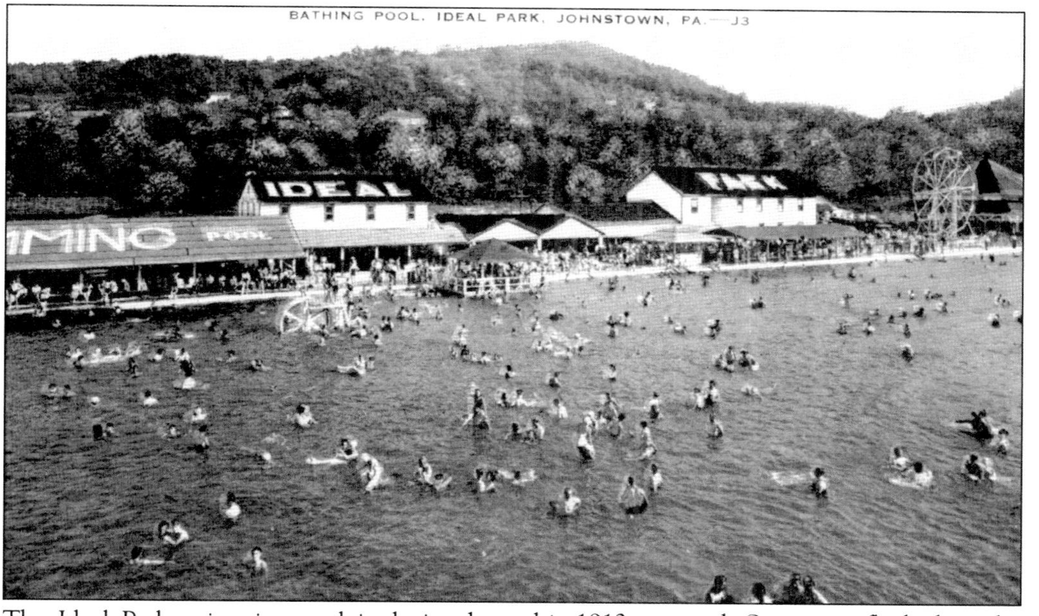

The Ideal Park swimming pool is depicted on this 1913 postcard. Swimmers flocked to the waterwheel, which rotated riders in Ferris wheel style, dumping them into the water. A triple-level diving board, assorted amusement rides, a concession stand, and a picnic area made a visit to the park an all-day event. Water pumped from Benscreek maintained the cleanliness of the pool and supported the water level. When Ideal Park became Fun City in the late 1940s, the water novelties and entertainment venues disappeared. Fun City was the last public pool in the area after rival Crystal Beach closed following the 1936 flood. (Courtesy of Jeanne D. Buck.)

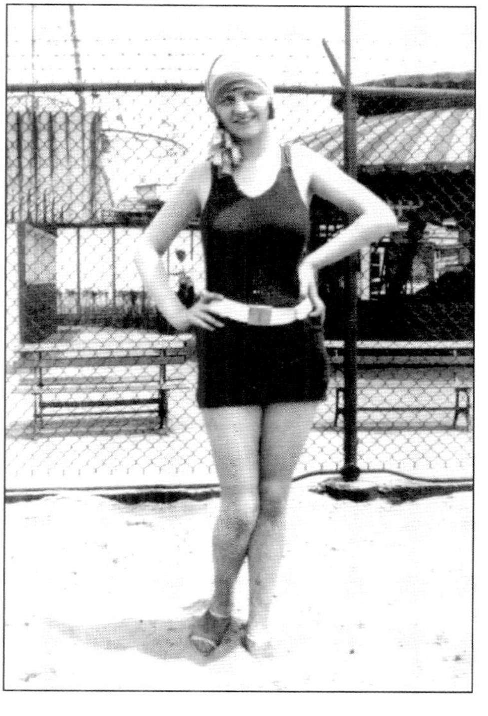

In this c. 1910 photograph, a charming beauty poses in her finest bathing attire at one of Johnstown's many swimming parks. (Courtesy of Robert Snavely.)

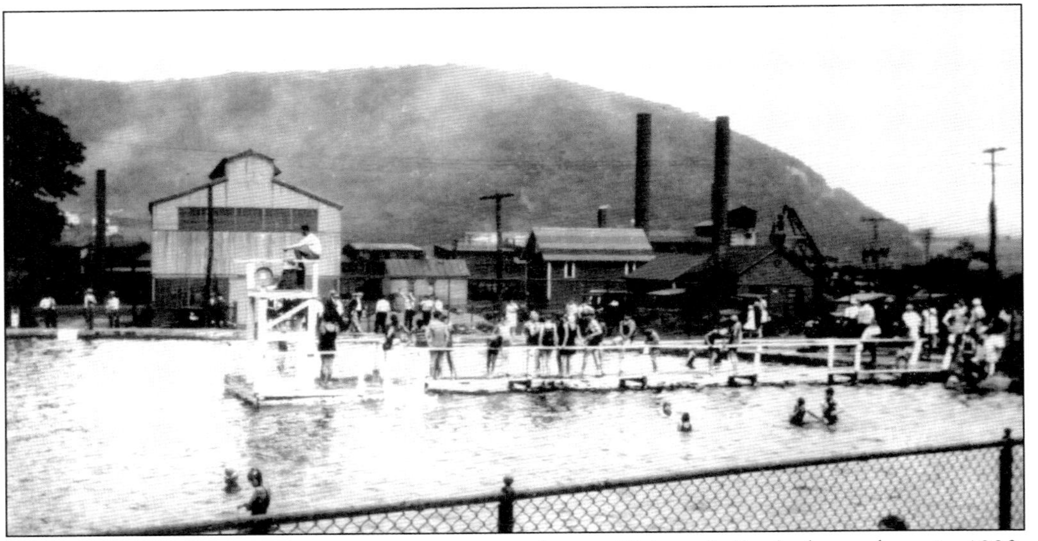

The best bargain in town, morning swims were free at Fichtner's Pool, shown here in 1923. Admission cost 10¢ after 12:00 noon. The pool, located off of Sheridan Street behind the Garfield Junior High School, was donated to the city in the 1930s by the Fichtners. The head lifeguard during the late 1940s was Herbert Pfuhl, who later became Johnstown's mayor. Swimmers plunged from the diving platform while mill smokestacks behind them pumped soot into the air. Faced with repair costs and expansion of the school, the city closed the pool c. 1975. (Courtesy of Robert Snavely.)

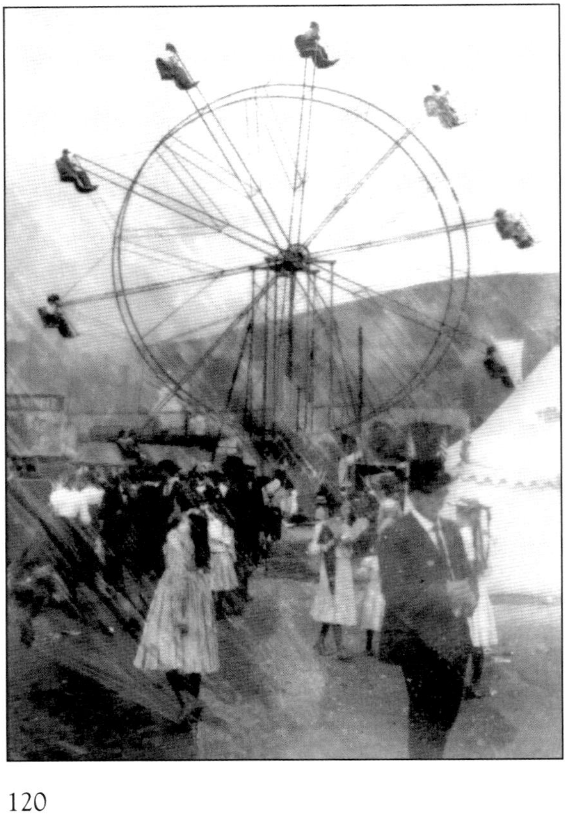

Named after Coney Island's New York attraction, Luna Park was a remarkable undertaking in the mid-1890s. Located in today's Roxbury Park, the park featured an impressive roller coaster, a carousel, and a Ferris wheel. Families picnicked among the shade trees. A racetrack enticed bets on a full scorecard. The teetering cars on this Ferris wheel, c. 1894, would never pass today's safety requirements. Amusement rides were independently owned, and proprietors rented space from the park. If a fee dispute arose, the ride owner packed up his attraction and moved to another city. (Courtesy of the Johnstown Area Heritage Association archives.)

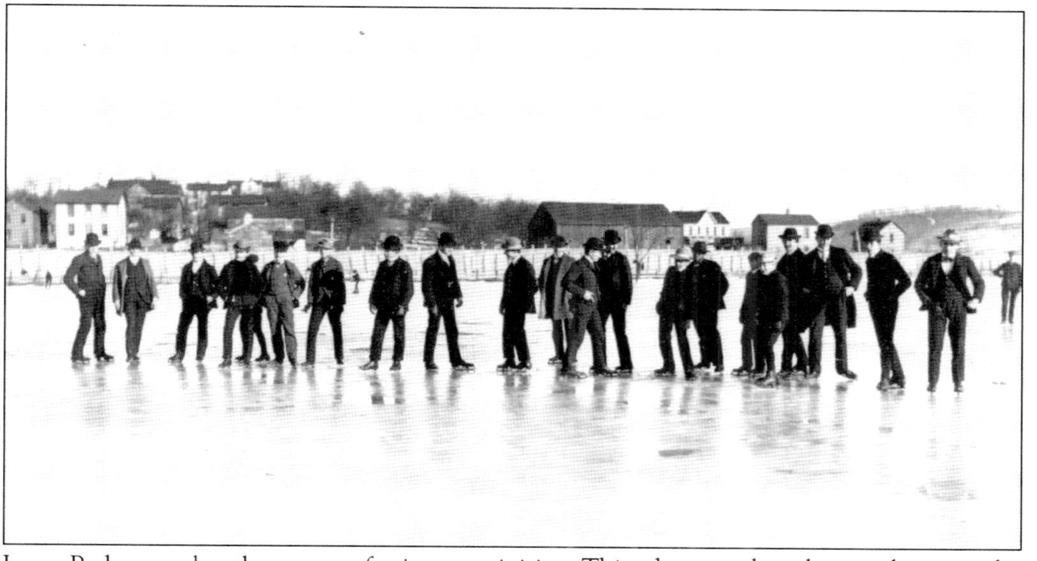

Luna Park was also the scene of winter activities. This photograph, taken perhaps in the mid-1890s, shows men skating at Luna's outdoor rink. The scene is notable for the less-than-warm-looking attire worn by the hearty skaters. Of course, a proper hat, preferably a nice derby, was the standard head covering all year-round. (Courtesy of the Johnstown Area Heritage Association archives.)

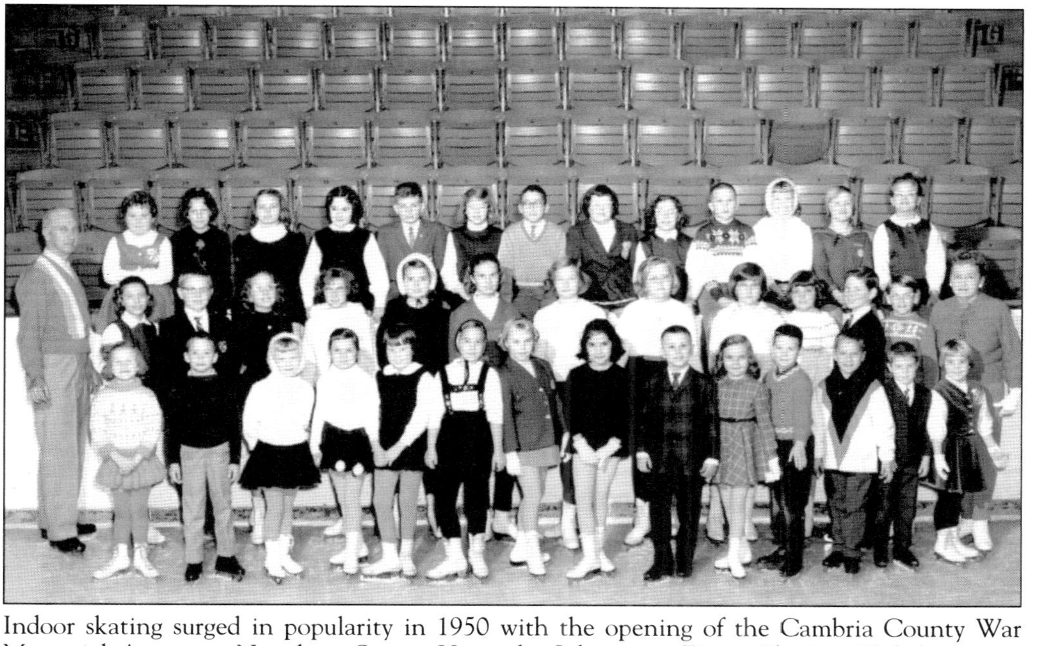

Indoor skating surged in popularity in 1950 with the opening of the Cambria County War Memorial Arena on Napoleon Street. Here, the Johnstown Figure Skating Club beginners strike a pose, showing off their best skating attire c. 1965. The club included skaters of all ages. When the resident hockey team was off-duty, skaters practiced the Dutch waltz, spins, and jumps. Members of the Ice Capades tutored students in between their own performances. Today, the club divides its time between the War Memorial Arena and Planet Ice on Jari Drive. (Courtesy of Jim Cover Jr.)

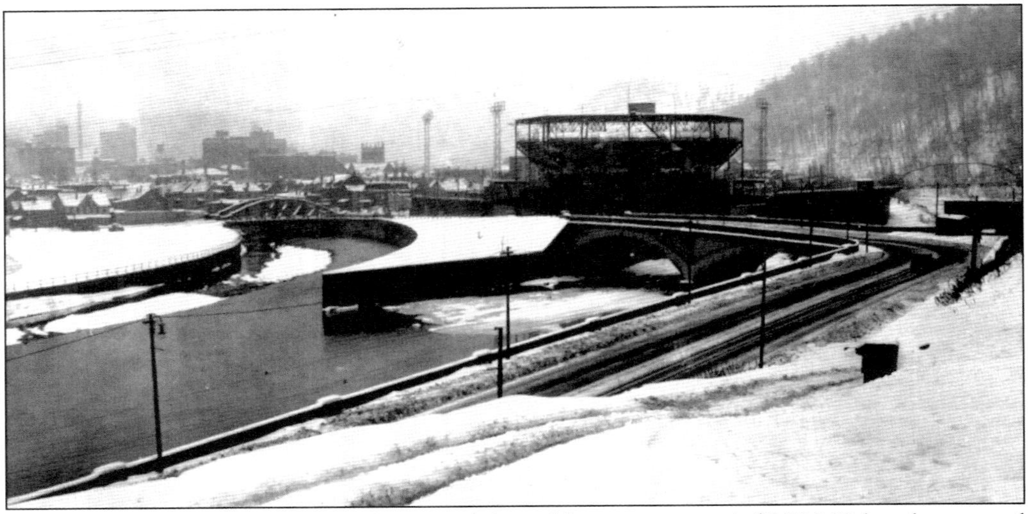

The Point Stadium sits on land designated for public recreation. A $250,000 bond approved by residents in 1925 supplied construction funding for the brick and steel structure. On July 5, 1926, the first echo of "Play ball!" resounded within its walls as the Johnstown Johnnies hosted Clarksburg in a doubleheader. The upper deck, seen here, was added in the 1930s to provide additional seating; it was dismantled in the 1960s. Fans flocked to see stars Babe Ruth and Satchel Paige take a swing toward the home run–taunting 400-foot right field straightway. Ruth met the challenge. (Courtesy of the Johnstown Area Heritage Association archives, photograph by Ted Pekich.)

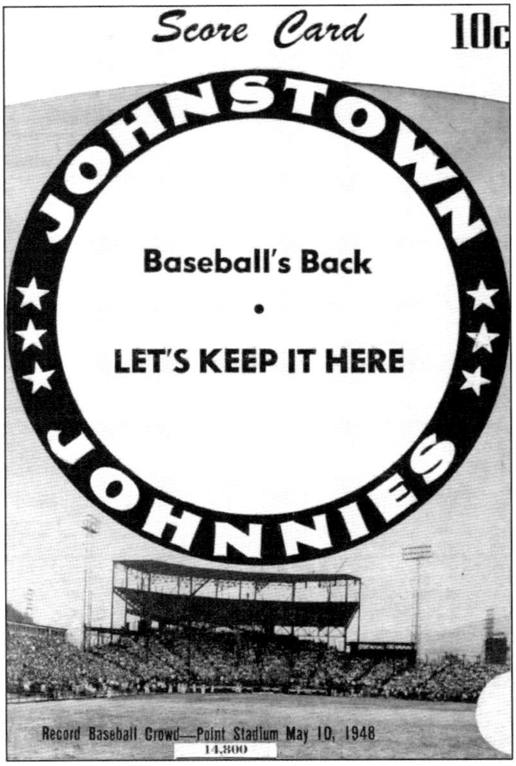

Unfortunately, the minor-league Johnstown Johnnies suffered an on-again, off-again existence. Playing their first game in 1926 as part of the Middle Atlantic League, the Johnnies went through reorganizations and league problems that led to breaks in the action. This 1948 official program heralds "Baseball's Back." However, as recently as 2003, the team was purchased and moved to Florence, Kentucky. If history repeats itself, optimists believe the Johnnies will be back again. (Courtesy of the Johnstown Area Heritage Association archives.)

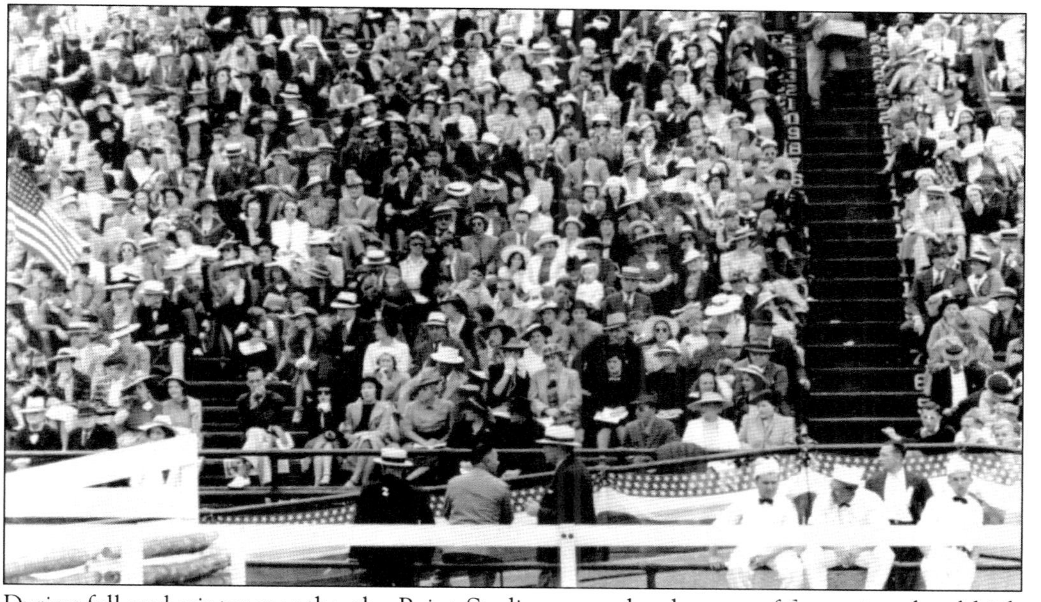

During fall and winter months, the Point Stadium served as home turf for various local high school teams, including Conemaugh, Dale, Franklin, and Catholic High (Bishop McCort). Crowds jammed together on metal bleachers to watch the Johnstown High School Trojans football team play ball at the Point until 2003, when a new high school stadium opened on school grounds, ending an era of Johnstown High football history. (Courtesy of the Johnstown Area Heritage Association archives.)

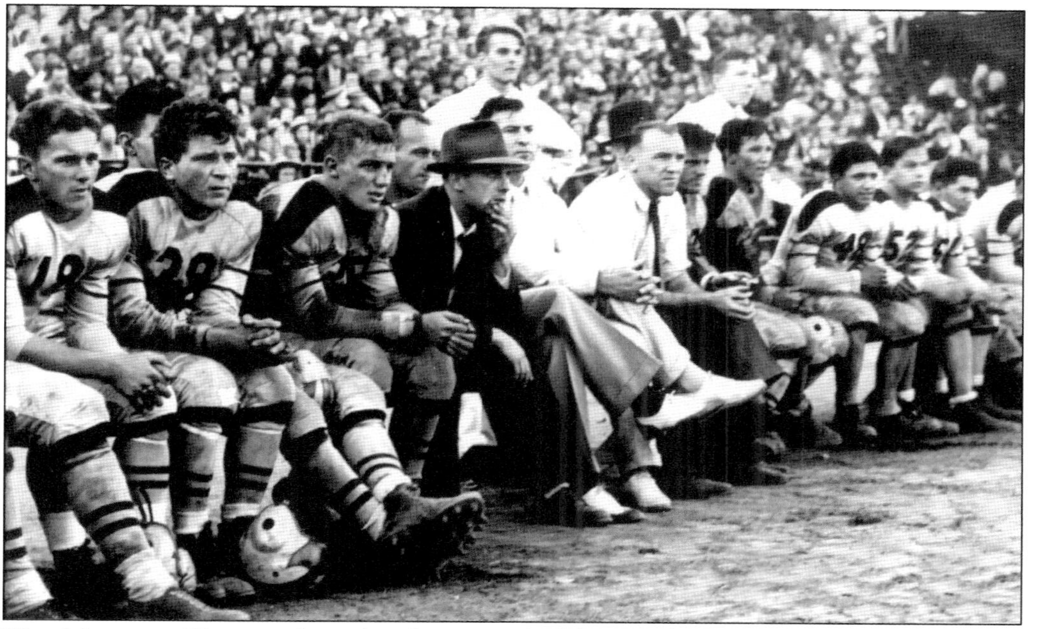

The Johnstown Trojans often played to a packed house when major rivals like Windber, Altoona, or McKeesport came to town. Stadium seating, combined with standing room, allowed 15,000 avid fans the opportunity to cheer their teams to victory c. the 1940s. (Courtesy of the Johnstown Area Heritage Association archives.)

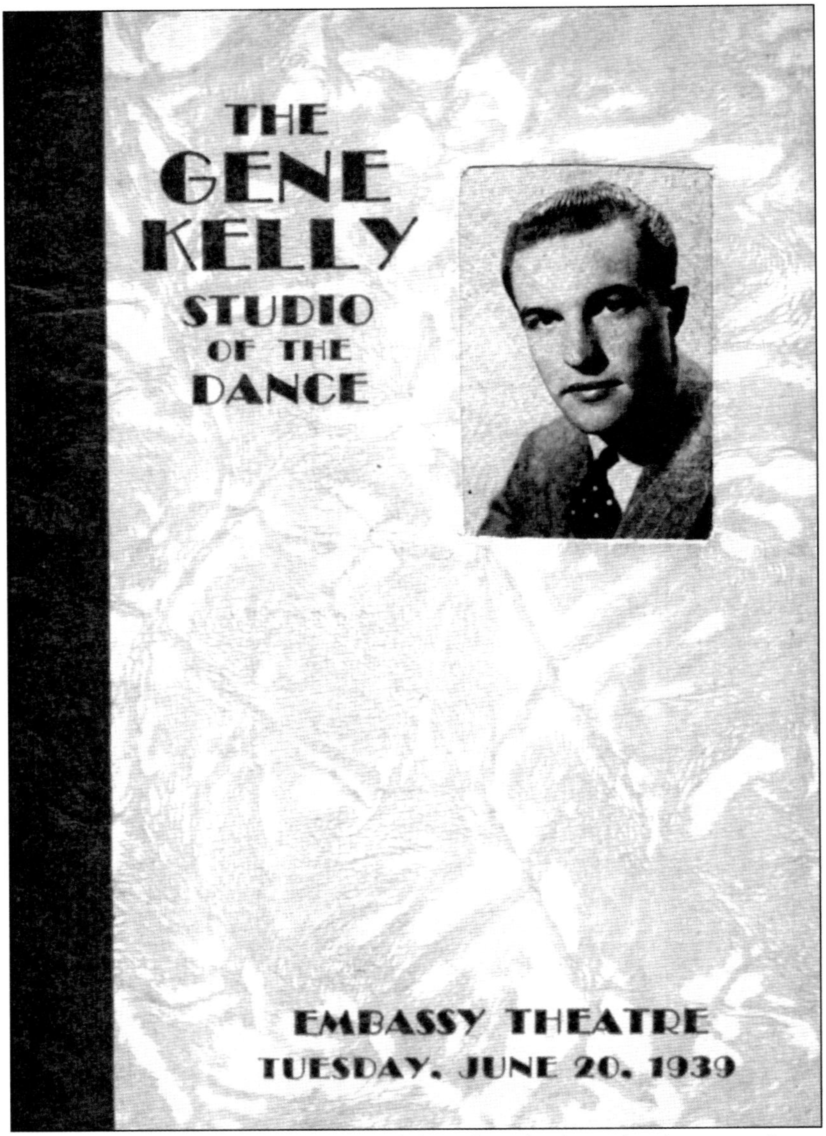

Johnstown's Gene Kelly Studio of the Dance debuted modestly at the American Legion Hall in 1929. Initially, Gene Kelly, still a teenager, taught weekend classes while attending Penn State University in State College, where he studied economics. After one year, he transferred to the main campus of the University of Pittsburgh to accommodate managing both his Pittsburgh and Johnstown schools. Believing he would attract additional students with a more pleasant location, Kelly moved the school to 443 Vine Street at Franklin Street c. 1931. Advertisements claimed that it was "Johnstown's most beautiful dance studio." Later, the school was moved to the second floor of another Franklin Street building that overlooked Central Park. Kelly's siblings Fred Kelly and Louise Kelly served as dancers-in-residence, and although his visits became infrequent as Hollywood called, Gene Kelly remained the dancer pictured in studio promotions. This is the front cover of the program for the *Gene Kelly Studio of the Dance* review held at the Embassy Theatre on June 20, 1939. The dance studio closed in the 1950s. (Courtesy of Jeanne D. Buck.)

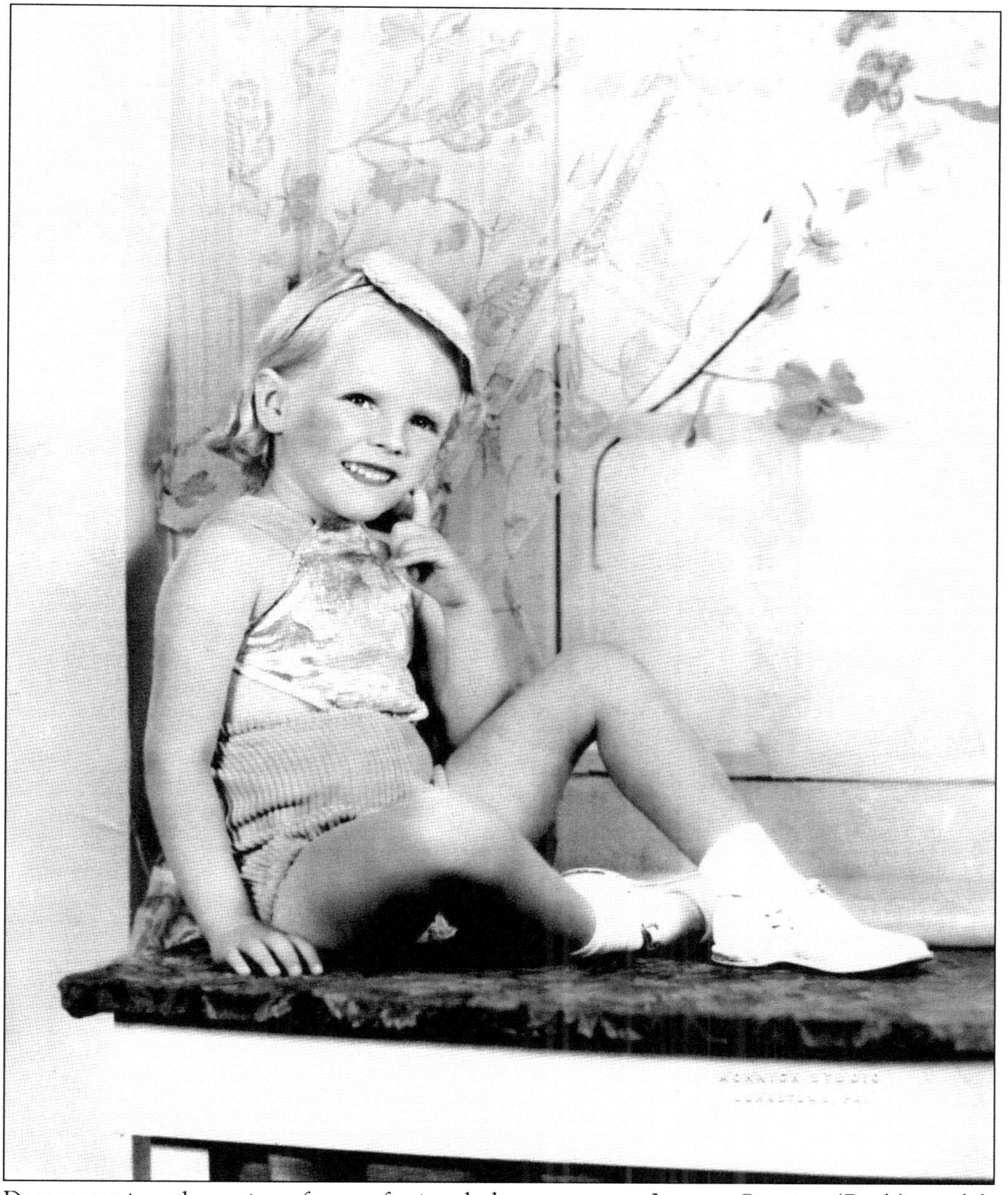

Demonstrating the poise of a professional dancer, young Jeanne Cousins (Buck) models the sparkly costume she wore for a tap-dance number in a 1934 Gene Kelly review at the Embassy Theater. Several of Kelly's Johnstown students made it to Broadway or accepted other professional dance opportunities. The instruction was serious, and Kelly's teaching philosophy revolved around each student properly mastering dance moves. His methods created a lifelong interest in dance among many of his students. (Courtesy of Jeanne D. Buck, Hornick Studio.)

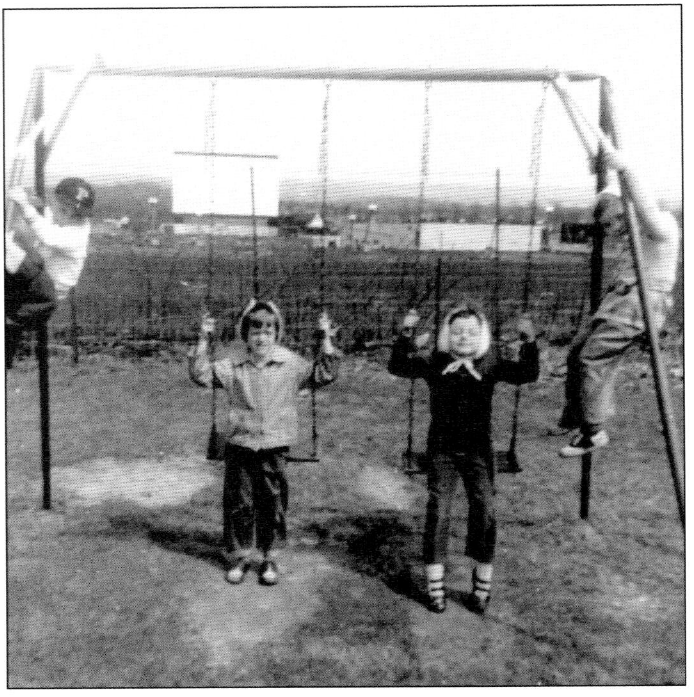

The backyards of houses along Judith and Willet Drives faced the Westmont Drive-In Theater, providing a bonus for youngsters who gathered on swing sets at dusk to watch the cartoons before the scheduled feature. The theater, which operated from 1952 to the early 1960s, was replaced by Westwood Plaza, a strip mall that included an indoor movie theater. (Author's collection.)

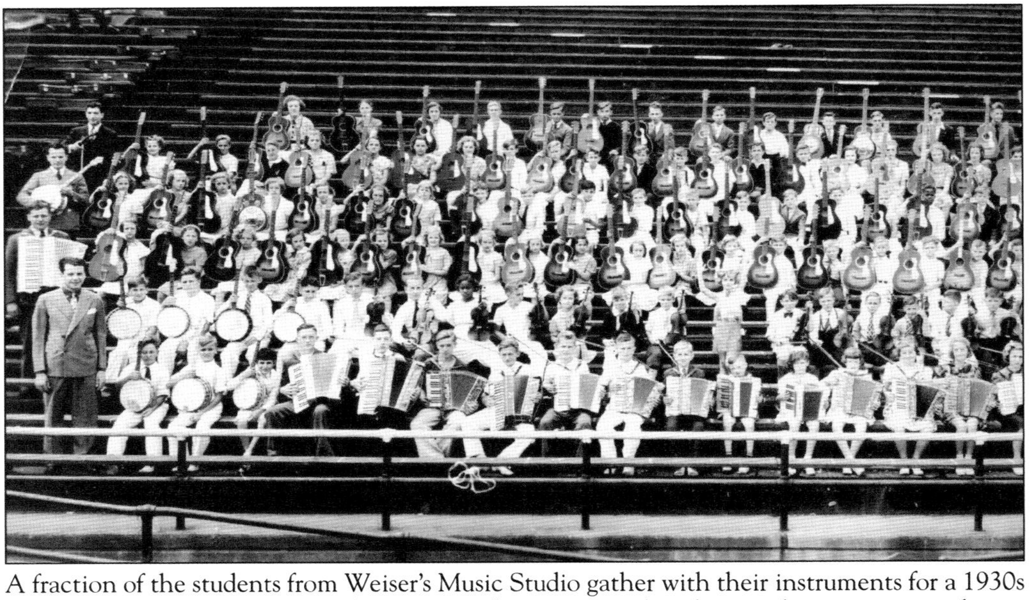

A fraction of the students from Weiser's Music Studio gather with their instruments for a 1930s photograph in the bleachers at the Point Stadium. Notice that the popular instruments chosen by this group were accordions, guitars, violins, and drums. (Courtesy of the Johnstown Area Heritage Association archives.)

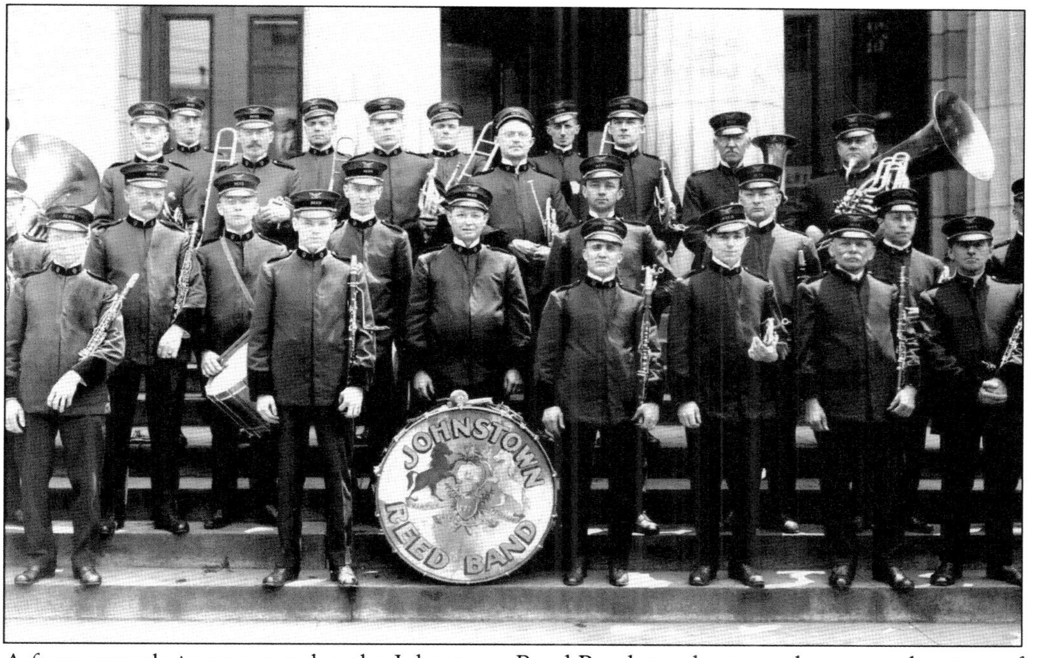

A former staple in area parades, the Johnstown Reed Band stands at parade rest on the steps of the old Market Street post office in 1925. Chartered in 1883, it became a concert band after World War I. Today, the band continues to entertain in summer performances on Thursday nights in Central Park. (Courtesy of the Johnstown Area Heritage Association archives.)

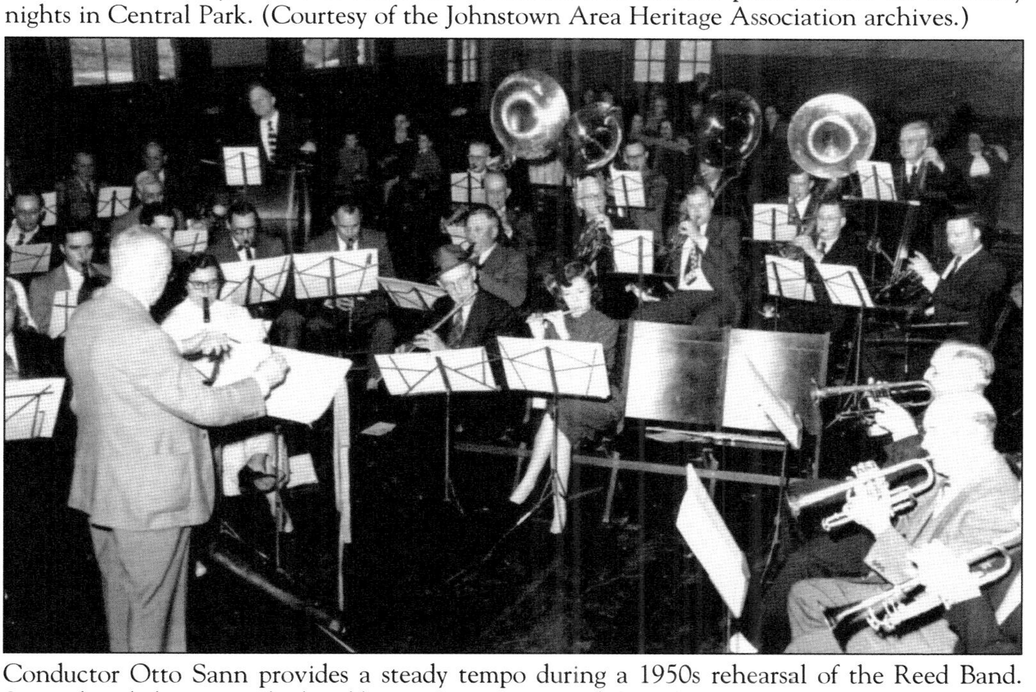

Conductor Otto Sann provides a steady tempo during a 1950s rehearsal of the Reed Band. Sann played clarinet in the band beginning in 1894 and then directed it for 46 years. Although he was somewhat of a local musical legend, his day job was in the engineering department of United States Steel. (Courtesy of the Geist family collection.)

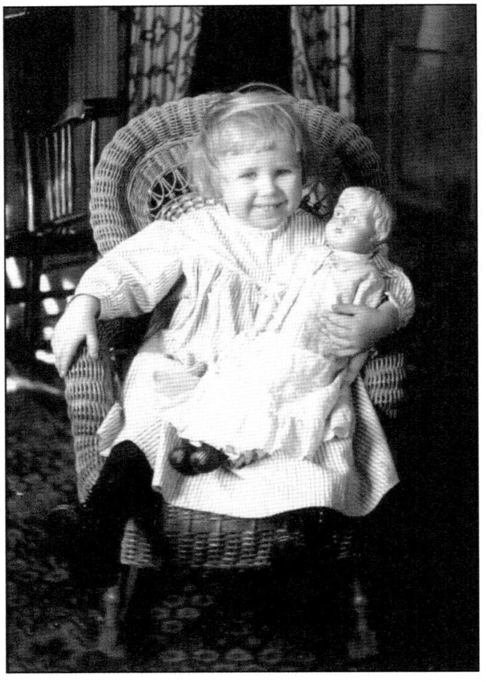

Three-year-old Vera Kemery, c. 1912, proves that no matter the era, the wide grin of a happy child is infectious. (Courtesy of Jeanne D. Buck.)

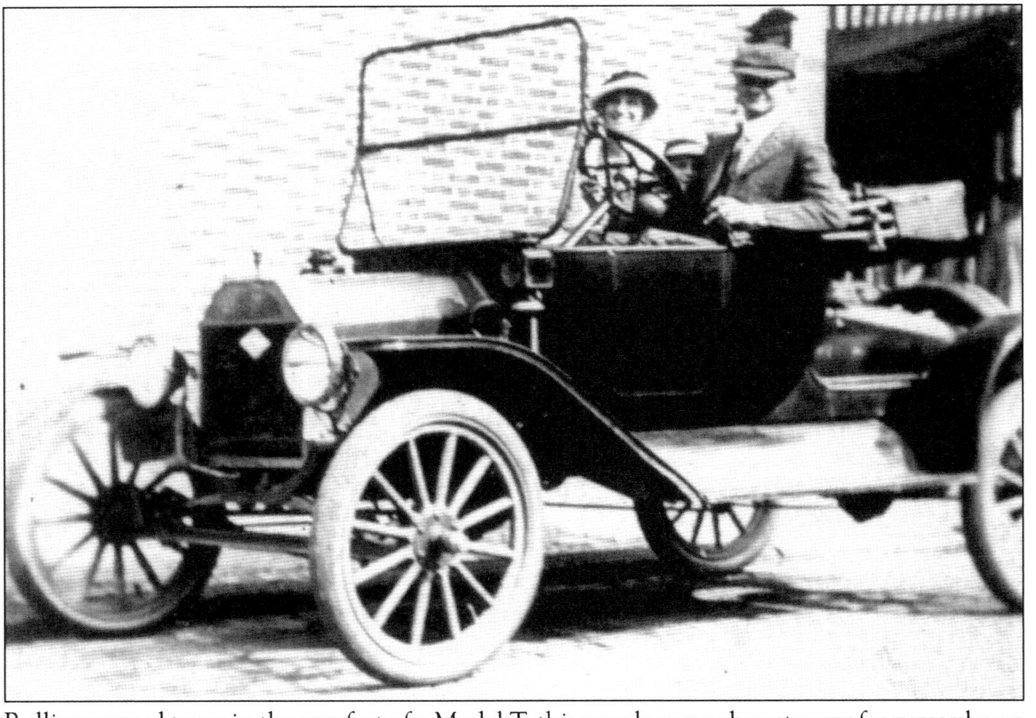

Rolling around town in the comfort of a Model T, this couple was a showstopper for passersby on F Street in 1916. Although the street is no longer paved with bricks and clothing and lifestyles have changed, Johnstown's residents continue to move into the future with old-fashioned optimism. (Courtesy of Robert Snavely.)